Restoring Pianolas

Restoring Pianolas

and other self-playing pianos

ARTHUR W. J. G. ORD-HUME

Illustrated by the author

London
GEORGE ALLEN & UNWIN
Boston   Sydney

George Allen & Unwin (Publishers) Ltd,
40 Museum Street, London WC1A 1LU, UK

George Allen & Unwin (Publishers) Ltd,
Park Lane, Hemel Hempstead, Herts HP2 4TE, UK

Allen & Unwin Inc.,
9 Winchester Terrace, Winchester, Mass 01890, USA

George Allen & Unwin Australia Pty Ltd,
8 Napier Street, North Sydney, NSW 2060, Australia

First published in 1983

British Library Cataloguing in Publication Data

Ord-Hume, Arthur
  Restoring pianolas.
1. Pianola – Conservation and restoration
I. Title
789.7'2   ML652
ISBN 0–04–789008–8

Set in 11 on 12 point Plantin by Nene Phototypesetters, Northampton
and printed in Great Britain by
The Alden Press, Oxford

Contents

List of Plates

List of Line Illustrations

Acknowledgements

I am grateful to the many friends and acquaintances who have helped me both in the gathering of information and in the furthering of my own knowledge and abilities in restoring instruments. Particular thanks go to the museums and both public and private collections which have provided assistance. A special word of thanks must go to what is probably the only national museum of mechanical instruments anywhere in the world which is sponsored by government and state grant – Holland's Nationaal Museum van Speelklok tot Pierement in Utrecht. Director, conservator and, above all, good friend and fellow enthusiast Dr J. J. L. Haspels has provided help and photographs, particularly the fine colour illustrations on the jacket.

To the owners of instruments which I have worked on or been invited to examine and allowed to photograph, my thanks again; the names appear in the list of picture credits.

Introduction

The purchaser of a player piano is forever endowed with optimism. His new treasure may be thirty, forty or even sixty years old, and has probably spent many years out of favour, perhaps relegated to a damp barn. Yet when he gets it and drags its bulk and massive dead weight into his house, he somehow expects it to perform perfectly, effortlessly and with the panache of a hidden keyboard virtuoso.

Alas! This is seldom the case. His instrument will most probably sit mute and desolate, reflecting the disappointment of its new owner. It may play badly, sporadically, or maybe the only sound will be a faint wheezing of leaking air. Rarely indeed will a newly unearthed relic surprise its finder with a passable performance without drastic and extensive attention.

Player pianos are contrived as delicately adjusted devices created out of wood, felt, rubberised cloth, tubing, springs, slides, screws and wire. Like every machine, they deteriorate with time, neglect, dampness and changes of temperature. Confronted with such a challenge, the new owner may understandably flinch at the thought of ever getting such an assortment of pieces to perform properly. This, though, need not be that much of a worry. A player piano responds to attention and, with patience, all but the most blatantly deteriorated instrument may be brought gratefully back to a fresh lease of life in the hands of the average enthusiast. As with all forms of restorative work, however, two qualities are paramount for the worker – patience and thoroughness. There are two ways to do every job in life – the quick way and the right way – and only one can be assured of leading to success. The mechanical piano, be it barrel-operated, planchette-playing, pneumatic push-up, player piano or reproducer, rewards its careful rebuilding and thus demands a high level of personal integrity from its restorer. In short, there are no short cuts to perfection.

Why should one devote a whole book to reviving these outdated and outmoded pieces of musical furniture? The truth is that there are many, many player pianos still lurking largely unattended and uncared for around the world and now, after the inescapable change of fashion which demeans an artefact and reduces it to worthlessness, they are now becoming collectable collectors' items. All these instruments, I venture to suggest, need some attention unless the previous owner has recently laboured long and hard on them. Restoration is a word which embraces a multitude of sins. It comes in all degrees and complexities from a kick at the cabinet and a drop of oil on the castors to a full pneumatic rebuild and return to 'as new' condition. Proper restoration is a job demanding skilled man-hours and is thus very expensive. Player piano engineers do not really exist today because few owners would be able to pay an economic price for their labours. This means that the player piano owner must fall back on his own abilities to bring an instrument back to life. This is not the daunting task it may at first appear as, for all their apparent complexity, player pianos are surprisingly simple things. Admittedly, the outward appearance of an apparent labyrinth of tubing and interior airways and valves must at first sight appear confusing if not downright frightening; yet the work involved in dismantling and restoration is nowhere near being beyond the means of the average handyman who has the ability to use both his hands and his brain. Once the principles are mastered, the rest is easy.

My own interest in the player piano has been long, although I clearly recall that my first meeting with one filled me with horror. Encounters with other examples over the years went largely unnoticed until one day I found one which would not work. Out of curiosity, I set about giving it a new lease of life. The lack of suitable reference material at that time necessitated my learning the hard way. Now, many pianos later, I still cannot claim to know all the answers for there are so many different styles of player. Even so, all work on the same principle and, once this is understood, the task is made easier.

There is also the so-called 'barrel organ' or street piano to be found. The terms 'barrel organ' and 'piano organ' both enriched the confusion surrounding these devices during their heydays. Although exposed to rough use and all weathers and consequently committed to a short working life, quite a few still survive. Today they are mainly used as charity fund-raisers although some find their way into private collections and museums. These, too, need care, attention and regular maintenance – often more, it must be said, than their indoor brothers.

I well remember the first barrel piano I saw and I recall the first one I had to work on. It seemed to leer at me in grotesque, silent challenge. As with the pneumatic players, I had to learn the hard way but now, many examples later, I believe I understand most of their problems and know my solutions to them.

And so the idea of this book is to pass on the gentle art of preserving these things. I also include a brief look at roll-playing reed organs since these have a similar form of action to the player piano.

Fundamentally, all player pianos ought to be the same. They have perforated paper rolls which cause the piano hammers to strike the strings. Unfortunately the operating mechanism and its controls are never quite alike in any two brands of player and this makes any attempt at detailing one particular instrument potentially confusing for the owner of another make. This remains as much of a limitation to this present book as it did with my previous book *Player Piano* published in 1970. The solution would be to compose a gargantuan handbook covering every single type of player ever made (which would be prodigously expensive and have a very small market). I have therefore decided that the best course of action is to concentrate on the restoration of the more common types of player and then describe briefly some of the characteristics you may find in other types of instrument. Hence this book includes details of different types of action and considerable specific detail on the actions most frequently encountered. The subject of reproducing pianos and their individual adjustment is not accorded extensive space because the component parts follow standard pneumatic player principles and can thus easily be understood, and there are extensive details of their regulation readily available elsewhere, particularly in the form of reprints of the original instruction or factory manuals.

Several sources of references are open to those who seek specialist aid. In America, the Vestal Press, operated by mechanical-music enthusiast Harvey Roehl, reprints many items of early player memorabilia, including servicing and data sheets. In Britain there is the

Musical Box Society of Great Britain, which is devoted to mechanical musical instruments of all sorts and publishes a quarterly magazine which often contains items of player piano interest. Then there is also the Player Piano Group, whose quarterly bulletin is an additional source of interest.

Music rolls are also back in production. Admittedly it is no longer the vast business that it was once, but there are new rolls available, and several sources specialise in recuts of old rolls for the majority of player and reproducing systems. And, for the real enthusiast who has the patience, there are several new home roll-perforating machines on the market with the aid of which the musical amateur can punch his own music for his player piano.

The challenge presented by a dilapidated instrument in need of a rebuild is far less demanding than that of trying to set down in an intelligent manner the processes of tackling the job. I only hope I have succeeded.

The companion volume to this book, *Pianola – the history of the self-playing piano*, describes in depth the history of the player piano from the very first automatic stringed instruments through to the development of the barrel piano for both domestic and street use. It then traces the development of the pneumatic player piano and describes the various inventions which together assisted the instrument in attaining perfection in later years as the reproducing piano. An important chapter looks at the music of the reproducing piano and assesses just how accurate we are in describing it as a 'faithful reproduction of the original performance'. Appendices look at the part played by the player piano in teaching pilots to fly complex Second-World-War bombers, and two rare pamphlets – one on Aeolian's World's Music series of rolls and another on the Ampico – are reproduced in facsimile. Together these two books represent an invaluable reference library on the history of the self-playing piano and its preservation.

LYRAPHONE PIANO-PLAYER

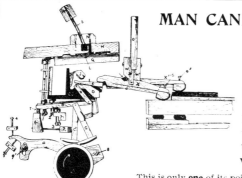

MAN CANNOT IMPROVE ON NATURE,

as was proved when Frankenstein produced his Monster ; but that

HE CAN EQUAL NATURE

has been evidenced by the wonderful "FLEXIBLE FINGERS" of the Lyraphone Piano=Player, by which remarkable invention this instrument is to=day in the proud position of being the ONLY one on the market with an absolutely "HUMAN TOUCH."

This is only **one** of its points of superiority over other piano-players—the chief one —but it has others ; among them being absolute control of tempo and expression, and ease of operating, the pedals only requiring a light uniform action, necessitating no extra exertion for shades of expression and tempo, these being absolutely independent of the pedalling ; in fact, so much so that electric motive power is ever more frequently being substituted for foot pedalling.

IN HAPPY HOMES

wholesome musical recreation is a vital feature. **YOUR** home can be made doubly attractive with one of these Lyraphones.

At the close of a busy day, what more restful pleasure can the tired business man find than in playing for himself a selection of such music as his mood requires? He can have that pleasure through his own efforts, and need never depend upon the skill of others. The Lyraphone will assist him. Its "flexible fingers" will attend to the difficult part—the manipulation of the keys. He can control everything—expression, tempo, pedals, etc.—and can play with the swing of the skilled artist. He, his wife, his son or his daughter can amuse and instruct themselves and each other, or their guests, without exertion and without the necessity of any previous musical training. In evidence, read the following two, of many, testimonials received from prominent business and professional men :

"I have now had a Lyraphone for nearly a year and do not hesitate to say that it is the best piano-player in every way on the market.

"The pedalling is easy ; the expression one can obtain from it is simply marvelous. I find that it is one of the greatest sources of pleasure and diversion a business man can have."

Yours truly,   JOHN M. LITTIG,
Pres. National Marine Bank, Baltimore.

"It gives me great pleasure to endorse the Lyraphone, the most finished attachment to the piano I have ever heard. The ability of this instrument to express music, to shade and modulate the tones, surely, to my mind, surpasses anything of the kind yet put upon the market.

"We have found the Lyraphone to be the most enjoyable addition to our country home."

Yours truly,   (Gen.) FELIX AGNUS, Proprietor of the "*Baltimore American.*"

AS AN EDUCATOR, the Lyraphone is unequaled, as it not only permits the finished and artistic performance of the most intricate and difficult music of the masters by any tyro without the years of drudgery entailed by learning the piano, but in the hands of the governess, the music-teacher, or the dancing-master, it is an invaluable adjunct to the teaching of singing and dancing. Read the following testimonials from prominent instructors of music :

"The Lyraphone piano-player plays everything with clearness and brilliancy of technique.

"Its flexible fingers are so marvelous that they put the boasted piano virtuoso to the blush.

"The Lyraphone will prove a boon to singers who wish to play their own accompaniments without the drudgery of years to learn piano playing. This I have tested with the utmost satisfaction with some of my pupils."

LEO KOFLER,
Instructor of Singing and Author of " The Art of Breathing as the Basis of Tone Production."

"The Lyraphone is certainly a very remarkable piano-player that appeals as readily to the musician as it does to the amateur.

"It can be readily adjusted to any pianoforte, and its wonderfully flexible fingers do the rest.

"The musician can give an expressive performance of a Beethoven or Mozart Sonata with all the desired subtleties of phrasing, tone color and tempi with the Lyraphone.

"Its advent means a quickened knowledge of the masterpiece by our little tots, without the fatigue of years of practice before they could otherwise become familiar with the compositions written by the masters who wrote for all time."

WM. F. T. MOLLENHAUER, Violin Virtuoso and Instructor.

The Lyraphone never hesitates. Does not have to be coaxed. Never gets nervous. It responds instantly. Never makes a mistake. Let the Lyraphone bring forth the melody from your silent piano. If your elder children who used to play it have grown up, married, and left the old home, let the younger ones enjoy its pleasures without any long course of study. **Buy them a Lyraphone.** Christmas will soon be here, and the important question arises—

What Shall I Give {HIM HER THEM} for Christmas ?

Let us answer this question for you.
GIVE A LYRAPHONE.

It is the ideal piano-player. **PRICE $225.00.** Electric motors from $25.00 to $35.00 extra. We have agents almost everywhere, but if not represented in your district, and if your local dealer does not carry Lyraphones in stock, address us direct.

N. B.—TO DEALERS : Agents wanted everywhere ; liberal terms offered for representation. It will pay you to send for catalogue and discount sheets.

SMITH LYRAPHONE COMPANY,   =   13 West Pratt Street, Baltimore, Md.

CHAPTER 1

Equipment for the Job

Before setting out on the restoration of an instrument, be it player piano or barrel piano, you will of course have to ensure that you have on hand certain tools and sundries in order that you can carry out the necessary work economically and adequately.

Now you can manage to overhaul an instrument with a few pretty basic tools but, if you want to be sure of making a good job and particularly if you are going to tackle more than just one instrument, then it is well worth investing in the right tools.

Always remember that cheap tools are the most expensive in the long run since you will end up having to replace them early on. Buy the very best you can get: it is false economy to do otherwise.

You will need a good, clear space in which to work. An outside lean-to will not do – it must be a clean and dry workroom, preferably well lit or, failing that, with ample provision for artificial light. A stout table or workbench will be needed, along with a random assortment of pieces of clean wood to use as packing and to aid in supporting components on the bench. And if you are planning on more than one piano, an absolutely invaluable device is a proper piano trolley. This is the name sometimes mistakenly given to a removal man's skid, which is a thick wooden board with four castors at the corners. This is not the same animal! A proper piano trolley has a pair of large-diameter central wheels and a smaller pair at each end. With the aid of this it is possible to move a piano up or down steps with ease and safety.

I assume that you have, for a start, a reasonably good set of hand tools. The minimum should include a large screwdriver having a ⅜ in. wide blade and a long (say 18 in.) shaft and a good, palm-sized handle; a few shorter and more average-sized screwdrivers and also a slender 'watchmakers'-type screwdriver with a ³⁄₁₆ in. wide blade. You will need an 8 oz hammer, a pair of heavy pliers, a pair of long-nosed pliers, a pair of round-nosed pliers (for forming the eye ends on music wire),* a pair of stout piano-wire cutters for music wire, a pair of side-cutters, and a wire brush. You will also need a pair of long, slender tweezers or forceps with legs about 8 in. long, a steel wire brush, some steel wire wool, a pair of heavy scissors, a carpenter's brace with screwdriver bit, sundry clean paint-brushes and a piano-tuning key or lever. This is properly termed a 'tuning hammer' and is a special socket-ended lever used to turn the tuning pins (wrest pins) for tuning the finished piano. If you have a small instrument you will probably find that you will need a tuning hammer with a rectangular socket end. The larger ones usually have the same size of tuning pin as an ordinary pianoforte. You must always use a properly fitting socket – never a spanner, adjustable or otherwise.

You could add to this list a set of piano-action regulating tools but I suggest that, unless you

---

* A proper piano-string looping tool is useful if you can afford the expense. It is a necessity if you have a lot of re-stringing work to do or if you plan to do more than one piano.

1

plan to go into things pretty deeply, you do not bother with these but give the task of overhauling and regulating the piano action itself to an expert. For this reason, then, this book does not concern itself with the actual regulation of pianos. There are several good books on this aspect of pianowork; one which is commendably clear is that by Art Reblitz, listed in the bibliography at the end of this book.

A set of tuning forks or a pitch-pipe will help you in tuning unless you are fortunate enough to possess perfect pitch or you have access to another keyboard instrument for pitch comparison. However, as we shall see, the question of pitch depends on the instrument and is not always as critical as in an instrument used in concert with others. Street pianos were often tuned to a different pitch, sometimes arbitrary!

Various other sundry items will be required as you proceed such as clean rags, graphite grease (for barrel piano cogs and clockwork motors), braided tape, pneumatic quality rubber cloth and so on. All of these I shall mention as we go along.

If you are going to work on reproducing pianos, then you will also need to have the proper servicing manual for the particular type of piano action you wish to work on, plus the correct test roll. These items are readily available.

Similarly, I have not included any advice on the restoration and refinishing of piano cabinetwork. This is much more akin to furniture restoration and there are any number of good books on that subject. All I would add is that any cabinet stripping and refinishing should be completed before the piano and player actions are replaced.

Two items of piano sundries will probably be needed – music wire and wrest pins. These are called up or specified in what, to the novice, may seem confusing terminology. The following tables should make it all clear.

COMPARATIVE TABLES OF MUSIC WIRE GAUGES, IMPERIAL AND METRIC DIAMETERS, STANDARD WIRE GAUGES AND APPROXIMATE LENGTH OF WIRE TO THE POUND IN FEET

Music Wire Gauge (MWG)	Inches	Millimetres	Feet length per pound	Standard Wire Gauge (S.W.G.)
00	·008	·213	5138	35
0	·009	·234	4716	34
1	·010	·254	3840	33
2	·011	·279	3415	32
3	·012	·305	2955	31
4	·013	·330	2581	30
5	·014	·356	2026	29
6	·016	·381	1553	28
7	·018	·432	1221	27
8	·020	·495	995	25
9	·022	·559	755	24
10	·024	·635	690	23
11	·026	·686	575	22
12	·029	·737	485	22
13	·031	·787	420	21
14	·033	·838	375	21
15	·035	·889	330	20
16	·037	·927	295	20
17	·038	·965	265	20
18	·040	1·016	235	19

Music Wire Gauge (MWG)	Inches	Millimetres	Feet length per pound	Standard Wire Gauge (S.W.G.)
19	·042	1·067	215	19
20	·044	1·105	200	19
21	·046	1·156	180	18
22	·048	1·206	165	18
23	·050	1·270	150	18
24	·053	1·372	130	17
25	·057	1·448	110	17
26	·061	1·550	95	16
27	·065	1·651	85	16
28	·069	1·753	75	15
29	·073	1·829	68	15
30	·077	1·930	61	14

WREST PIN DIAMETER (GAUGE) AND LENGTH CHART

Gauge No.	Dia. (ins)	Dia. (mm)	Length (ins)	Length (mm)
1	$^{17}/_{64}$	6·75	2	51
			$2\frac{1}{4}$	57
			$2\frac{3}{8}$	60
			$2\frac{1}{2}$	64
1/0	—	6·95	2	51
			$2\frac{1}{4}$	57
			$2\frac{3}{8}$	60
			$2\frac{1}{2}$	64
2/0	$^{9}/_{32}$	7·10	2	51
			$2\frac{1}{4}$	57
			$2\frac{3}{8}$	60
			$2\frac{1}{2}$	64
3/0	—	7·25	2	51
			$2\frac{1}{4}$	57
			$2\frac{3}{8}$	60
			$2\frac{1}{2}$	64
4/0	$^{19}/_{64}$	7·50	2	51
			$2\frac{1}{4}$	57
			$2\frac{3}{8}$	60
			$2\frac{1}{2}$	64

CHAPTER 2

Rebuilding the Barrel Piano

The barrel-playing piano is a very simple instrument. Although it was made in a number of sizes from the tiny Hicks-style portable through to the cart-mounted street and café clockwork varieties, it remained essentially a basic mechanism and as such its restoration is a relatively straightforward exercise. Directly descended from the 17th century clockwork spinets of Augsburg and the magnificent string-playing musical clocks of the 18th and early 19th century, its workings are easily followed. However, as with all mechanisms, regardless whether they are simple or complex, a thorough understanding of the way the instrument operates is essential if overhaul and restoration is to be successful. Before tackling the job, then, have a good look at the illustrations in this chapter and make sure that you follow the way the mechanism actually operates. Of prime concern is the relative position of the barrel to the keyframe; this is the main factor to observe if proper playing of the piano is to be achieved. Once you have grasped this, repair and regulation are largely a matter of applied common sense.

There are three types of barrel piano that you are likely to encounter. First is the small and very simple Hicks-type of portable piano, hand-operated and capable of being dismantled on the kitchen table. Then there is the large, hand-turned street barrel piano of comparable size and proportion to the conventional pianoforte. The third type is the clockwork café or public-house type of piano. A variation of this is the piano-orchestrion, sometimes of piano proportions but more usually in tall, vertical format and always characterised by the addition of a percussion department comprising instruments such as drum (occasionally bass and side drums), tubular bells, glockenspiel or xylophone, triangle, cymbal, castanets and tambourine. These various types are illustrated in Fig. 1.

To begin with, then, we shall take a look at the little portable street barrel piano of the type associated with the Bristol family of makers, Hicks (Fig. 2). This instrument is small enough to tackle on the workbench or kitchen table and if we can understand how this operates and become familiar with its parts and its principles, we are halfway along the road to tackling the larger instruments.

When you have one of these to restore, begin by carrying out a detailed examination to determine exactly what work must be done to bring it back to perfect playing condition, then see what parts, if any, must be made. Finally, assess what work needs to be done to the case to restore its appearance. Since most of these very early portable pianos can be classified as rarities and antiques, remember that your aim should be to restore, conserve and preserve. Resist the temptation to try to improve on the original in any way. And, as a matter of good museum practice, keep a record of the work you do, write it or type it out on a piece of paper

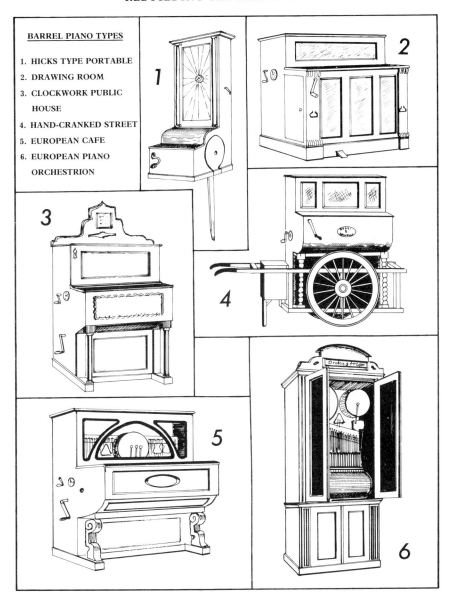

BARREL PIANO TYPES

1. HICKS TYPE PORTABLE
2. DRAWING ROOM
3. CLOCKWORK PUBLIC
   HOUSE
4. HAND-CRANKED STREET
5. EUROPEAN CAFE
6. EUROPEAN PIANO
   ORCHESTRION

Figure 1   Various types of mechanically-played barrel pianos

with your name, address and date and conceal it somewhere in the instrument for the benefit of a later owner or restorer. With large instruments, you can easily seal this document in an envelope and pin it behind the soundboard to one of the posts. If new parts have to be made, always try to preserve the original which you are replacing. Later generations may learn something from the original which is not apparent to you today.

Begin by dismantling the instrument. The barrel access door on the right-hand side of the

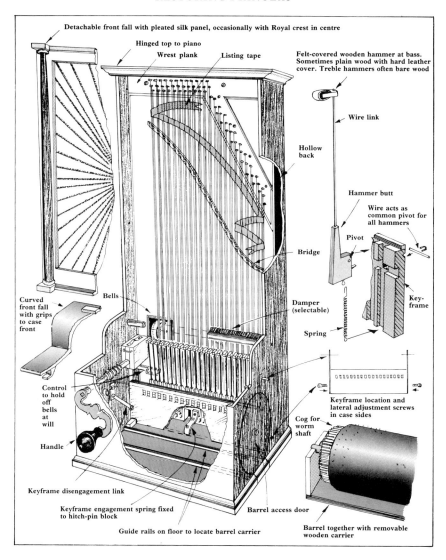

Detachable front fall with pleated silk panel, occasionally with Royal crest in centre

Hinged top to piano

Wrest plank

Listing tape

Felt-covered wooden hammer at bass. Sometimes plain wood with hard leather cover. Treble hammers often bare wood

Wire link

Hollow back

Hammer butt

Wire acts as common pivot for all hammers

Pivot

Bridge

Key-frame

Bells

Curved front fall with grips to case front

Damper (selectable)

Spring

Control to hold off bells at will

Handle

Keyframe location and lateral adjustment screws in case sides

Cog for worm shaft

Keyframe disengagement link

Keyframe engagement spring fixed to hitch-pin block

Barrel access door

Guide rails on floor to locate barrel carrier

Barrel together with removable wooden carrier

Figure 2   The English portable street piano of the type made by Hicks in Bristol

case is usually secured either by a wire which passes down through the case side (seen when the front panel and barrel lid are removed) or by a turn-button on the inside of the door. You will see that this door has two little locating studs protruding from its flat bottom edge which engage in holes in the bottom of the case side. Since this door provides the end bearing for the barrel, its security is vital and if these studs are missing or if the holes into which they fit are oversize you will have to make good the deficiency with new studs made of sawn-off short wire nails or by inserting a new strip of wood into the case into which you can bore new holes.

The action of the keyframe is controlled by a cam on the outside left of the case. Turning the cam pushes the keyframe away from the barrel, so moving the tails of the hammers away from the barrel pins. This is so that, when the barrel is shifted, there is no fear of hammer tails and barrel pins making contact and becoming broken or bent. The keyframe must be moved to this 'free' position before shifting the barrel and if it does not move – due, say, to the linkage being loose, missing or broken – then you must push the frame back against its spring with a long screwdriver and hold it there while the barrel is withdrawn from the other side of the case.

Take out the door and you will now be able to see the end of the barrel. Usually this is supported in a wooden cradle to facilitate sliding the barrel in and out, but sometimes the cradle is missing. Its absence does not affect the working of the instrument, although it is a good idea to make up a simple cradle so that, when the door is removed, the barrel does not drop down on the pins at that end.

Hold the barrel end by the protruding spindle with the right hand, raise the tune-selecting knife (Fig. 3) on the other end of the case with the left hand, and draw out the barrel,

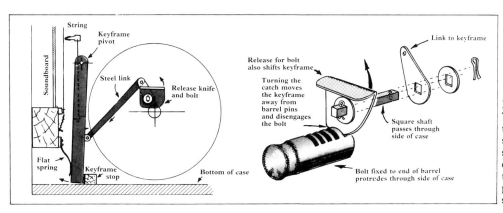

Figure 3
The Hicks-type barrel shifting system for changing tunes on portable street pianos

watching carefully to see that the pins do not foul the case round the doorway. Remove all loose dust and dirt with a brush. Because barrels are made of softwood, they are often found to be infested with woodworm. More often than not this can be cured and all made well again. At this stage it is a good plan to treat any infestation with a proprietary worm-killer. Use this liberally and let it soak well into any infected parts, particularly the barrel ends and the drive cog. Because several applications will be needed to do this job properly and because it is advisable to allow a day or so between each treatment, the sooner you apply the first treatment the better.

With the barrel out of the instrument, you can now remove the crank handle by turning it anticlockwise while holding the worm-shaft still. Originally, these handles were threaded on to the end of the worm-shaft as far as a protruding stop so that they could be removed easily without the handle having become 'thread-bound'. Sometimes this protruding dog is missing and you may have to apply a little force to unscrew the handle. Now take off the bearing block which supports the inside end of the worm-shaft. This is fixed with two screws from the outside of the left of the case. When the block is free, a little juggling is often necessary to free both it and the worm-shaft from the case, the worm-shaft having to be moved back a little to free it from its bearing in the case front.

7

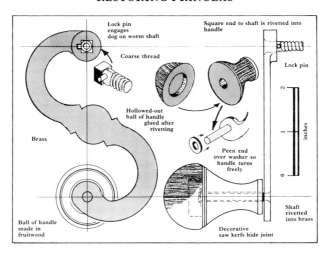

Figure 4   How to make a new handle for the portable street barrel piano

Disconnect the tune-selecting knife, the keyframe linkage and the cam and set them aside for cleaning. All the brass parts, including the handle and worm-shaft, can be treated with any suitable metal polish. Stubborn dirt stains – common enough on these parts – can be removed with a brass wire brush or the application of a piece of fine, worn emery-cloth lubricated with metal polish.

The keyframe is next on the list and this is taken out by springing the right-hand-side strip clear of its pivot in the case. Insert the blade of a screwdriver between the strip and the case and twist gently to do this. The frame can now be turned a little to clear the bearing, disengaged from the pivot at the other end, and lifted clear of the case.

You are now left with the empty piano case complete with the stringed portion or 'strung back'. If the strings are all present and in fairly good condition, there is no need to remove them unless the wrest plank is badly split or the wrest-pins loose. The wrest-pins should all protrude from the wrest-plank at the same angle – a little above the horizontal. If any are at variance with this norm, it is a good indication that the pins have become loose in worn, oversize holes, or that the wrest-plank itself is split.

Most of these pianos employed a strung back having twenty-three notes. On most instruments the tuning scale was marked above each pin, there normally being three strings to each note over the tenor and treble parts of the scale, the bass notes having two or just one string. Only the bass notes are what is called 'wrapped'. Wrapped strings have copper wire coiled round them so that they vibrate at a low frequency without having to be so loose that they flop around.

Assuming that the piano is in the worst condition, we will continue to strip the instrument but do bear in mind that, if the instrument is basically sound at this point, there is no need to proceed further and you can continue with replacing any broken or missing strings, tuning and reassembly.

As in full-size pianos, the strings are not all of the same thickness: usually at least three different gauges of wire are used, the thinnest for the highest notes. Again, the bass notes are wrapped strings, so these have to be considered separately. If possible, measure the gauge of

8

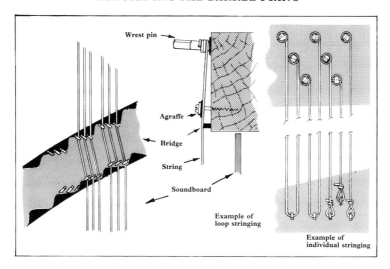

Figure 5   Details of piano stringing

the wires before removing them, or at any rate keep specimen strings and mark which groups of notes used the same gauge of wire. There are some more points to make on wire later on.

To remove a string, slacken off the wrest-pin first, unhook the string from its lower peg (hitch-pin) at the bottom of the strung back, and then uncoil it from the wrest-pin. It is not advisable to remove the actual wrest-pin unless it is so loose that it can be pulled out with the fingers. This is because the wrest-pin was originally a very tight fit in the board and its unnecessary removal will make it looser on replacement. Again, if the pins are taken out to be cleaned (they are often rusty), do not clean the portion which fits into the wood.

If the wrest-pins are loose the piano will not stay in tune, since the tension of each string will exert a torque greater than the frictional resistance offered by its wrest-pin in the wrest-plank. Resistance can often be improved by removing the pin and thoroughly rubbing the shank with powdered resin. If the wrest-plank holes are slightly oversize and the pins still turn, then you must carefully redrill them very slightly larger, making sure that the drill goes in at the proper angle. Fit new oversize pins which you can get from the piano sundries supplier. Should the new pins be a little too long, you may legitimately drill the holes sufficiently deep so that the string hole on the new pin lines up with those in the other pins. If the wrest-plank holes are very badly oversize, ream them out to a clean, circular shape and plug them with a hardwood peg well glued in. Trim this off flush with the plank when dry and drill slightly undersize to take the pin. At all times when removing wrest-pins use plenty of powdered resin on them before replacing. Remember, by the way, that the shanks of these pins are, in fact, slightly threaded and so they should be screwed in with the tuning key.

But to return to the dismantling of the piano. With all the strings removed, brush out all the accumulation of dust and dirt from inside the instrument. You may choose to scrub the inside of the case with a little water and detergent, but do not overwet the wood or allow it to soak up too much moisture. Again, do not wash the actual soundboard, which is of thin spruce or clear pine. Wiping it with a damp cloth and detergent should be sufficient to restore its brilliance. You can rub down the sound-board with fine sandpaper and revarnish it if you

9

wish. Stains are best removed by scraping with the grain, using a single-edged razor-blade before sanding.

Examine the bridge very carefully for secureness, cracks and missing bridge pins. It must be securely glued to the soundboard and the pins which align each string must be all present and correct. Missing or broken ones can be replaced by panel pins but these must be inserted at the proper angle. Do not try to knock them to the proper angle after driving them in straight – that will split the bridge.

If the soundboard is cracked or split, it must be restored to one homogeneous mass since it is the sound resonator and amplifier of the piano and splits will diminish the volume of sound produced, make parts of the scale sound 'dead' and, in bad cases, cause a disagreeable vibration or buzzing sound. Ideally, try always to work from the back of the soundboard. This means removing it by carefully prising off the small wooden moulding around its boundaries and then easing the whole board out. In some early pianos, though, it was firmly glued into place and cannot be taken out. If the back of the piano is cased and veneered, as in early ones, you can only work from the front, raking out narrow cracks and forcing in hot brown glue and thin strips of softwood filling. If you can get to the back of the board, glue a patch of short-grained wood veneer about ½ in. or ¾ in. wide over the split. Wipe surplus glue from the front face of the soundboard with a damp cloth and leave to set. Do not, incidentally, nail or tack the veneer strip, but press it with weights or wedges of scrap wood to

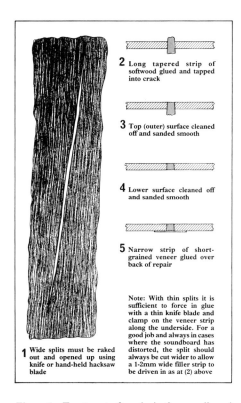

1 Wide splits must be raked out and opened up using knife or hand-held hacksaw blade

2 Long tapered strip of softwood glued and tapped into crack

3 Top (outer) surface cleaned off and sanded smooth

4 Lower surface cleaned off and sanded smooth

5 Narrow strip of short-grained veneer glued over back of repair

Note: With thin splits it is sufficient to force in glue with a thin knife blade and clamp on the veneer strip along the underside. For a good job and always in cases where the soundboard has distorted, the split should always be cut wider to allow a 1-2mm wide filler strip to be driven in as at (2) above

Figure 6   Treatment of cracks in the soundboard

10

exert setting pressure. See that in packing to apply setting pressure you do not distort or dish the soundboard.

In the case of bad splits, proceed as above but force in shaped strips of well glued softwood. When set, remove surplus wood and glue with the bevelled edge of a broad wood chisel.

Sometimes the soundboard is badly bowed. Usually there is not much you can do about that and, so long as the bow does not touch the strings and still allows the strings to press down on the bridge with a reasonable bearing (see Fig. 7), it is better to leave it alone. Where,

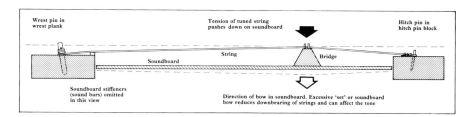

Figure 7   String bearing on the soundboard

though, bowing is excessive, remove the soundbars from the back, straighten them or, if very bad, remake them, and refit. Should that not be possible, make a new soundboard from top-quality boat-builder's clear pine or sitka spruce. Follow the grain direction, dimensions and, particularly, the thickness of the original.

Examine the wrest-plank for splits, in particular around the pin holes. If there are any they may loosen the wrest-pins to a greater or lesser extent. I have mentioned that if the wrest-pins are slightly loose, you can probably rectify the problem by rubbing powdered resin on them, and that if they are very much oversize and distorted, allowing the pins to pull downwards under the tension of the strings, you should plug the holes and rebore. Splits come in two sorts: the facing of the wrest-plank is a veneer about $1/16$ in. thick and this sometimes cracks. This is not very serious although it often looks worse than it is. You can fill up these cracks with hot brown glue. Much more serious, however, are deep splits where the pins have acted as wedges to split open the plank along its grain. Here the best remedy is to fit a new plank using straight, well seasoned and very dry maple, beech or ash. Failing that, proceed as before by gluing hardwood plugs into the pin holes, force very hot glue (or synthetic resin glue) into the splits and then clamp the whole lot up very tightly for a week or so to dry out. Then redrill for the pins through the centre of the plugs. This sometimes works, but if the problem is bad enough to call for this treatment, then replacement of the whole plank is the only really satisfactory solution. Sometimes only part of a plank may be affected, so this technique is certainly worth trying first. After plugging a wrest-pin hole, always drill the new hole in exactly the same position or, if you have to alter the position, adjust it upwards or downwards – *never* to one side, which would throw the string out of alignment with the hammers. A cake icing syringe or a hypodermic syringe (a glass one, not plastic) is ideal for forcing glue into awkward placcs.

Where no splits in the wrest-plank are obvious, but the wrest-pins are still loose, a preparation available from piano-tuners and sundries stockists will tighten them up. To apply this, you must again lay the case down so that the wrest-plank is horizontal and then paint the special liquid round the loose pins, leaving it overnight to soak in and do its job.

The next job is restringing. Equip yourself with a 1-ounce coil of each of the necessary gauges of wire for the unwrapped strings. Cut each string about 6 inches longer than is required and form a small eye on one end with the round-nosed pliers. See that the loose end is securely wrapped round the body of the wire as otherwise it will unwind under the tension needed to tune it.

Begin with the longest unwrapped string and hook it on to its proper peg at the bottom of the harp.* Lead the wire straight up to the wrest-pin – make sure that you line up with the right one – and cut the wire exactly 1¾ inches longer so that you have that much wire protruding above the pin. Take a pair of flat pliers and bend over the last ⅜ inch to a right angle. Thread this bent end through the hole in the wrest-pin and, using the tuner's key, turn the pin in a clockwise direction to take most of the slack out of the wire. You will find that the amount of overlength on the wire gives you about two and a half turns on the pin. The exact number is immaterial – two to three is usual – but they should all be the same. See that the coils lie side by side and do not overlap each other. Before applying the last half turn of tension, tap the end of the wrest-pin with a hammer to make sure that it is properly home in the wrest-plank. Now thread the lower end of the wire around its proper bridge pins. This serves to stop off the length of string which is capable of producing the desired note for given tension. Bring each string just tight and no more until all the wires are in place. Proceed with all the strings in this manner, lining each one properly in place on the wrest-plank and also its bridge pins.

A word now about the gauge of wires on these pianos. Without overstepping the limits of justifiable restoration, one can decidedly alter the tone by restringing with slightly thinner wire. The effect is to brighten the tone and often to accentuate the treble and tenor registers – these last frequently being 'woolly'. It is entirely up to the restorer what he does here, but I have been agreeably surprised at the improved tone achieved by restringing a 23-note Hicks piano with strings two gauges thinner throughout (for 36-gauge wire I used 38-gauge). Needless to say, you should not try to use thinner wire for the wrapped bass strings as these are best left as intended. A major reason for restringing with a slightly thinner wire is to reduce the strain on an elderly piano. There are other things which you can do, legitimately, to amend tonality and these will be discussed further on.

Wrapped bass strings are readily obtainable and, since it is not possible to cut down regular pianoforte strings because of the resultant loosening of the winding, it is far better to get a piano repair merchant to make them up for you. He will need to know the gauge of the music wire and also the gauge of the copper winding plus the exact distance from the eye end (hitch-pin) to the wrest-pin. Ideally the original string should be given as a pattern. Larger merchants will usually make you a new string whilst you wait. Confide in them that you are restoring a barrel piano – a little cultivated interest will generally get you a better and quicker service!

The next stage is tuning, and this is a job which will take several days – sometimes a week – to do properly, for the strings must be allowed to stretch and the piano harp-frame allowed to move. The combined load on the wrest-plank when all the strings are tensioned is quite considerable and it is perfectly normal for the plank to warp a little. Excessive deformation now or at any time in its previous career will result in splitting or tearing away from the supports.

* The term 'harp' here is used to refer to the strung portion of the piano which, in full-sized instruments, is also referred to as the 'strung back'.

The technique of tuning these street pianos is somewhat arbitrary. They were never intended to produce concert music, nor were they intended to be tuned to a set pitch. The fact that the notes may be lettered to the scale again means little for you can call any pitch of sound 'C', for example, and create a perfect scale to that note. Remember that the divisions of the scale in music are indications of the relationship of one note to another in a series and that relationship remains constant regardless of the basis from which the scale starts. This cannot, of course, apply to *consort* music otherwise one would have a jarring clash of sound and so for this type of music the first step in the scale must no longer be arbitrary but is defined very precisely by the number of cycles which a string vibrates in a second. That first step in the scale (or any other step defined as being a precise distance in pitch above or below it) is qualified by the number of cycles and can be identified by the use of a tuning fork or a pitch-pipe. What you actually call a note is of interest purely where the instrument is to perform music with other instruments or with a singer. For this reason, it is sometimes not only difficult but quite impossible to tune a street piano to the correct concert pitch of the notes shown on the wrest-plank.

The tuner therefore has to lay out the foundations for his scale without necessarily being influenced too much by his letter 'C' tuning fork and the note 'C' on the normal piano.* When tackling a piano which has some or all of its original strings still *in situ*, it is sometimes possible to find the scale basis by plucking the bass notes, for these are the least likely to have got out of tune as they are subjected to less tension. From this a note can be found – preferably C – from which to set off a tenor C or middle C. If the piano harp is badly warped or if it has been split, it is a good idea and perfectly acceptable to lower the pitch slightly (throughout the instrument, of course) to reduce the tension of the strings.

After you have found the strings on the harp lettered 'C' and tuned them to a pitch (note that I am not necessarily saying that these should be to concert pitch C), proceed up the scale. For the non-musical, the tonic sol-fa scale is quite helpful in identifying pitch intervals and this corresponds to normal musical notation as follows, starting the scale from C:

C	C♯	D	D♯	E	F	F♯	G	G♯	A	B♭	B	C
doh		ray		me	fah		soh		lah		te	doh

Because the scale starts and stops with the letter C, we have set out an octave. At this point, do not worry about the intermediate notes (the black notes on the pianoforte), which are C♯, D♯, F♯, G♯ and B♭. Just concentrate on the 'natural' notes of the scale.

A treatise on piano tuning is out of place here and I intend only to set out the rudiments of the science. For those who wish to delve much further into the art and the skills, there are several good handbooks on the subject. Back, however, to our amateur tuning which will suffice for the street piano. The chances are that we shall end up with an instrument that sounds better than it did at the time it was first made in spite of our limited experience and skills.

---

*Note that very early instruments (pre-1880) will have been tuned to a different pitch and instruments of a much earlier era may be tuned to a different temperament. As regards the establishment of the scale, I am reminded of the words of Pietro Aaron in his *Toscanello in Musica*, written soon after 1500. He says: 'You must first consider the string or degree called C, giving it whatever pitch you please . . .'

If you can tune to a pitch-pipe, so much the better. But if you have had to set off your own scale, then you must usually resort to what we will call comparative tuning. Briefly, this consists of producing notes which are in perfect concord with each other.* If you have a good ear for music and for pitch, you will easily be able to detect the notes which fall in concordance and the steps are as follows, starting with the foundation of C.

C	E and D
C and E	D and B
C and G	C and F
E and C (octave)	F and A

Begin by concentrating on one octave and tune all the naturals in that – this means the 'white' notes as listed above. Now you can proceed downwards from the 'middle C', and then upwards to the treble. You can do this easily by tuning in octave unison, one note at a time, from the foundation notes you have already established in the centre of the piano harp. At this point, go back and check through that first octave to see that it is still in tune. The tension may have warped the wrest-plank slightly, so flattening the pitch of the notes. If this has happened, retune to the same principles.

Now you can tune the sharps and any flats. Few of the small pianos are fully chromatic, that is to say few of them have all thirteen notes in the scale, and so you will only have to bother with perhaps F♯ and G♯ and C♯.

Once you have tuned all the sharps and flats in the foundation octave, tune those in the octaves above and below. If you have restrung the harp, it is better to set the instrument on one side for a day or two and allow the strings to stretch and the frame to accustom itself to the strain.

Do remember one of the fundamentals of piano tuning, and that is that the tuning lever has to be treated gently when 'pulling up' a string. The higher up the scale you go, the greater the tension of the strings relative to their length and gauge and also the less you must turn the lever to adjust them. Also, because the string is in two parts (the part between the wrest-pin and the bridge and that between the bridge and the hitch-pin), it is necessary to overtighten the string a semitone and then bring it down to the correct pitch to help to even out the tension in the two halves. Even so, a piano needs frequent adjustment until it will hold its tune for a reasonable length of time and this is because the bridge pins effectively break the string into two lengths and it takes a while for both halves to assume the same tension.

As I have said, a treatise on piano tuning here is unwise. To tune a concert grand requires a practised ear and several years of training. Because you can tune a barrel piano does not mean you are a piano tuner. You are an amateur and may remain so for good! I recommend reading the little book *How to Tune a Piano* by H. Staunton Woodman.

Before leaving the subject of tuning, I would add that the barrel piano, with its wooden frame, will not hold its tune for long. I expect to have to tune my own instruments at least once a week, particularly if they are in regular use since the act of hammering a string helps to stretch the string and loosen the wrest-pins a fraction. Not that you will have to lay your foundations all over again – it is just a question of a little polishing up of the pitch here and there and need take no more than fifteen minutes.

---

*This is not strictly true since to tune to perfect pitch there must be very slight variations. For the street piano with its problems of remaining in perfect tune for very long, though, I feel we can overlook these.

Next you must service the keyframe. The Hicks and Distin type used very long, thin, brass springs on the hammers – shown in Fig. 2 – and these frequently become brittle with age and disintegrate. Whilst a very good temporary repair is the ubiquitous rubber band, this is neither permanent nor practical and you should make new springs. Use the thinnest possible music wire (called 'oo' in music wire gauge or ·008 inch in diameter) and wrap your new spring around a piece of 16 standard wire gauge (s.w.g.) piano wire, obtainable from a model-maker's store. Ideally, you should hold the thick wire in the chuck of a slow-turning drill and wind on the music wire to make a tight, even-coiled spring of sufficient length (about ½ inch less than the overall length between hammer and spring-peg).* Slide the new spring off the wire mandrel. Form the loop ends and fit the new spring, noting that at the hammer end it is fixed with a thread loop. If the loop is broken, make a new one of button-thread poked through with a needle and knotted into place.

All the hammers should have the same spring tension – this is important. When the springs have become weak, either shorten them if they will take such treatment without breaking or make new ones. See that the hammers move freely in their slots in the frame. Do not remove them unless absolutely necessary (this is achieved by withdrawing the hinge wire) as this will necessitate the probable undoing of all the springs, risking breakage. If the hammers are stiff, pump powdered graphite into the gaps on each side to lubricate. Never use oil or grease – this will clog them even worse and attract dust and dirt. The ideal graphite to use is of the type sold by locksmiths to free and lubricate door locks and it usually comes in a puff-container. It is marketed in Britain under several brand names, one of which is Foliac.

Now look at the hammer heads. If they are leather-covered, see that the leather is properly attached – it frequently springs away at the top and bottom of the hammer. If the leather is grooved where it has been in prolonged contact with the music strings, then you may be able to tease it with a fine wire brush. On larger instruments which use felt-covered hammers similar to those on a pianoforte, you can 'needle' the felt or reshape the hammers with a file as described later on. If the leather facings are very hard, as is quite usual on the older instruments, it is better to replace all the leathers using skin of matching quality and thickness. Remember that the harder the surface of the skin, the more strident the tone: the softer the skin, the more mellow the sound produced. Usually you will find that a thin chrome leather or fully stretched skin makes a good replacement. On larger and heavier hammers you can use a piece of thin kangaroo skin of the type used for making bellows flap-valves in the pneumatic player piano. Never re-cover just one or two hammers: do the lot, otherwise the tone will be uneven.

See that the keyframe hinge-pivot support arms are not loose and at the same time check that the strip steel spring in the bottom of the case which pushes the frame out from the back is in good order. Renew the strip of thick and fairly hard felt against which all the hammers rest. The old stuff often goes rock hard and lets the hammers lie badly. Replace with a good piano felt. Also renew the pads on the blocks in the case bottom against which the keyframe rests when backed away from the barrel.

A frequent point of wear and damage is at the hammer tails. These are made of a hardened steel and are consequently very brittle: they may sometimes be bent slightly but respond to rough treatment by breaking off. Once a hammer tail is broken off flush with the wooden

---

* You must hold the thin wire in stout leather gloves during winding otherwise it will slice through your flesh by friction. Be warned!

15

hammer butt, the chances are that you will not be able to grasp the stump with the pliers to draw it out. By far the most satisfactory means of repairing hammer tails in this state is to cut away a little wood all around the broken pin using a modelling knife or scalpel until enough of the metal is exposed to enable you to get a grip on it with fine pliers or even the side cutters. Gently ease out the root of the pin, twisting it a little as it comes to free it from the inevitable rusting in the wood. Make your replacement from hard steel stock or from thick piano wire, which you can grind up to square section on a small grindstone. Do not let the hardened wire get too hot in this process, otherwise you will destroy the hardness and temper. Alternatively, you can use an ordinary 2 inch wire nail, again grinding it up to the proper cross-section on the grindstone or with a flat file. Now harden it by heating it to blood red, quenching it in water, polishing it on fine emery, reheating to a light straw colour and then quickly quenching in oil. Because wire nails are made of low-carbon steel, this will leave the new pin slightly more flexible to allow for any gentle bending necessary in realignment while at the same time being sufficiently hard on the surface. Now fill the hole in the wooden hammer butt with synthetic resin glue such as Araldite and press in the new pin. See that it lines up exactly with all the others along the keyframe and that it is spaced equally with all the others. Leave the glue to set for the proper length of time, file up the point to the correct protrusion by lining up with a straightedge and a rule, refit the hammer frame, reconnect the linkage which provides for moving the frame in and out while changing the tune, and see that it is properly pressed by the case spring.

The next operation is to attend to the barrel or cylinder. Wash the surface by brushing it with benzine applied liberally to the surface. Remember that benzine is highly inflammable: do not smoke and preferably do this job out in the open air. I do not recommend using petrol for this job since it leaves a deposit on the paper covering to the barrel. While the benzine is on the barrel, look to see if there is a watermark date visible in the paper – there sometimes is! If the barrel is fitted into a carrier, see that it is not loose or broken and make good any slack joints. The carrier should slide easily in the rails provided for it in the bottom of the case. See that the tune-changing stud is tightly fixed to the barrel but *do not turn it* as this will throw the registration of the tunes out of true.

Any badly bent barrel pins should now be straightened with fine, flat pliers. The pins were almost always made of thick, fairly soft, brass wire, so there is little danger of their breaking off.

At this point, carry out any final treatment of the case which you think necessary. To finish cases, French polish or wax polish should be used rather than paint or varnish.

Refit the brasswork to the case (tune-change knife and so on), and refit the crank-handle and worm-drive shaft, firmly screwing its block to the case. See to it that the sprung, adjustable bearing piece for the inside bearing of the worm-shaft is working properly – this is intended to diminish wear and tear on the barrel cog by keeping the worm in firm contact with it.

One tricky job may yet remain to be done to the barrel. Sometimes the wooden barrel cog-teeth become worn away. Where worm has infested the barrel, the cog-teeth may have been weakened so much that they have crumbled to a useless state. If the cog is extensively crumbled, then the only solution is to carve up a new cog from a beech log whose centre becomes the barrel axis. Make certain that the new cog is precisely the same diameter as the old one. If you cannot make a new one yourself, a cabinetmaker should be able to oblige but he will want the barrel as a guide. Show him the delicate pins and then wrap them in foam plastic packing so as not to damage them.

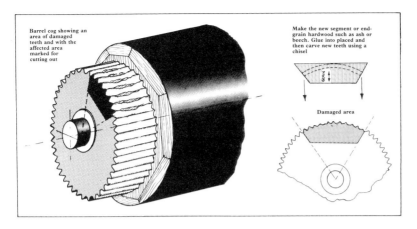

Barrel cog showing an area of damaged teeth and with the affected area marked for cutting out

Make the new segment or end-grain hardwood such as ash or beech. Glue into placed and then carve new teeth using a chisel

Damaged area

Figure 8   How to repair a section of worn barrel drive cog

Where the cogs are only partly worn, you can make a new insert yourself, spiling off the profile for the new piece from part of the existing cog. Where one or two teeth only are damaged, you can cut in a new tooth by notching the cog and gluing in a strip of straight-grained ash or beech, carving it to shape when set. The illustration Fig. 8 shows these steps clearly.

Fit the barrel back into the piano, seeing that it is located properly in the bearing provided for the brass pivots at each side. The right-hand bearing is in the barrel access door. If these bearings are loose or sloppy, then the instrument will not work properly and you should have new ones made to fit into the woodwork. There should be about $\frac{1}{64}$ inch maximum side play in the bearings – some play is not only unavoidable but actually desirable otherwise the access door cannot be angled into its location when supporting the barrel bearing.

Check two things at this point – first that the keyframe does in fact clear the barrel pins when in the proper position, and second that the keyframe is parallel to the barrel and not leaning closer to one end than the other. If the former applies, you must adjust the linkage and probably make a new connecting link of slightly different size. If the latter is the case, then there are two small wooden blocks in the case bottom against which the keyframe is encouraged to rest by its spring. One or both of these may be missing, or they may need replacing. This is easy – they are only small pieces of $\frac{1}{2}$ inch square lumber. Face each one with a leather or felt pad.

With the tune-selector knife engaged in the first slot in the barrel stud, see that the hammer tails are in line with the pins. Play the instrument and see that it performs a recognisable tune and is not in fact playing part of two tunes at once. On some instruments, there is a small screw through the side of the case with which the keyframe can be moved laterally just sufficient to bring the hammer tails into register with the barrel pins. Where this is not fitted, you must pack one or the other of the keyframe pivots with a thin washer to move the frame over a little.

It is quite likely that the instrument will sound very tinny and devoid of resonance. This is because the hammers, instead of just striking the strings and springing back clear of them, are remaining in contact after striking, so muting the strings. Earlier I mentioned the

17

importance of having all the hammer springs of the same strength so that the hammers all offered the same resistance to the barrel pins on the hammer tails. Now you must ensure that the hammers, when at rest, are not touching the strings. As the hammer heads are fixed to stiff wires which pierce the hammer block, all you have to do is to bend the hammers to achieve a nominal clearance of about ¹/₁₆ inch. When bending the hammers, bend the wire by holding the end of the wire close to the hammer block and do not, for example, take hold of the hammer head and try to use it to lever the wire. This will split the head and can crack the block. Bend only the wire.

At this point the piano will begin to produce acceptable music. Bear in mind that the hammer tails must lie in a straight line parallel to the axis of the barrel both in plan and elevation, that the pins must be straight in the barrel and that the hammer tails must all be firm in their blocks.

The last job on the mechanism is to damp off the 'dead' portion of the music strings above the bridge. This is done by threading cotton tape through the strings as shown in the illustration (Fig. 9). Use ⅝ inch or ¾ inch wide cotton bias binding in red or crimson to

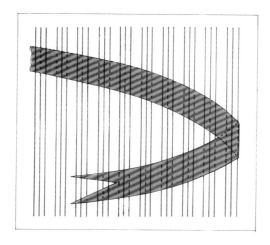

Figure 9   How listing tape is threaded through the non-sounding parts of the strings

match the original. The tape is easily threaded between the strings with a wire hook. The fish-mouth ends serve both for decoration and to prevent fraying. The proper name for this tape is 'listing' and without it no barrel piano will play clearly.

Your portable barrel piano should now play perfectly. Where a damper is fitted, it is usually nothing more complicated than a round wooden rod traversing the strings just above the hammers and carrying in a slot along its length a strip of felt. The rod, protruding through the case side, has a knob by which it can be turned to press the felt strip on to the strings. You may have to replace tattered or moth-eaten felt here. Some pianos were also equipped with two small bells of indeterminate pitch which were secured on a bracket let into a cut-out in the soundboard and struck by the two hammers at the extreme left. There was usually a method of disconnecting these during playing – generally a knob on the left outside of the case which rotated a U-shaped wire against the hammer connecting wires, so pushing them clear of the barrel pins which controlled them.

18

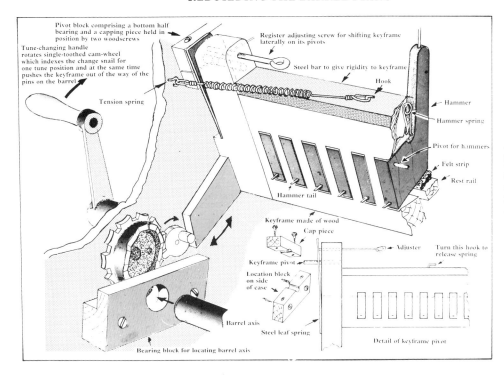

Pivot block comprising a bottom half
bearing and a capping piece held in
position by two woodscrews

Register adjusting screw for shifting keyframe
laterally on its pivots

Tune-changing handle
rotates single-toothed cam-wheel
which indexes the change snail for
one tune position and at the same time
pushes the keyframe out of the way of the
pins on the barrel

Steel bar to give rigidity to keyframe

Hook

Tension spring

Hammer

Hammer spring

Pivot for hammers

Felt strip

Rest rail

Hammer tail

Keyframe made of wood

Cap piece

Adjuster

Turn this hook to
release spring

Keyframe pivot

Location block
on side
of case

Barrel axis

Steel leaf spring

Detail of keyframe pivot

Bearing block for locating barrel axis

Figure 10
How tunes
are changed
on the
larger type
of street
barrel piano

LARGE STREET PIANOS

I have so far been describing the portable barrel piano. Once you have mastered the action of the little piano and understood both the principles and practice of overhaul and repair of such instruments, it is but a small step to the much larger street barrel pianos, café or clockwork pianos and piano orchestrions. All contrive to achieve the same end – the striking of strings by hammers controlled from pins on a barrel. And all may be treated by the intelligent application of the foregoing. There are notable differences and some important points to watch, so let us now look at the popular street piano of the type usually seen on a handcart.

The illustration Fig. 10 shows the operation of the tune-changing mechanism of the large street piano. A progressive snail cam shifts the barrel 'odd numbers' one way and then back on 'even numbers'. Because the instrument is so much bigger than the small piano, yet since the relative distances between the rows of pins for the tunes are small, it is easier to get out of adjustment, out of register and consequently out of order.

To strip the instrument, first of all you must open the door in the right end of the case. This door is doweled into the case at the bottom and is locked in the proper position by one or sometimes two stout, wooden turn-buttons. The door also carries a stiff leaf-spring to hold the barrel firmly against the change cams at the other end of the case, and the right-hand barrel axis bearing.

On the left-hand side of the case will be found a handle. Turning this handle produces two effects. As you can see from Fig. 10, it works exactly the same way as a Geneva stopwork on a clock spring motor. One rotation of the handle indexes the snail cam one position. However, as well as doing this, it also lifts the keyframe away from the barrel for the duration of the critical lateral shift of the barrel from one snail cam to the next, so avoiding the chance of damage to the barrel pins and the hammer tails. Thanks to this contrivance, it is possible to change tunes in the middle of playing the instrument without fear of damage, since the keyframe is only lowered to the barrel pins again when the lateral shift is completed. Set this handle in such a position that the keyframe is at the limit of its travel away from the barrel and see that, in fact, the pins are clear. If they are not, then you can wedge the frame further away by using one or more large screwdrivers pushed between case block and keyframe at each end.

There is no knife or bolt to secure the barrel – it is now quite free to be removed. Some barrels originally had carriers or cradles but these may have been lost or discarded. The removal of the barrel is best achieved with an extra person to guide the far end of the barrel while you gently lift and pull from the right end. Watch that you do not lift the barrel so much that the pins catch on the access door surround. When the barrel is out of the piano, lay it on the floor, preferably on sacks or cloth so that the pins will not be damaged.

To remove the keyframe, the first step is to take off the tension spring which connects the left end of the frame to the left side of the case. This spring is looped around a stout wire lug threaded into the iron capping of the keyframe. Hold this lug firmly in the pliers and rotate it anticlockwise for 180° so that it is in line with the loop of the spring. Put a piece of cloth over the spring and hold the coiled part firmly while springing the loop from the lug with a screwdriver. The spring is then easily unhooked from the case side. This is shown in Fig. 10.

Remove the two large wire springs which hold the keyframe in contact with the tune-change cam. These stout wire springs usually have their top ends bent over to form a handle and they are fixed to the case as shown in the drawing. Hold the spring by the handle, push it forward, move it towards the centre of the piano to disengage the screwhead locating its upper portion, let it back and then jigger it off the large centre pivot-screw which passes through its two or three centre coils. Remember which spring came from which end – it will save time and frustration on reassembly.

Now unscrew the two small capping pieces from the keyframe pivots. The frame is now free to be lifted out. However, it is comparatively heavy, awkward and a tight fit in the case and, whilst with practice you can take it out singlehanded, you would be better advised to have someone to help. Ensure that the hammers do not jam between the strings as you get it free and, most important, avoid the hammer tails: not only do they have a certain habit of catching in the clothing, they may also be murderously sharp if the piano has had a lot of use, and can slice the flesh.

Pianos fitted with tremolo arrangements are but a little more complicated to strip and the techniques are largely a matter of common sense since I assume none to be foolhardy enough to meddle with even the simplest mechanism unless they can recognise a screw, a bolt or a wire and take the necessary action to suit the task.

Where the strings are all present, but rusted, you can largely restore the tone by giving them a stiff brushing with the wire brush. However, bad rusting does really call for restringing, particularly in the extreme treble register where the strings, even at their best, tend to sound 'dead'. Rusting deadens their tone still further.

The stringing of these pianos is different from that of the smaller ones, and tends more to follow the styles used in the conventional piano. Better made instruments have strings which end only at the wrest-pin, the other end forming a U-turn round the bottom peg and then coming back up to the wrest-plank again. This means that one broken string requires the replacement of the adjacent strings also, since it is one continuous piece of wire. These pianos also feature a continuous pressure bar or agraffe which holds all the strings down firmly before the wrest-pins and ensures contact with the first bridge. The illustration Fig. 5 (page 9) shows these points.

Bass strings – the wrapped ones – are single strands per run with eye ends on the bottom pegs. Badly corroded or broken ones must be replaced with new ones. Again, use the old one, where present, as a pattern for the string-maker to copy.

Clear away any broken strings and proceed to give the inside of the case a thorough clean. Where the harp or strung back is not in bad condition, you can, as before, proceed immediately with reassembly. However, as with the smaller piano, we must consider every eventuality in the process of resurrection.

Just as with the smaller piano, pay particular attention to the soundboard and see that it is not split and that the diagonal bracings which are glued to its back (the soundbars) are all secure and not loose at the ends or in the middle. Loose soundbars will cause a nasty rattling sound and can often be detected by tapping the soundboard all over with a padded hammer and listening to it reverberating. If the wrest-plank, described in the next paragraph, has come away from its attachments and has tipped forward, then the top edge of the soundboard may be bowed or crushed and you will have to remove the soundboard and re-glue the lipping piece by means of which it is secured to the case. Do note, by the way, that the soundboard must 'float' within the case by a certain amount and for this reason it is only attached rigidly at the sides and top, its other portions being no more than located. Many pianos have been altered during their lives and hence the soundboard and bridges may show signs of modification. If you can see where bridge positions have been altered or parts (invariably at the bottom end) removed or repositioned, do not try to bring the piano back to its pre-modification condition as it will not play properly. The soundboard alterations will have resulted in changes to the tuning which will have influenced the way the music is pinned to the barrel. Clean off the surface of the soundboard and give it a coat of copal varnish or, if you prefer, rub it well down and give one or two coats of clear polyurethane varnish.

Now for the wrest-plank. Street pianos were exposed to all kinds of weather, including changes in temperature, rain, and damp fog, not to mention snow and roasting hot sun. The most highly stressed part of the instrument was the strung back itself and changes in temperature and humidity caused the total force of the string pull to vary. Whilst this was contemporarily noticed as 'going out of tune', the effects may remain today as a cracked or split wrest-plank. A plank in such condition will neither be stiff enough to resist the string pull nor will it hold its wrest-pins tightly in place. It must be repaired or, in extreme cases, replaced.

Another thing which is sometimes found is where the total string tension has resulted in the wrest-plank coming adrift from its supports at either side and from the posts at the back, and tipping forward. In this condition, you have a lot of work to do.

Whatever work has to be done to the plank, first we must find out exactly how it is made. The majority were made of well seasoned hardwood, usually beech and sometimes maple or ash, with a front face of vertical-grained hardwood, such as oak, and the whole covered with a horizontal-grained veneer occasionally of a wood such as bird's-eye maple.

The effect of having two, three and even four or more lines of wrest-pins closely spaced along it served literally as the thin end of a wedge hell-bent on splitting the timber. I must admit to having had the horrifying and frustrating experience of seeing a wrest-plank on a newly strung and tuned piano gradually start to split and, as I watched powerless to do a thing, the crack spread across the centre two feet of timber! The plank is surprisingly deep and thick; in fact one wonders, on seeing it exposed for the first time, how on earth it could ever split. This demonstrates the terrific load of the strings.

Where the plank had developed cracks across its width, it is sometimes possible to close these together using clamps and long coachbolts. To do this, remove all the piano strings and the wrest-pins. The back of the piano will be found to comprise a detachable frame of thin wood covered in cloth. Removal of this will expose the heavy wooden posts which support the wrest-plank. Check very carefully round the points of contact between plank and these posts for looseness or opened joints. You may find it necessary to remove the soundboard to gain better access to the wrest-plank. Where cracks show evidence of such separation, open them as wide as you can without using excessive force, force in synthetic resin glue (I use Croid, but be careful: many of these glues can give you dermatitis if you get them on your fingers) and clamp up tightly using very large G-clamps or sash-cramps.

If you have to remove the plank completely, this is easily done so long as you take extra pains to see that you do not cause any other damage to the piano.

Use a broad chisel and a heavy hammer to separate the glued joints between plank and posts and the shaped pieces of heavy hardwood packing between the posts. Note that for this job you must have the soundboard out of the piano before starting. Try to remove the wrest-plank in one piece but, if you cut it, measure several distances across it before cutting and make marks so that the precise length of the plank can be re-established when the two pieces are lined up together after removal.

Select well seasoned beech for the replacement plank and keep it indoors in a warm room for three months or so before you start to work with it. I once had the experience of replanking two pianos with wood which I considered to be properly dry. Both pianos worked loose again within months, so take time over sorting out and drying the wood. See that the fresh timber is not warped, bent, twisted or otherwise distorted either in length or width.

Take the old plank and lay it on a bench and stretch over it a wide sheet of thick tracing paper. Using a solid wax marking crayon (the thing which used to be used by shoemakers and was called heel-ball*), rub all over the paper on the plank as if you were making a brass rubbing. This will transfer the position of all the wrest-pin holes and other marks on the old plank as well as the exact profile of the plank itself – its edges. This is important since some planks may taper and others have cut-outs in them for percussion instruments such as nested bells. The reason for using a wide piece of tracing paper is so that the paper itself cannot distort excessively and produce errors when it comes to applying the paper pattern to the new plank.

With the new piece of wood lying flat on the bench, do not at once cut it to final dimensions, but leave it oversize on all faces and edges except thickness until you have fitted the cladding and the veneer. I use a 5 or 6 millimetre planking of ash or oak. Because ash is easier to obtain planed to precise thicknesses, you may prefer to use ash for this job. Try to obtain your planks as wide as possible – about 6 inches if you can, although width is not critical. Cut the planks of ash into pieces the same length as the width of the wrest-plank, and lay them across the face. Compare the general layout of the plank to the rubbing of the old one and try to avoid getting the joints in the cladding where you will later on be drilling for pins. Some alignment may well be impossible: just try to avoid too much of it. Now mark the

* Heel-ball is a polishing mixture used by shoemakers and consists of a solidified mass of hard wax and lamp-black.

22

pieces of ash in pencil with a number and a mark to show which is the top of the outermost face. Gather them all together and plane up the edges so that they are quite square.

Liberally coat the face of the wrest-plank with synthetic resin glue and begin reassembling the ash planks to it, making sure that you properly glue the butt joints between each piece. When all the pieces are in position, press them together end to end with bench wedges and wipe surplus glue from the upper surface with a damp cloth. Lay a sheet of thin plastic over the whole and now place a length of smooth, flat timber on top. Clamp this sandwich together at closely spaced intervals. Leave the whole thing to dry for at least a week.

Unclamp the sandwich, remove the clamping wood and the plastic sheet and thoroughly sand the surface of the ash cross-planking using, ideally, a power sander of the orbital type. Take your new piece of veneer and glue this into place. You can either use one of the patent dry 'glue-films' for this (in which case you iron on the veneer using a hot smoothing iron), or you can use synthetic resin glue spread very evenly on to the plank. Roll the veneer into position on the glued surface and smooth it initially with the palm of the hand. Now take a squeegee roller and roll all over the veneer exerting pressure to force out air bubbles and surplus glue. At a pinch you can do this with an empty beer bottle or a pastrycook's rolling pin. Once again clamp up the whole thing and leave it to dry.

Take the newly laminated wrest-plank complete with clamps and clamping boards and put it somewhere dry and warm for as long as you can – a few weeks in a domestic airing cupboard would be ideal.

During the time this is taking place, you can always work on the case of the piano, stripping off the old finish with a proprietary paint-stripper and then rubbing down the bare wood prior to refinishing it either in black paint or whatever you choose. More on this a little later on.

Once the plank is dry, sand the veneer face and apply one coat of polyurethane varnish. When dry, give it an even, thin coat of artist's rubber cement (this is used in drawing and art offices for sticking down paper on artwork and in Britain goes under the trade name of Cow Gum). Apply a thin coat of the same solution to the back of the tracing paper rubbing of the old plank. Do not use any conventional 'wet' glue or paste as this will make the paper expand and destroy the accuracy of your work. Once the two gummed surfaces have become tacky, carefully position the tracing paper rubbing over the new wood. Get someone to help you do this as once the gummed paper touches the gummed wood it will instantly stick. When the paper is aligned in the proper position, begin by pressing one end onto the wood and then, keeping the other end lifted up, rub the hand along the paper, pressing the paper down smoothly until the full length is stuck to the wood. Cut off surplus paper overhanging the edges of the wood and now cut the plank to the drawings, ideally using a power saw to cut through paper and plank. Work accurately and, if the edge of the original plank was chamfered, reproduce this chamfer most accurately.

To drill the wrest-pin holes, you should ideally use a drill mounted in a stand as this will enable you to set the necessary angle for the holes so that all are at the same inclination. You will also be able to set the drill stop on the drill press so that each hole is the right depth. You can do this with a hand-held electric drill, but it requires a steady hand, patience and, without doubt, some sort of angle gauge. The drill should be slightly less in diameter than the diameter of the wrest-pins you will be using – about 7 to 10 thousandths of an inch smaller. You can make an effective depth gauge by slipping a tight-fitting length of rubber tube over the drill and cutting it off to the proper length: this will show the right depth without defacing

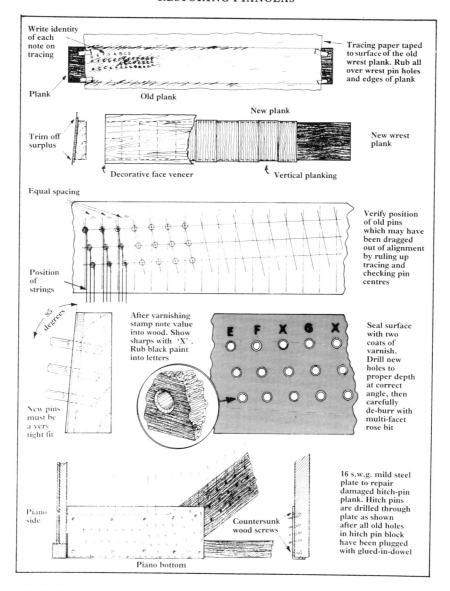

Figure 11   Making a new wrest-plank, marking and drilling off for the pins, and repairing the hitch-pin
block

the timber. Do not drill the hole longer (deeper) than is necessary and always use a new, sharp drill. Once a drill has been resharpened, unless it has been done on a proper engineer's drill-sharpening machine, it may well no longer be accurate enough to drill a hole of the correct size.

Once all the holes are drilled, check against both the rubbing and the original that you have not left anything off. Now peel off the paper pattern and rub the surplus rubber cement off the drilled and prepared plank with your fingers. It will come away quite cleanly without recourse to special removal techniques to leave the varnished wood beneath. Slightly counterbore all the holes with a 120° rose bit held in a carpenter's brace.

To glue the new plank into the piano, prepare everything first during a 'dry run' so that when you come to gluing up you have everything to hand – the right clamps, the proper wooden packing and clamping pieces and the right tools. Mix up your glue and, to save your hands from contamination with the adhesive, wear either thin rubber gloves or disposable plastic gloves.

This is the point where you can spoil all your good work through carelessness, so take great pains to see that the new plank is properly seated and well glued into position. The back posts and their intercostal blocks must all be firmly fixed one to another as well as to the plank.

Leave the glued-up piano for a week to dry before attempting to unclamp. Remove surplus glue and generally clean up round the new work. Now the original, old plank had the tuning scale impressed into the wood with metal punches and for a really professional job you should buy a set of ¼ inch metal letter punches and copy the markings of the old plank onto the new. The method is to take, for example, the C punch, make sure that you position it against the right set of wrest-pin holes, and give it a tap with the hammer. Just how hard you hit it will be determined by practice on a scrap piece of wood. For sharps it was fairly common with some makers to use the letter 'X' so that C, C sharp, D, D sharp, E would appear as C, X, D, X, E and so on. Once you have marked all the string-tuning instructions, take a clean piece of cotton rag and put a tiny quantity of black enamel paint on it. Roll the cloth into a ball and rub it over each letter you have stamped into the varnished wood. The black paint will fill or stain the bruised wood in the letter, making it easier to read. Finally, give the whole plank a second coat of varnish, taking care to see that it does not trickle into the wrest-pin holes.

Once a hole is drilled into wood, it gradually starts to close up a little as the wood fibres recover. Take a hand reamer the same finish size as the original drill and clear out each wrest-pin hole, taking care not to enlarge it above its intended diameter.

The next task is to examine the hitch-pins. These are the pins at the bottom of the piano below the soundboard to which the other ends of the strings are attached. The treble end of the piano also has a diagonal hitch-pin block and this should be checked for splits, cracks and looseness in exactly the same way as the wrest-plank. Any repair work follows the same pattern. However, partially loose hitch-pins can be fixed securely and a partially split hitch-pin block made good by facing it with a 16 gauge steel plate. This should be bent up so that there is a 2-inch wide lower flange which can fit under the hitch-pin block and be securely screwed into place. The positions of the actual hitch-pins are transferred to the metal and drilled through at an angle as before. New hitch-pins can be made by cutting about 1¼ inches off the pointed end of a 4-inch wire nail and using these points hammered well into the timber through the steel plate so that about ⅜ inch protrudes.

Once all this is done and the soundboard replaced, you can begin restringing. If you plan on doing more than one piano, or if you want to make a particularly neat job of your piano, I strongly recommend buying a piano-wire looping tool. This makes forming the eye end on the very stiff piano wire a simple task and gives your work that professional touch.

Buy your new music wire from a piano sundries house in half-pound coils for the bass strings, and 4-ounce coils for the treble. The treble wires being shorter, you will not use so much wire as you will for the full-length bass strings.

Stringing is a job which gives you sore fingers. Start at the bottom end and work your way up to the treble, observing the illustration Fig. 5 as your guide. Do not at this stage attempt to bring the new strings up to any tuned pitch. Place the new wrest-pins in their holes as you go – this will allow you more room to manoeuvre than if you put them all in first. Start the pin by tapping it in with a hammer until the wire hole is about half an inch from the wood surface. Cut the new wire 2 inches longer than the hitch-pin to wrest-pin distance with the wire located on the hitch-pin, form a right-angle bend in the last $\frac{3}{8}$ inch of the wire, push this into the wrest-pin wire hole and, using the tuning hammer, wind the pin in, coiling the wire round and down the pin as you go. See that the angled end does not slip out of the wrest-pin, and see that the coils are tight but not superimposed. The bottom coil should be about 1 millimetre from the surface of the wrest-plank. If it is more than this, tap the pin again with the hammer.

When all the strings are in place, thread each wire around its correct bridge pins and then weave the listing through the 'dead' part of the strings as with the smaller piano. Now bring the piano roughly up to tune so that the strings can stretch. Do this working from the middle outwards in both directions and do it roughly: this is called 'chipping up' and is purely a means of applying tension to the newly strung back to give it a chance to settle down.

Now back to the case and its refinishing. Where the winding handle fits into the case, oil-sodden wood is almost always present. Make good any really bad pieces of timber by dovetailing in fresh wood. Many of these street pianos were varnished and imitation-grained and most received so many coats of paint and varnish during their lives that a covering of paint $\frac{1}{16}$ inch thick is not uncommon. A few were done up very attractively with enamels and decorative lining with barrows to match but these are the exception rather than the rule. There was nothing special about the wood used, so do not enthusiastically scrape down to bare wood and expect to find anything more exotic than fairly clean pine. One of the best modern treatments I have seen on a street piano is one which probably demands far more work than any other – thorough sanding to a dead smooth surface followed by a black mirror finish like a normal piano. Since the casework is usually well knocked about, chipped and split, such a labour of love is seldom justifiable and the best and simplest finish is probably to strip down to the bare wood, apply a dark stain and then several coats of copal varnish. When the final coat has hardened properly, rub it all over with fine wire wool to produce a slightly matt surface. This will enable you to rub in a final coat of household wax polish which will give the casework an attractive finish without the garish gloss of a varnish finish. Alternatively you can apply an undercoat of paint and then put on a brush-grained finish using scumble, finishing off with polyurethane varnish.

Now tackle the keyframe. There can be more work to do on this than on the rest of the instrument put together, so begin by examining carefully to detect the following points: (1) broken or bent hammer tails; (2) broken hammer blocks; (3) loose hammer-head wires; (4) bent, damaged or split hammer heads; (5) loose, missing or badly ribbed felts on the hammers; (6) weak, broken or missing hammer springs.

Quite often, the hammers in a street piano are found either to be very tight and difficult to move in the keyframe, or so loose and rattling that the barrel pins push the hammers sideways rather than allowing them to be drawn back and strike the piano strings. The first job is to disconnect all the hairpin springs to the hammers using a special tool shaped as in Fig. 12.

Provided that the keyframe is dry, tight hammers can be freed by rubbing graphite in powder form on the hammer butts. Loose hammers can be packed out by sticking small pieces of gummed brown paper on the butt flanks and then rubbing in graphite. Much of the trouble in a well-worn piano stems from the actual hammer axis being worn. This is a long

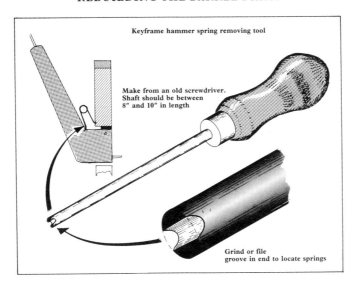

Keyframe hammer spring removing tool

Make from an old screwdriver.
Shaft should be between
8″ and 10″ in length

Grind or file
groove in end to locate springs

Figure 12   Keyframe hammer-spring removing tool

strip of brass wire which is threaded through the keyframe and all the hammers so that they can pivot on it.

Carefully clamp the keyframe in the bench vice, number the hammers from one end to the other, and unbend the ends of the brass pivot wire. Grasp one end in the jaws of a good solid pair of pliers and twist and pull to withdraw the whole length of wire. Often some considerable force is needed to do this because, over a long period of use, the friction of the hammers wears away at the contact area of the wire, virtually turning it into a sort of multi-throw camshaft. In very severe cases you may be forced to sacrifice one or more hammers by breaking them out so that you can cut through the wire hinge and pull out from each end.

Once the hinge is out you can set about treating the hammer butts. Where they are loose you will invariably find that their flanks are rounded and they must be sanded down using fine paper resting on a sheet of glass to provide a flat surface to rub against. The small amount of wood you remove can be made up by one or two layers of brown sticky paper stuck on. Once the hammer butt has been brought up to the right width so that it is once more a reasonably tight fit in its slot in the keyframe, lightly moisten each side of the butt by breathing on it and then rub powdered graphite into the paper.

Carefully measure the diameter (gauge) of the wire hinge you have removed. It is usually about 18 s.w.g. Obtain a length of 16 s.w.g. piano wire from a model shop: it is sold in straight lengths of about three feet. Using a grindstone or carborundum stone, form two cutting edges on end end just as if you were sharpening a drill. Put the other end of the wire in the chuck of the electric drill and very gently drill through the pivot points using the piano wire cutter to ream and polish the bore. If the wire is not long enough, work through from each end. Finally cut off the last inch or so of the piano wire to include the cutter you have just used and put this short piece in the drill. Now ream through each hammer butt one at a time. The new pivot hinge will be a piece of 16 s.w.g. brass wire (or whatever the gauge of the piano wire reamer was) which must be pointed on one end and then gently pushed into the pivot hole, engaging the hammers one at a time.

Where hammer tails are bent out of alignment, they can usually be eased back into position by gently bending them with a pair of heavy pliers. Remember, though, that these tails are extremely hard and brittle. Where you are confronted with a broken one, diligent use of side-cutters and end-snips will usually produce part of the metal which you can gently twist and pull until it comes out. In obstinate cases, you may have to pare away a little wood at the sides to get a good grip on the pin. Make your new hammer tail from square-sectioned silver-steel or tool steel (I find that ⅛ inch square is just about right for the job) and glue it firmly into place with Araldite synthetic resin.

The hammer butt may be broken through shearing along the grain. If so, and the two mating faces are complete and clean, repair is not too difficult. You will need two long thin brass screws, preferably round-headed and 1½ inches in length by ³/₃₂ inch in shank diameter. Have a helper hold the top half of the hammer butt firmly in place and drill two ¹/₁₆ inch diameter holes from the underside (see Fig. 13). The holes should be the same depth

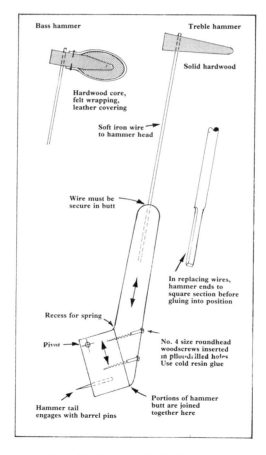

Figure 13 Repairs to broken hammers

as the length of the screws. Now drill both holes $^3/_{32}$ inch in diameter for a depth of not quite an inch. This ensures that the screws will hold the wood without expanding it and so causing the hammer to bind in its slot in the keyframe. Apply a little glue to the mating wood faces – not so much that it will be forced out in excess to cement the hammer butt into the keyframe. Work the two parts together a little to exclude air bubbles and then screw up tightly. Wipe excess glue off the flanks and put a thin strip of waxed paper between the hammer butt and keyframe slot on both sides so that they will not stick while drying out. Ideally this job should be done by removing the hammers in the manner suggested above.

The wire extensions which fit into the top of the shank or butt and carry the actual hammer heads sometimes break off or come loose at the butt. They are made of soft iron wire and, where they have come loose, remove the wire and replace it into a hole filled with Araldite adhesive. Wipe off the excess adhesive before it sets. Where the wire has broken off, try to ease out the stub end in the manner described earlier for hammer tails. The other end of the wire is usually threaded into the hammer head. Make a new wire from soft iron or mild steel. I have found that the wire of wire coat-hangers is just the right diameter and ductility for most jobs. Cut a straight length which is long enough and hammer a flat portion onto both ends. Incidentally you can also use the welding filler rod used by oxyacetylene welders, although that is obviously more expensive: coat-hangers are for free! Remember that the wire should fit about 1½ inches deep into the hammer shank or butt. Glue the new wire in well, make certain both butt and hammer head are in the right plane (not twisted) and set aside to dry.

The hammer heads usually have felt covers like normal pianos, or felt with a leather strip around the outside. These vary from maker to maker and most makers used plain wooden hammers of hardwood for the treble hammers or where a tremolo effect was fitted. However, the bass and tenor hammers were invariably felted. The intervening years often cause the felt to spring free from the wooden part of the hammer head and it must be replaced or glued back and held down until set, using a large spring paper-clip. Where the part of the hammer which touches the musical strings is compressed or deeply ribbed, you should carefully dress the felt back into shape using a new flat file. Use a second-cut file and work round the hammer head in one direction only – towards the striking face – from the top and then from the bottom. Fig. 14 shows the operation.

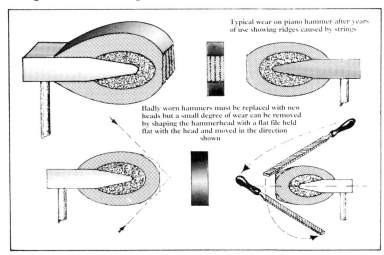

Figure 14
How to reshape
worn hammer heads

29

The hammer springs are next for examination. These are like large safety pins and can be removed, if necessary, with a pair of long-nosed pliers. Any missing or broken ones must be replaced using thick piano wire obtainable from model engineers' shops. Use the tool shown in Fig. 12 to reconnect the springs to the hammers: by the way, do not try to withdraw the hammer axis wire with the springs still connected to the hammers. The outcome should be spectacular!

Draw back all the hammers and see that approximately the same resistance and force applies to each one. Any slow or sluggish hammers will affect the playing of the piano and, where they are stiff through friction in the frame rather than because of flaccid springs, you should liberally apply powdered graphite to the hammer flanks. Remember, never use oil or grease.

Between the hammers and the keyframe there is a strip of felt upon which the hammers sit when at rest. If this felt is hardened or moth-eaten, the hammers will not sit evenly at rest and, more important, the hammer tails may scrape the tune barrel. To examine the felt, hold all the hammers forward with a strip of stiff wood. Tease up the felt with a wire brush if it can be re-used, otherwise strip it off and replace it with a length of 3/16 inch thick hard piano felt available from a piano sundries dealer.

If the piano is to play properly, the hammer tails must be perfectly in line and must all protrude by exactly the same amount. If their ends are rounded through constant use over a long period, the tendency will be for the barrel pins to push them sideways, so wearing away the hammer butts and the pivot wire. Hone these points absolutely dead in line laterally and as regards protrusion. Use a carborundum stone but take great care not to slice your fingers if the stone slips. I have spilled much blood on street pianos – and always on these blasted tails!

Finally, look over the keyframe for other damage or defects. The extension lever on the left side which engages with the tune-changing mechanism must be a good tight fit; it is screwed to the main keyframe member.

Before putting the keyframe back into the piano, check over the tune-changing mechanism and see that it works properly. It should be lubricated with a good graphite grease. If the bearing for the changing handle is worn so that the handle is sloppy, take off the handle, remove the shaft and make a new bearing.

Replace the keyframe on the half-trunnions in the case sides, screw back the trunnion-bearing capping pieces, replace the two stout wire springs which press the frame against the changing mechanism and reconnect the tension spring which pulls the frame up against the left side. Hook this over the lug on the keyframe and turn the lug back clockwise to hold it securely. Turn the tune-changing handle to see that the mechanism works properly and then set it so that the keyframe is held out in the between-tune position so the barrel can be replaced.

Treatment of the barrel is more or less as described for the portable piano, except that, being bigger and stouter, the wooden cog is less likely to have succumbed to wear. Any woodworm can be treated and any bent pins straightened.

Gently slide the barrel back into the instrument, taking care not to catch the pins on the access door or on the hammer tails. At the end of its travel, check to see that the arbor is located properly on the changing cam and that the drive-worm is correctly engaged in the barrel cog. The end of the barrel may need to be lifted slightly to get it into the proper position.

See that the stout leaf-spring in the access door which pushes the barrel against the change mechanism is free and able to do its job. A light film of grease should be applied with the finger to the working face of this through the hole on the inside. Note that this end bearing of the barrel is adjustable on the access door, for the wooden block, screwed inside the door to support the barrel arbor, can be loosened and moved a fraction up and down and from side to side. Unless playing the piano shows that the barrel is in the wrong position, it is extremely unwise to upset the setting of this bearing, so leave it well alone.

Refit the door and lock it with the turn-buttons. Reconnect the special wire spring which presses down on to the rear bearing of the winding handle. This must be a very stiff fit as if it is loose (or absent) the worm-drive will rapidly wear away the barrel cog teeth. Let back the keyframe with the change lever, and play the piano. At the end-of-tune position, stop and check that when the hammers are at rest they are just short of the strings, otherwise, as before, the strings will be muted. They are easily bent into the right position.

The piano must now be put into registration, so wind the tune-change handle until the barrel is at its farthest-left position. This should mean that the farthest-right pins are now in the playing position – play the piano and check. If they are not, then the keyframe must be moved laterally, using the horizontal, eye-ended adjuster at the left end of it. This must only be done at the end-of-tune position otherwise pins and tails will be broken. Once the last tune on the right of the barrel has been accurately registered, turn the tune-changer until the barrel is at its farthest to the right, so bringing the last set of pins on the left end of the barrel under the hammer-tails. Play this one and make any necessary adjustments to the lateral position of the keyframe. Note that quite frequently you must strike a practical medium between all the tunes on the barrel so that they all play with more or less equal success.

The fore-and-aft position of the keyframe is also important. If the hammer tails are too close to the barrel, rapidly repeated notes will not be sounded properly, as there is insufficient space or time for the hammer to fly to the strings before the tail catches on the next barrel pin. If the hammer tails are too far away, the sound will be weak and sporadic. Adjustment for this is by the two vertical, eye-ended adjusters, one each end of the keyframe. Make sure that the keyframe is parallel with the face of the barrel – a visual check, looking down behind the barrel, will show this. See that the hammers clear the strings by about $\frac{1}{16}$ inch when at rest and do not 'block' them, so preventing them from vibrating.

It will probably be necessary to polish up the tuning at this point. It is advisable with these instruments to 'stretch' the octaves a shade in the extreme treble; this means tuning the top four or five notes a fraction sharp. Because these top strings are so short, they tend to sound percussive and their often indeterminate tone can be helped by this marginal sharpening.

CLOCKWORK OR AUTOMATIC PIANOS

The mechanism of the 'automatic' piano (one driven by a clockwork motor and probably coin-operated) is basically the same, with the exception that there is no crank-handle to play the instrument. An additional handle is fixed usually to the left side of the case, to wind the clockwork.

One word of warning here. The springs used in clockwork pianos are very powerful indeed and any unskilled attempt at dismantling the motor can result in the release of a coil of steel of such power that it could cause very serious injury. If the spring is broken, and unless you are a competent engineer, I do not advise you to try to repair it yourself. It is safer to give it to some small engineering workshop to put right. Usually, when a spring does break, it fails at either the inside end (the piece which hooks on to the arbor) or the outer end where it is looped and riveted round one of the assembly posts of the motor cage.

The motor should be cleaned and this can usually be done without taking it from the instrument. Do not try to dismantle the gear train and the endless screw carrying the governor. If you tamper with this, any power left in the motor will immediately be released and the least that can happen is stripped gears and a broken spring. If it is necessary for some reason to dismantle the governor, then let the motor run right down against its Geneva stopwork and only remove the governor when there is no longer any force in the motor to turn it. Lubricate the motor with grease.

Coin-operated automatics are in no way complex devices. The coin drops down through the piano in a chute until it finally falls into a pan or other form of receptacle which is counter-balanced on an arm. When the coin lands in the receptacle, it tilts the mounting lever, freeing a detent from a check on the governor. Automatics usually play twice (occasionally three times) for one coin and, after the set number of turns, the coin is ejected and the receptacle and its lever return to the 'stop' position, so stopping the works. The number of revolutions and the instruction to start or stop the mechanism come entirely from the motor unit and not from the barrel or any part of it, so it is important that the barrel be inserted in exactly the right position. If this is not done, the music will stop and start in the middle of the tune. Examination of the barrel will show one point on its periphery where there is a clear line along it, devoid of pins. This is the start/stop position and usually you will see also small prick marks or ink dashes to mark the alignment of the hammer tails at the start of the first tune position.

Positioning the barrel is thus very important. Instead of being rotated by a wide, coarse-threaded wooden cog, the barrel carries on its left end a large diameter gear-wheel, comparatively narrow, which meshes with a wide pinion carried in the top of the clockwork motor. (Note that I refer here to the more common type of automatic with the motor fixed at the left end under the barrel; other types will be similar in general arrangement, although slightly different in detail.)

First see exactly where the stop/start position on the barrel is and gently slide the barrel into the case. You will need to lift up the left end of it to seat it on the drive pinion and at this point see that, when the keyframe is lowered into the playing position, the hammer tails will fall more or less exactly into the centre of the 'no-man's-land' of the barrel. If it does not, then index the barrel one tooth at a time until this is reached – you can easily do this by repositioning the barrel (with the keyframe held clear, of course).

The final check on this positioning is to locate the barrel completely – that is, with the door closed to support the right-hand barrel arbor – and play the instrument. The music should stop exactly at the end-of-tune position with none of the hammers partly lifted.

If the piano plays too slowly or too fast, then you can regulate the speed by the adjustment of the collar which prevents the governor from flying out too far. To make the music play faster, you must allow the governor to fly out farther, so the collar is moved farther down the endless screw carrying the governor. To make the music slower, you must restrict the fly of the governor by moving the collar farther up the shaft.

When it comes to piano orchestrions and other varieties of the barrel-operated piano, the foregoing words will form a basis of the intelligence and skills needed to tackle the job. Watch for controls such as automatic dampers for *piano* and *forte* playing, special keys to bring on effects, and the careful adjustment of percussion linkages to achieve optimum results in playing. All tend to be individual in design to the many various makers, so my words can be no more than general.

In conclusion, we will examine some of the things which can go wrong with barrel pianos, both hand-turned and clockwork.

Piano will not play, although barrel is turning.   Keyframe held off so that the hammer tails are not engaging. Cause might be dirt, stiffness or the breakage of the springs which press the keyframe against the tune-changing trip lever.

Barrel will not turn, or turns sporadically when handle is turned to play.   This means that the drive-worm on the handle shaft is slipping and can be due to badly worn barrel cog teeth or to the breakage of the spring-loaded inner bearing (on small pianos), allowing the drive-shaft to ride up.

Clockwork piano plays jerkily.   Spring not wound enough (or the Geneva stopwork is wrongly positioned so that the motor cannot be wound enough, or the spring has been shortened/replaced by one too weak). Might also be that the keyframe is too closely engaged with the barrel, so putting a very great load on both the barrel pins and the hammer tails.

Music barrel shows fresh scoring from hammer tails.   Keyframe too close to barrel or the hammer-rest felt has become hard and compressed, so allowing the odd hammer to come too far back. Rectification is to adjust the positioning of the keyframe or remove it altogether and refelt the rest-rail. This used to be adjusted by many piano hirers by packing between the compressed felt and the keyframe with scraps of card. This is no proper repair!

Instrument plays discordantly.   Keyframe not in register with barrel pins or the hammer tails are bent, so picking up pins from the next tune. Check the hammer tails carefully for vertical and lateral alignment. Note that all the tails must also be exactly the same length otherwise some notes will sound late due to the hammer being held back longer by the barrel pins. The barrel pins must also be straight.

Instrument plays nine tunes perfectly and the last (or first) tune unmelodiously.   This means that the keyframe is registered one complete tune out of position and you must take the barrel back to the first tune position, check the registration, then repeat the checks at the last tune position. This is a very common fault with pianos where a previous repairer has failed to appreciate what he has done wrong – or omitted to do.

Clockwork piano plays with excessive mechanical noise.   Badly worn gears in motor-drive or, most likely, the stop/start detent is not disengaging fully from the governor sprag, causing a rapid 'tick' as the piano plays. Adjustment is to regulate the coin-tray arm or bend the governor sprag slightly.

Repetitive notes do not sound – hammers stop short of strings.   This means that the keyframe is too close to the barrel. Adjust the two vertical, eye-ended adjusters. Note that, on tremolo arrangements, every note has its own individual hammer adjustment.

Music sounds dead, particularly in the treble.   This may be due to very rusted strings which are now useless and must be replaced, or due to the fact that the hammers are striking the strings too close to the bridge. It is practice for the hammer to strike the strings at a distance between $1/7$ and $1/8$ of their length (this is the 'speaking length' between the bridges, of course), to produce the best and purest tone. Demonstrate

33

this on a string near the centre of the piano by plucking the string at various positions along its length. Barrel-piano makers were not so fussy about this fact, but a dead string usually means that you must make the hammer hit the string a little farther out from its end. Try resetting the hammer by bending the wire slightly whilst maintaining the correct clearance between the hammer and the string when at rest – about $\frac{1}{16}$ inch.

Music sounds dead and tinny in places. Check the hammer clearance. If the hammers are actually touching the strings when at rest, the string is muted or 'blocked' and cannot sing out. Bring all hammers to within $\frac{1}{16}$ inch of the strings.

If you have understood all these points, and appreciate how the barrel piano works, then you can confidently tackle similar barrel-operated percussion instruments. One golden rule, and this applies to all mechanisms. It is better to spend time thinking about the job carefully before starting work than to dash ahead and risk irrevocable damage by over enthusiasm and lack of understanding.

F. VERHERTBRUGGE

125, Boulevard de Ménilmontant - PARIS (xxᵉ)

Pianos Électriques

Pianos Automatiques

Orchestrions & Orgues

MUSIQUE PERFORÉE

pour toutes les Marques

CHAPTER 3

Rebuilding the Player Piano

The player piano is a carefully engineered, precision-made piece of mechanism (the player) installed in a well developed and carefully designed instrument (the piano). The degree of care and precision used in the creation of both player mechanism and piano naturally depends to some extent on the maker of each and one can be safe in saying that a good action was seldom married to a cheap piano and, likewise, the top-quality pianos always made use of the finest player actions.

Other than the very few electrically operated, non-pneumatic actions such as the Tel-Electric (as distinct from electrically *pumped* actions found in some expression pianos and reproducers), player pianos operate by creating a chamber of reduced air pressure within the instrument into which air at atmospheric pressure is allowed to leak through carefully regulated paths. In entering the low-pressure area, these leaks of atmospheric pressure are gainfully employed in operating some function of the player action on their way.

It is easy to see that for a given volume of low-pressure space there can only be a designed number of such leaks before 'power' is lost and the ability of the low-pressure area to maintain itself under the barrage of air leaking in becomes diminished. In other words, if air is allowed to enter elsewhere than through the proper places, or if ill fitting or damaged pieces are used to control the air leaks, then more of the atmosphere will rush in in its attempt to equalise the pressure inside the instrument than the action was designed for. Result: the player will not operate properly and fast pedalling will be needed to try to compensate.

This means that the restorer must take great pains to see that his workmanship is thorough and careful. Attachment and assembly must always call for care and foresight to ensure that no leaks exist except those intended (through the tracker bar holes, through the motor and so on). The importance of this cannot be overemphasised and failure to understand this means that you will never make a good restorer. 'Good enough' just isn't adequate.

The player piano had one unfortunate secondary characteristic in that it works in exactly the same way as a vacuum cleaner. It draws air in from all around it and passes it back into the atmosphere, having extracted the dust particles on the journey and deposited them over its internal passages and valves. Dust and dirt are thus the main day-to-day enemies of the instrument.

The player action of a piano cannot make the piano play any better than the piano is capable of playing. If the piano is a poorly made specimen or suffers from certain inherent defects as a piano, then, no matter how good or how perfect the player action, it cannot improve the performance of the instrument. For this reason, the first task in overhaul must be to overhaul the piano itself or, if this is beyond your capability, to have the work carried

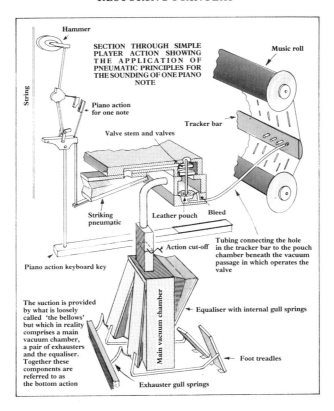

Figure 15   Section through a simple single-valve pneumatic player action

out for you by a professional piano restorer who will thoroughly check and regulate the piano action and see that there is neither lost motion nor irregularity in it.

Buying a player piano should therefore be prefaced by a careful examination of the instrument *as a piano* in addition to its condition and capabilities as a mechanical interpretor. A damaged frame, poor soundboard or badly worn key action, incorrect down-bearing of the strings on the bridge and soundboard or excessively worn and trimmed hammers are features which will increase the amount of work involved in restoring as well as putting up the cost. Never discard a piano – somebody somewhere will want it and will be able to restore it.

It is always preferable to buy an instrument by a good maker so that you can be fairly certain of its potential. Many players are still in working order or are advertised, hopefully, as 'needing slight attention' – a piece of vendor's jargon used to describe a valetudinarian piano in need of anything extending from the reconnection of a loose tube to a total rebuild. Even more players are of unsound action, tubercular-bellowed and faint-hearted. Restoration can thus take anything from a few hours up to many weeks of work. For the present, I am assuming the worst and therefore will go right through the procedure of stripping, repairing and regulation. Naturally, if a player is in fair order, it would be foolish to dismantle the thing completely. Nevertheless it is always a good idea to remove the player action, clean both it and the piano, check over the piano and tune it, and then replace and regulate the player action.

Often one is confronted by a player piano which is advertised as 'fully overhauled'. Now this is a description which, unfortunately, frequently means anything but fully overhauled. No player piano can be described thus unless it can be sworn that certain minimum work has been done. Briefly, the minimum work needed to warrant the description 'fully overhauled' should include:

(a)   Dismantling and thorough cleaning of the action and removal of rust from all player parts, repainting or replating as required
(b)   Replacement of all rubber tubing and rubber hoses by suitable new material
(c)   Recovering all pneumatic motors including action pneumatics, tracking mechanism motors, pneumatic pedal action motors, roll-drive/rewind motor, etc.
(d)   Removal of all valves, cleaning and resurfacing as necessary
(e)   Renewal of all pouches using suitable replacement material
(f)   Rebushing all felted bearings in roll-drive motor, control rods and suchlike
(g)   Renewal of all jointing gaskets, air strainer felts and action pads
(h)   Regulation of player action to piano so that all notes play at equal volume both at softest and loudest extremes, and repeat as rapidly as called for on the tester roll

The expert action restorer will relacquer all woodwork, polish all screwheads, even replace damaged transfers (decals) so that the action looks like new again. Regulation includes the correct adjustment of wind motors, expression and tracking mechanisms and all player action systems and accessories.

Evidence of this work having been carried out must preface the purchase of an instrument which the vendor claims to be 'fully restored'. Anything short of this and the whole action is suspect and will require complete dismantling and examination.

TOOLS AND MATERIALS FOR THE JOB

In Chapter 1 I listed the majority of basic tools needed for the overhaul of various automatic or self-playing pianos. To service pneumatic actions, you will also find it useful to have a pair of long-nosed pliers and one of those extremely useful right-angled screwdrivers. This is an odd-looking thing but it is indispensible for tackling screws in awkward places (and, believe me, a player piano is full of such things). The tool comprises a cranked rod having a 45° blade at one end and a 90° blade at the other. You should also have certain specialist tools for attending to the piano action but I suggest that you may care to leave this side of things to the hands of a specialist in pianos themselves unless you are well versed in the practicalities of piano overhaul, in which case you will already have these piano tools and know how to use them.

For player action work you will require a good sharp pair of scissors – ideally barber's narrow, pointed scissors – a selection of paintbrushes to be used for dusting and glue-spreading, a broad putty knife or decorator's wallpaper stripping spatula for easing pneumatics from the stack and for helping to peel off old rubber cloth, and a sharp scalpel for cutting leather and pneumatic cloth *in situ*. Most important of all, you should buy a tracker-bar sucker from a player-piano sundries house. This looks like a large bicycle pump with a specially moulded rubber end cap to fit over the tracker bar. The difference is that instead of blowing it sucks and is used for drawing dirt and dust out of the tracker-bar ducts. If you intend to restore more than one player, a power sander can be useful for the speedy removal of old pneumatic cloth from the small pneumatic motors.

As for materials, you will be using thin leather for pouches and seals, and rubber cloth for pneumatics and bellows. The leather for pouches is soft, supple, airtight and very thin and no other quality but *tan pouch leather* will do the job. Leather for gaskets is quite thick and is usually white or buff and is called 'half-strained' or 'unstrained', which means that it has not been stretched in processing and is thus easy to form. The leather strips used as flap valves on bellows exhausters, usually tacked at one end and held taught on springs at the other, are made of kangaroo skin, a fairly thick material with a hard exterior which resists deformation.

Rubber cloth comes in several types and grades. The original quality cloth as used by Aeolian in America was made to a very high standard indeed and modern cloths have not matched this quality either in durability or in airtightness. A few years ago, an American player-piano supplies company traced the original manufacturers, had them hunt out the old specification and make a batch of fresh material which is outstandingly good. Rubber cloth comes in a number of grades. The thinnest (for action pneumatics) is called tosh or sometimes pneumatic cloth. This normally has a black rubber coating on a white cotton fabric. A thicker grade is used for the roll drive motor pneumatics and this has a much coarser weave to the fabric. Bellows cloth is normally a heavy twill-like fabric, rubber-impregnated, and a heavier grade is made which is a double thickness of rubber-impregnated fabric bonded together with rubber. Note that ordinary rubber, unreinforced with cloth, such as latex rubber, is unsuitable due to the extreme pliancy and short service life. Never be tempted to use thinner or thicker grades of rubberised cloth since these changes will undoubtedly affect the response of the action and most definitely the durability of the finished job. Rubber cloth and leathers can be bought from the specialist sundries houses or from any piano or organ supplies firm. Piano felts, leather buttons for limit adjusters, tubing and all such parts can be found in the same places.

A word about rubber tubing. There are two types of rubber – red and black. Now black tubing contains a high percentage of carbon and this causes the rubber to harden and deteriorate far quicker than the red quality. There is very little difference in price and red rubber tubing has almost twice the life of black tube under normal conditions. However, under very warm, unventilated conditions, red rubber can go hard and brittle through a process of self-vulcanising, described further on. Tubes used to transfer vacuum from bellows to action are normally of fabric-reinforced rubber hose and this is the same quality as car radiator pipe. Unlike tracker-bar and service tubing, which can be stretched on to a pipe or nipple, the main suction trunks are not so flexible and are held firm by hose clips. The Jubilee clip is an ideal replacement for the original wire clips.

Many people have retubed pianos using plastic or neoprene tubing on the grounds that it is often cheaper and certainly more durable than rubber. Be that as it may, these substances are affected by temperature, tending towards being hard and inflexible in cold weather and the opposite in summertime. Also, they are not endowed with the same properties of stretching as rubber, which means that once fitted to a nipple they can develop a 'set' and work loose or leak. On the point that it will outlast rubber, I would say that it is more than likely that a player action should receive fairly thorough attention probably every ten to fifteen years of its life. Rubber tube can certainly last that time and it is no great hardship to retube the action on such occasions if necessary. It is probable that there will always be two schools of thought on this subject, so it must be left to the restorer as to which he chooses.

38

A vital accessory is a proper player piano test roll, which is available for either 65- or 88-note actions. These rolls are specially contrived to provide a thorough test for the operation of the action for each note, as well as demonstrating the proper valve setting and bleed hole size which will ensure that the note will repeat adequately and quickly. The roll is also used to regulate the speed of the player action in conjunction with the air motor and the tempo-control scale.

Test rolls are still available today from good piano-sundries houses the world over. They are not expensive and you cannot hope to do your job properly without one. Reproducing pianos, as we shall see in the next chapter, require to have their own special tester rolls.

Generally speaking, the materials from which player actions were made are durable and suffer only from attrition due to age. However, this cannot be said of all actions. The all-wood actions of the early days of the player very soon gave way to metal, first with the use of metal valve seats and parts, then with the all-metal action assembly which just had to be screwed on to a valve board. It is with these part-metal and all-metal actions that the problems of corrosion arise. Usually the only indication of a problem is that the action requires a great deal of pumping and only plays softly, indicating that there is a massive leak somewhere. With valve seats swollen through corrosion, the leak may be very small for each valve but multiplied throughout the stack.

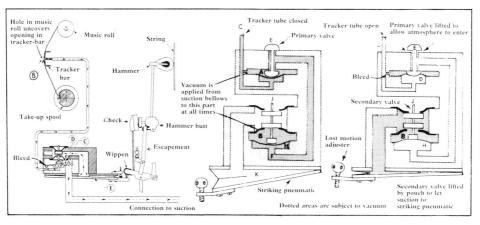

Figure 16   Section through Aeolian single-valve action and sections through the two-valve system showing how valves interact

The corrosion of nickel plated steel parts which are in contact with other metals or with leather appears inevitable yet often it does not occur for half a century or more until the moisture conditions are just right.

A particularly severe case was brought to my attention recently concerning a fine Brinsmead upright which had lost power over a period of a year or so. Examination of the valve board in the stack revealed that the plated valve seat had reacted with the leather valve bearing on it, producing a surface swelling of corrosion products. A thin nickel plated disc on top of the leather had also been reduced to powdery brittleness (see Plate 30).

Reparation in this case was a lengthy process involving the removal and dismantling of all the valve units and the renewal of the leather faces. The actual valve seat whose sealing surface was spoiled was gently rubbed smooth on a sheet of very fine emery cloth laid on a sheet of glass, care being taken not to rub more on one side of the seat than the other. Once this was done, a fine artists' paintbrush was used to apply a very thin coat of polyurethane varnish just around the seating surface of the valve seat pressing. The disintegrated metal disc on the valve stem assembly was in this case dispensed with, although it could have been replaced with a glued-on thin fibre disc.

Always, before dismantling valves in this manner, measure the distances between the various faces carefully so that the valves can all be assembled correctly, otherwise you could be in for some problems in adjustment.

Metal unit actions suffer equally from this form of corrosion and certain American-made actions which were formed out of a zinc-rich alloy called Mazak are often found in very poor shape today. The worst of these, though, can usually be restored satisfactorily by the careful worker. The use of the polyurethane varnish helps to give more body to the damaged valve seat while at the same time inhibiting further corrosion by filling the pores of the metal. In punching out new leather discs for valves, by the way, do use a proper wad punch. These can be bought from most good tool stores and are supplied, usually, unsharpened, so you will have to grind these up very carefully on a sharpening stone. Keep the punch sharp at all times and cut out your new leather discs by hammering the punch on the leather while it is supported by a smooth and clean hardwood board.

Incidentally, it is a mistake to try to improve the seal of the valve by increasing its size. The reason why this is self-defeating is simple. The effectiveness of the seal is a function of how hard the leather seal is pressed against the valve seat. The smaller the area of contact, the greater the effective pressure, but the larger the area the less the pressure and the less effective the seal. There is another reason for maintaining the proper dimensions: if you vary the size of the valve you will affect the pressure of the air working on the whole valve which will show up in a deterioration of the response of the player action. Follow the size of the original piece in every respect, and similarly do not make the valve heavier or lighter in any way – too heavy and it won't lift, too light and it won't close. The people who built player actions generally knew just what they were about.

REMOVING THE PLAYER ACTION

Now to start work on the piano, beginning with its dismantling. The first job is to unscrew and remove the bottom panel (to expose the bellows system), the upper front fall, the fall-board and the top of the piano. This will expose the complete workings. Removal of the player action necessitates the disconnecting of the controls to the hand levers and varies in detail from instrument to instrument. The pneumatic stack is fixed into place by screws or by two thumb-nuts, one each side, and usually by a central bracket or long stud into the piano frame. Take off the air hose connecting the bellows department with the stack or chest and now take out the chest and set it on your workbench so that it is lying front face downwards. Take care in getting the chest out: tilt it inwards at the top while gently easing it out from the bottom so that the pneumatics clear the wippens. Note that the action comes out with spool box and tubing complete.

The bellows are removed, once you have removed the control linkages, by undoing the bolts holding the centre board into place. Wooden spacing blocks are sometimes used in each side and these, too, must be removed. The bellows can now be withdrawn complete.

Before proceeding further, this is the point where you should have an experienced piano-tuner come and regulate the piano action, take up any lost motion in the key-to-hammer action, and also put it into tune. It is important that lost motion be rectified here and now, while the key action is readily accessible. A thorough overhaul of the piano is absolutely vital if anything like perfection is to be sought. Rusted or otherwise corroded piano strings will always sound dull and it is well worth having them replaced. Hammers which are deeply grooved may need replacing if it is not possible to needle the felt back to life or reshape them. The action should be checked carefully for moth, since moth grubs cause more damage to pianos than may be appreciated. The grubs hatch in the felts and systematically eat their way through. This reduces the felt to a hard, lumpy mass, non-existent in places, and makes all the hammers lie at different positions. The throw of each hammer is thus different and the action noisy. Where traces of moth are present it is vital that all felts be replaced. It is utterly false economy to ignore these points and then spend much time and effort on the player action only to have it work fitfully due to a bad or damaged piano action. It is your instrument – take pride in it from the start if you intend to restore it.

Once the piano itself has been overhauled, you can either close it up or cover it with a dust sheet until the player action is ready to be replaced. To leave a piano open can do nothing but harm.

We can now start work on the player action. The assembly known as the upper action comprises two parts – the valve chest and the pneumatic stack – which are usually connected by woodscrews or screwed brackets. The dismantling of the action will call for a certain amount of careful examination, as manufacturers constructed their actions along different principles. Removing the front board and the top board, where fitted, will reveal the primary valve tops and the screws which secure the pieces forming the lower ducts and airways. Fig. 17 shows the Standard Player Action in part-section and from this can be seen the valve chest and the pneumatic stack which must be separated.

Begin by removing the action linkages which run between the striking fingers and the pneumatics. On most actions these are fixed to the pneumatics with small metal brackets, held in place by woodscrews. Others, like the Aeolian, use wooden brackets. Disconnect all these brackets but do not remove them from their wire links unless it is necessary to clean or replace them. The decks carrying the pneumatics can now be unscrewed from their common location board and the fixing screws can normally be found running from the front of the location board back into the decks. Before this, however, mark each deck clearly at one end, say 'a', 'b' and 'c', to aid reassembly. Now mark each individual pneumatic with a ball-point pen or similar, to ensure that each may be replaced in exactly the original position. Always number from left front (bass) to right (treble) to avoid confusion.

The seal between the decks and the location board (which also carries the secondary valves board) is normally of soft leather. Occasionally, a previous repairer may have thoughtlessly glued them together, in which case you must split them apart carefully using a broad-bladed knife. Never use a narrow chisel or screwdriver to separate glued parts – this will compress the wood locally and forever spoil the seal. Use a putty-knife.

Carefully remove the decks one at a time, remembering that time spent thinking about each move beforehand can show the proper way to complete a job and also aid reassembly later.

Skill comes with practice. Never be guilty of fooling yourself. Take your time – it will pay in the long run.

Examine the pneumatics for deterioration, hardening of the rubber cloth and flaking of the

41

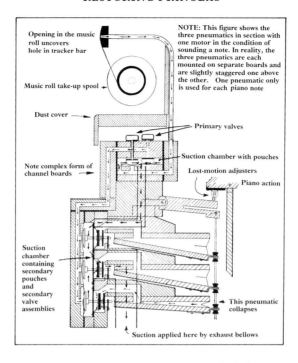

Figure 17   The Standard Player Action, popular in America

rubberised surface due to the hard surface cracking. If the cloth crackles when fingered, it is useless and must be renewed. In checking these pneumatics, do not deceive yourself into believing that perhaps they are all right when in fact they are suspect. Nothing is more exasperating than to complete the replacement of a player action only to find that careless work dictates that it must all be torn apart once more. If the rubberised cloth on one pneumatic has deteriorated, it is both a safe assumption and a wise decision to consider that all of the pneumatics must be re-covered. At the most it adds eight hours' work to your task – if you are practised in the art it will take you much less. The risk you run by leaving them alone is that, at any time, one or more notes may just cease to play and the whole player action lose power. It is a quirk of personalised mechanisms of all sorts that they always choose to malfunction when their proud owners are demonstrating them to an admiring (or critical!) audience. Rest assured that your carelessly restored player piano will pack up on you just when you are hopefully serenading someone of importance.

Occasionally one does find that just one or two pneumatics have sustained physical damage, although the remainder of the stack is genuinely serviceable. If it is not possible to remove the defective pneumatic for re-covering, and if the hole is small, it can be patched using a small disc of rubberized cloth at least twice the size of the damaged part. Glue only around the edge of the patch – never glue in the centre as this will result in a stiff lump being formed which may well affect the operation of the pneumatic.

Now comes the removal of the individual pneumatics. On some actions these are attached with woodscrews, occasionally only accessible after removal of a leather patch on the moving board. On others, though, they are glued on a leather strip and can easily be torn off, but in

42

some cases the pneumatics have been glued directly onto the boards with hot animal glue, which tends to be rather brittle. Drive the point of the putty-knife between the deck and the pneumatic, taking care not to allow it to dig into the wood. A few taps with a hammer are usually enough to cause the pneumatic to crack free. A word of warning here. A number of players, including those of European origin, and also some player organs which employ single-valve systems, have the pneumatics screwed to the deck from underneath. This type of attachment is easily recognised from the fact that there is a white soft-leather seal between deck and pneumatics, and they all come free as soon as the fixing screws are removed from beneath; glue was not used. Generally, glued pneumatics are the sign of a cheap player action made down to a price for a budget-priced instrument.

In removing these glued pneumatics, you may find some are more obstinate than others. These should be left until last so that, with the others out of the way, you can approach them from three and perhaps four sides. If they still prove unwilling to separate from the deck, paint methylated spirits round the edges of the glue line or tear open the pneumatic, fold the hinged board back, place a penny centrally on the fixed board and rest a hot soldering-iron on top. The transmitted heat will soften the glued joint after a few minutes.

Once you have taken off all the pneumatics, resist the temptation to clean off the deck and remove the old glue from the pneumatics, as the slightly irregular surface is matched on both deck and pneumatic and is necessary to provide a fresh seal on regluing.

Rubberised cloth is available in several thicknesses and only the thinnest must be used for re-covering the pneumatics. Before removing the old cloth from them, find one which still has its cloth reasonably intact and open the motor fully so that the cloth is taut. Measure the span of the motor in this position; this is the width which the newly covered motors must measure on completion. Remove the old cloth by sanding, ideally on a belt sander.

If this is not available, you can hold a sheet of medium sandpaper flat on a level table surface and, gripping the pneumatic tightly in the other hand, rub it briskly up and down the paper a few times. This will effectively remove the old cloth down to the wood, the folded cloth in the middle being pulled out afterwards. Try not to damage the fabric hinge to the pneumatic boards as this is invariably intact and in any case is covered by the rubber cloth. Incidentally, do not try to dispense with this hinge: without it, when the pneumatic is re-covered, the folded cloth will prevent the pneumatic from shutting properly.

Cut your new rubberised pneumatic cloth into strips just a little wider than the finished span required and long enough to wrap right around the pneumatic with an overlap of about $\frac{3}{8}$ inch at the back, or hinge, edge. Some repair men advocate tearing the new cloth into strips to save time. If you do this, allow at least an extra $\frac{1}{8}$ inch in width so that the ragged edge which invariably remains may be removed completely afterwards, since the act of tearing strains the rubberised fibres and can affect the airtightness.

Re-covering pneumatics, all 88 of them in a full-scale instrument and 65 in a 65-note player, may at first sight appear to be a time-consuming and tedious task. In reality, it is not so and if you apply a 'production line' technique you can complete the lot in an evening. While some player restorers today advocate the use of Evostik Resin W white woodworking glue for the job, I prefer to use the original hot brown glue for this task. One of the best ones available is cabinetmaker's Pearl glue, which comes in pellet form. This you must dissolve with water to which has been added a few drops of methylated spirits (denatured alcohol). The glue must be heated and applied hot and thin – more on that in a moment. Another good glue to use is Duraglue, which comes in a tin ready mixed and only needs heating. Avoid using clear glues or synthetics because these will ruin the chances of success for any subsequent repairer. Do bear in mind that, properly looked after, a player piano should last indefinitely if it is rebuilt, say, every 20 years or so, and thus you must always give a thought to the ease with which your work can be replaced in the future.

Dissolve your glue in a small jar and place the container in an old saucepan full of hot water to keep the glue soft. It should be maintained at the consistency of thin syrup; any thicker and it will not spread properly; any thinner and it will not adhere. Keep the mix right by occasionally adding a very little water to the glue. You will end up getting glue on your fingers which you will find yourself using as glue spreaders. For this reason, work close to the kitchen sink so you can rinse hands frequently. Keeping the glue pan on a stove or hot-plate is also a good idea. Beware the use of meths and gas jets in proximity.

Lay all the strips of cloth on the table so that none is overlapping and mark approximately the centre of each length. See that all the pneumatic boards are clean and not cracked or split (remembering, with glued-on motors, not to clean off the surface which is later to be glued back on the deck). With a small stiffish brush, apply glue evenly to the open ends of the boards of the first pneumatic and then press them firmly on to the cloth (rubber side on the outside, of course), moving them slightly so as to exclude any trapped air. The boards should now be standing vertically at the approximate centre of the strip, as shown in the illustration Fig. 18.

This work is all very important. You should apply the coating of glue evenly but neither too thickly nor too sparsely. Cover the surface with glue and then gently smear the surface with the finger to spread it. Try not to let any get on to the inside edges of the boards and certainly do not allow any to run over the inside of the boards or over the cloth. Glue on the inside edge will form a hard ridge; glue on the free portions of the cloth will harden it. Either will inhibit the free movement of the pneumatic in use. It all sounds involved, yet in the time taken to read these words you may complete the covering of several pneumatics.

After you have glued all the open boards to the strips, go back to the first one you worked on, lay it on its side, glue the edges and lay the cloth evenly over the upper edges, taking care

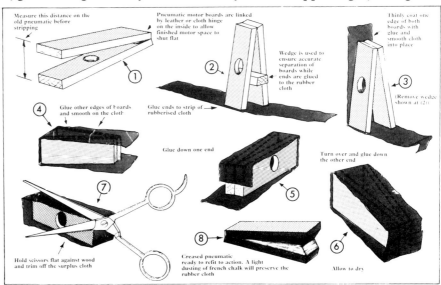

Figure 18
Steps in re-covering
pneumatic motors
using rubberised
cloth

not to overstretch the cloth whilst at the same time ensuring that it is properly down at the corners. Turn the pneumatic over and repeat the process on the other side, completing the job by gluing and lapping the ends of the cloth to the hinge edge of the pneumatic. The lap should be between ¼ and ½ inch. Set this on one side to dry, so placing it that it will not stick to the table. Proceed in this fashion through all the pneumatics. Now take a hot, damp cloth and quickly wipe the edges of all the pneumatics, keeping the cloth hot and moist from time to time, to remove any excess glue (it is difficult to avoid transferring some glue from the fingers to the outside of the cloth) which might cause tackiness. A player left in a moist atmosphere, bad at the best of times, may well have its motors gum up through neglect of this point.

Once they have all been wiped off, return to the first one again and trim it along all its edges, using a pair of long, narrow-bladed scissors. I use special barber's scissors, which are readily available from good hardware shops, and by the use of which a whole edge can be cut in one go. The final job is creasing, which is done by opening the pneumatic fully and then pushing in the sides with the thumb and middle finger whilst the forefinger pushes in the top. Press the motor firmly closed; this will induce a permanent crease in the new cloth. Finally, lightly dust french chalk over the rubberised surface of each pneumatic. This ensures that there is no chance of the cloth sticking in the folds.

To replace the pneumatic motors on their decks, first of all sort them out to follow the original marking or numbering for each deck. Where they have to be glued on, obtain some spring clamps or large Bulldog clips wide enough to clamp the pneumatic to the deck. Apply hot glue to the mating surface of the first pneumatic, press it into place and exclude all air bubbles, then apply the clamp. Avoid overtightening and, if you resort to using G-clamps, make sure you put a block of wood between the jaw of the clamp and the pneumatic to spread the pressure, and do not tighten more than is necessary to hold steady while the glue sets. In actions where the pneumatics are not glued but held in position by woodscrews, tease up the intervening leather seal with a wire suede-brush before refitting the motors. Once all the decks have been attended to and their motors replaced, put them to one side and attend to the valve chest assembly.

The state and condition of the valves, their operating pouches and the vents or bleed-holes is vital to the operation of the player action and thus you must use meticulous care in completing the steps of reconditioning.

There are many different styles of player action and, while all have the same salient features and ultimate function, the details of assembly vary greatly and some thought must be devoted to the way an action interprets the principles and to how best to take it apart. Dismantle the chest, setting each piece on a clean, clear bench. It is a good idea to cover your working surface with white or brown paper; it not only looks neater but it makes it easier to trace and find small parts which may otherwise hide themselves by camouflage.

Begin work on the pouch board. If the leather pouches are cracked, torn or hardened in any way, then you must replace the lot. Fortunately, this special leather, being closed up in the dark and with limited access to air, retains its life much longer than might be imagined. Pouches in good condition should feel smooth and pliable. Run the finger tip around the inner surface. Again, don't try to fool yourself that they are serviceable if there is any doubt. Gently press your finger on a pouch and just see if you can push your finger through the leather by exerting a little force. Good leather will easily resist tearing in this way. On some single-valve actions, the leather will have, glued to its centre, a disc of thick cardboard which engages with the button on the end of the valve stem to prevent its ultimate penetration of the leather. Most player actions used a fibre disc or washer for this purpose. Where a pouch is defective, pull off these discs and clean off any remnants of the old leather from their undersides together with the old glue and set them aside for subsequent replacement. Removing the old leather from the board is best done with a flat scraper. Work down to the bare wood where each leather pouch disc was originally glued. Thoroughly dust off the board and clear the bleed-holes of leather and glue dust. Ideally, use a vacuum cleaner for this, alternatively sucking and blowing (by reversing the hose in the cleaner) through the vents and also through the pouch recesses.

In cases where the pouches are not readily accessible and where it is believed that they may be in such good condition that it does not justify massive dismantling to get to them, each one can be tested by using a length of rubber tube. Arrange the position of the pouch board so that the valves are vertical and gently blow through the tube. The pouch should inflate and move the valves easily. Its operation must be prompt, sensitive and quite free.

The bleeds – they are often found as small, brass pressings fitted into the pouch board, adjacent to the pouches – must be clear of dirt. Some actions, particularly early ones, used discs of stiff paper or celluloid, stuck flat over a hole in the pouch board. These discs would have a small central piercing through which the air could pass.

Pouch leather is soft, thin brown skiver and is obtainable from piano sundries houses and also from organ builders. It is expensive and in short supply. In spite of this, don't be tempted to use substitutes. You might use a thicker white skin, but it will be at the expense of the promptness of sounding and the rapid repetition of the action. The merest puff of air has to be able to operate the pouch.

The leather must be cut into discs approximately ⅜ inch greater in diameter than the diameter of the pouch borings in the pouch board. Originally, these discs were punched but, unless you have a press and a sharp punch, you will be better off with a pair of sharp scissors. Examine the leather closely for imperfections and rough, hard patches on the underside. The edges of a skin often include irregular material having sharp variations in thickness and also small holes. Obviously, you must not use these pieces. Make a pattern in stiff card and mark round it on the leather using a ball-point pen. Carefully cut out each leather disc.

I must stress the importance of careful gluing. If too much glue is used to fix the leather discs over the pouches, it will form a hard rim around the inside, reduce the effect of the pouch, limit its movement and generally spoil the performance of the action operated by that particular pouch and valve. You should spread the glue around the pouch opening with the forefinger and in such a way that the extreme edge of the opening remains dry and unglued. Aim to apply a ring of glue around the opening – if it spreads outside the area it is of no consequence. By using the finger, fairly even glue coverage can be achieved. Place the leather disc centrally in the hole and with the left forefinger press it gently down in the extreme middle so that it touches the bottom of the pouch boring. With the fingers of the right hand, gently and evenly smooth out the edge of the disc so that it lies flat and unwrinkled. You can make up a tool to do this so that each pouch is dished exactly the same. Make it from hardwood and machine a dome on the end 1/32 inch less in diameter than the pouch boring, and about 1/32 inch less than the depth of the bore. The sketch (Fig. 19) shows such a tool. You will appreciate that, as the valves should all move an equal distance in the performance of their duties, the pouches should all move a similar amount, one to the other. If you find that successive leather discs overlap, this is quite acceptable so long as the edge of one disc does

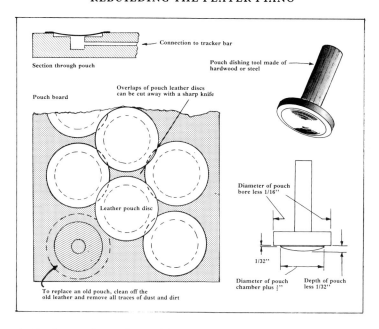

Figure 19   Leather pouches on the pouch board must be dished using a tool like the one shown

not actually come to the edge of an adjacent bore or become glued near the vital unsupported part of an existing, adjacent pouch-disc leather. Where this happens, it is perfectly acceptable to trim a piece off the leather. Do not let glue get on to the free leather of the pouch, and, if you make a mistake in positioning a disc so that it gets glue on the vital part underneath, then scrap it and use another or thoroughly wipe it off with a damp cloth.

A word on sealing pouches. Many makers of player actions applied a sealing compound to the surfaces of leather pouches to remove the inevitable and natural porosity of the thin skin and so improve the efficiency of the action. It is impossible to tell from examination whether pouches were sealed when new. Early Duo-Art actions had their pouches sealed with a film of white of egg, but, with the coming of rubber solution, this was used instead. Now I am in two minds about sealing and its advantages, so it is up to you whether you choose to seal or otherwise. If you use rubber solution, the film must be applied very thinly indeed, using the finger and concentrating around the edge of the pouch where the leather is subjected to the most strain during flexing. After sealing and when the solution is quite dry, lightly dust french chalk over the pouches and then remove all the loose chalk using a soft brush and a vacuum cleaner.

Refit the card or fibre central valve-contact discs to the leather where originally used and now refit the valve stack over the pouch board. Do not overtighten the screws or strip the screw threads in the wooden pieces. Adopt the policy of always inserting the screws by hand and starting them as far as you can go with your fingers. In tightening screws, start at each end alternately and tighten adjacent ones in opposite rows gradually so as to close the boards evenly and without strain. An engineer refits the cylinder head to a motor-car engine in the same fashion so that mating faces do not distort or gasket joints leak. Apply the same care and principle to the screwing of wooden pieces where the joint must be tight. Where leather is

47

used to face a joint, it is always glued with the natural outside surface to the wood, the soft, furry side (the inside or nap) being the one which seals to the mating component dry and without need of glue. When you have such a seal to replace, strip off the old leather and clean off any residue, particularly any traces of the peeled or skived surface of the old leather.

Your new piece of leather should be soft white skin, free from hard lumps or ridges on its surface. Ideally you should adopt the organ-builder's technique of sanding the soft inner side of the skin and then rubbing powdered chalk into it but, as this refinement is seldom found in piano actions, you can be excused from following suit.

If the piece is to be used to face, say, a windway with an opening in it, or if the piece has screw holes in it, cut neither the opening nor the holes before gluing. Using hot brown glue such as Duraglue, coat the wood evenly and then press the leather, natural outside to the glue, and apply hand pressure until the glue will hold it – normally a couple of moments. Trim off the outer edges with a very sharp modelling knife and then cut round the openings. Where the screw holes are, cut out a small square hole with the point of the knife.

Whilst you can use ordinary modelling knives in this work, it is well worth buying a proper surgical scalpel. You can buy these from both artists' and drawing-office supplies shops and chemists. The blades to use are No. 11, which are slender, pointed – and surgically sharp.

Back to the assembly of the valve chest to the pouch board. Now, since each make of action differs in detail, the only guidance I can give here is that the sequence of operations in dismantling should now be reversed. The regulation and adjustment of the valves can be made at this point. This is made easy on some actions by the valve stem being threaded so that the valve head may be screwed up or down a little. With the pouches in the normal, 'silent' position, the pad or button which is provided on the end of the valve should be just a fraction clear of the pouch disc. If you can pass a strip of thin notepaper between pouch disc and valve button without the valve being lifted from its seat, this is ideal. The final adjustment of primary and secondary valves is dealt with further on but there is one point to watch and this is that, if the valves were originally locked to the screwed stem with a drop of shellac or glue and if you have disturbed them, then you must relock them with a spot of glue.

At this point you can replace the pneumatic decks, making sure that the securing screws are all replaced and tightened evenly. Do not rely on the screws to draw up the wooden pieces by their threads alone – this way you can easily strip the threads in the timber. Hold each pneumatic deck in the correct position, start the screws by hand and tighten them evenly, gently drawing the deck back into place. It goes without saying that all dirt and dust must first be removed from all mating surfaces, otherwise the seal of the joint will be affected.

After refitting all the decks, you must now replace the connecting links attached to the pneumatics. These are carried on a bar or guide and if you removed this bar earlier you must replace it now. Where the links are attached to metal brackets, each is now screwed back on to its pneumatic and the trick here is to place a drop of hot glue between the metal link and the wood before bringing the two pieces together and tightening up the little woodscrews. Naturally the metal is not glued to the wood by the hot glue, but the glue, being forced out from under the link, forms a reinforcing key to steady the links from sideways play and prevents them from working loose. With wooden brackets, this is not necessary.

Replace all cover boards and refit any control levers and their cranks ('squares') to the underside of the action, as necessary. The action can now be retubed, as the last job before fitting back into the piano. The matter of the type of tubing to use – plastic or rubber – has been covered earlier in this chapter. Although at first sight the mass of tubing and its

◄ PLATE 1
This miniature portable street barrel piano plays eight tunes on 17 notes. Seen here with its fretted front panel, curved barrel fall removed and top lid open, this really small example, under two feet high, is not representative of the usual Hicks-type instrument depicted in Plate 2. It does, though, follow the design exactly.

PLATE 2 ►
Typical Hicks or Bristol-style portable street piano with pleated silk front and central Royal Crest and polished veneered case. These softly-playing instruments were produced by several makers in both Bristol and, later, London.

▼ PLATE 3
The domestic barrel-and-finger pianoforte first appeared during the first half of the nineteenth century but few survive to this day. Here is one, below, dating from the closing years of the last century. It may be played either by hand or automatically from the handle at the right.

▲ PLATE 4
An interesting feature of this clockwork piano, seen in full in Plate 11, is its automatic 'soft' pedal. A damper runs the full width of the piano and carries a strip of felt. When a special keyframe key is lifted by the staple-like bridges at the far left end of the barrel, this felt is placed between hammers and strings to mute the sound.

◀ PLATE 5

A tremolo piano made in London by Tomasso in unrestored condition. The tremolo action, contained in the long horizontal box at the right of the keyframe, is driven by helical gears. Connected to the drive shaft at the left is a pinion meshing with a second pinion on a transverse shaft carrying a bevel gear on the end. This meshes with a shaft which runs in front of the strings but behind the hammers and to which is attached the cam mechanism which causes the hammers to beat continuously on the string. To achieve this, the tremolo hammers are worked not by normal barrel pins but by long staples or bridges, which can be seen forming rather more than the second half of the barrel's length.

▼ PLATE 6

A Spanish barrel piano in the author's workshop. Note the irregularity of the hammers. As the hard felt strip on which the hammer butts normally rest is compressed, so the hammers lean further towards the strings and so the operator has progressively bent all the wires back to keep the heads from blocking the strings. The wrest pins are almost all horizontal instead of leaning inwards to the plank, so indicating that over the years the tension on this wood-framed instrument has pulled them all level and so split the wrestplank. The soundboard itself has been crushed along its top by the pressure from the plank and the bearing has almost entirely gone, meaning that the soundboard has been bowed away from the string pressure.

◄ PLATE 7
A detailed examination of the wrestplank shows clearly that the strings have indeed pulled the wrest pins downwards, severely splitting the plank. It is impossible to do anything with this and no amount of plugging and redrilling will be any good. The only solution is to strip the instrument, remove the old plank and glue in a new one. The hitchpin block at the bottom of the piano will almost certainly have split as well.

▼ PLATE 8
The first step is to remove the hinged top of the piano, which is usually glued on. Often the string tension will have been so much that the glue is already cracked. Use a broad chisel or brick bolster to lever off the top. Remove the barrel, the keyframe and all loose components. Here the instrument is ready for the next stage, which is removal of the strings, tuning or wrest pins, and then removal of the soundboard.

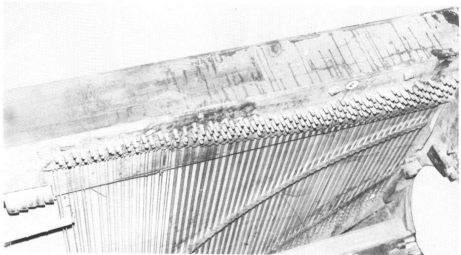

▼ PLATE 9
In the illustration below, the piano is upside down and a new hitchpin block has been glued in. The old block will be used as a pattern for drilling the pin holes. The same procedure is adopted for replacing the wrestplank. See that the packing pieces between the upright posts of the piano back are tightly glued. Always use the largest clamps possible and suitable scrap wood caul blocks to spread the load.

▲ PLATE 10
Rear view of a French clockwork café piano showing the stout
vertical posts, in this case angled like a fan to allow space for
the clockwork motor in this narrow and very compact
specimen.

▲ PLATE 11
The English type of clockwork piano as used in
public houses and places of entertainment. Note
how the instrument is made to appear taller by
extending the sides and back above the wrest
plank. Fitted with an automatic 'soft' mute (see
Plate 4), this finely restored instrument plays ten
popular tunes and is set in motion by the insertion
of an old penny into the coin chute. The horizontal
fall and the front and top are removed for the
picture.

▲ PLATE 12
Made by Crubois of Granville, France, this early twentieth-century café piano
plays on 51 notes and is drum, triangle and castanets accompaniment. The barrels
were interchangeable and the café proprietor could have his repertoire of tunes
changed every week by the piano-renting agency.

PLATE 13 ▶
The more sophisticated barrel pianos incorporated bass drum, side drum,
cymbal, xylophone and mandoline-hammer accompaniment. These barrel-
operated piano orchestrions were enormously popular in Europe and this one,
made in Central Europe early in the present century, would have been a star
attraction in a café or beer hall.

◀ PLATE 14
The early piano player was a separate instrument which could be set before an ordinary pianoforte in order to play it via mechanical fingers. Short-lived in popularity and overtaken by the player-piano, these 'push-ups' as they became known are often well worth restoring. This is a Pianola marketed in London by the Orchestrelle Company.

▼ PLATE 15
There were a number of low-cost player conversions for normal pianos. This one, the Classic (invented by G. A. Smith, British Patent No. 2852, 1914) folded away behind the front fall, compressing the whole mechanism into a small space with the valve chest under the keyboard. Tracker tubes pass down between the keys which are pared away to clear the brass nipples. Conversions such as this 65-note example are curios but seldom make good instruments.

▲ PLATE 16
Another view of the Classic, above, with the take-up spool swung down into the playing position. The back of the front fall, removed for these pictures, is carved away to allow clearance for the mechanism in so confined a space. Conversions of this type include connecting an 88-note tracker bar to a 65-note stack (valve chest) so that full-scale music rolls could be played. Notes at the top and bottom were played in octaves by T-tubes.

PLATE 17 ▶
Looking up under a 1920s Broadwood grand at that maker's unit valve player system. Each note has a square valve box, a collapsing pneumatic and a wire push–pull rod. Fortunately superseded by a more conventional action, this was a slow action, hard to service and with poor repetition.

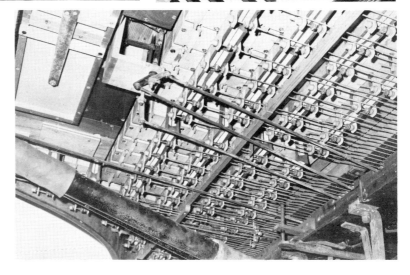

◄ PLATE 18
The Boyd Pistonola with its slim all-metal action made for a very space-saving installation. The multi-cylinder roll motor, right of centre, was like a car engine in miniature as regards design. The action also operated vertically instead of the generally horizontal lift of the wedge-shaped pneumatic action. This enabled the tiny carbon pistons to exert a direct lift on the action, saving power and making a prompt-speaking player action. However, while the Pistonola and its sister action the Terpreter were good players when properly adjusted, they are hard to service and regulate as corrosion in the alloy cylinders means that the self-lubricating pistons lose their smooth action. An elegant system, but one dogged by servicing problems.

PLATE 19 ►
Aeolian's Pianola action was produced in a variety of forms for a very long time. Usually with three decks or rows of pneumatic motors in the chest, occasionally two, and made with both single- and double-valve actions, good basic design and production quality makes the Pianola one of the easiest to restore. This is an early example with a 65/88-note dual tracker bar. The two control rods have quick-release spring clips to make it simple to disconnect without having to remove parts. The air motor is a triple seesaw giving the smoothness of a six-pneumatic motor. Power to the valve chest comes through two large rubber hoses at the left (bass) end.

◄ PLATE 20
In Germany, Aeolian's Berlin-based branch was named the Choralian Company and this installed the Pianola action into a number of German-made pianos including the Ibach seen here. The action, a later version of that seen in the picture above, is a normal 88-note model and was manufactured in Germany. Choralian also produced a German-made Duo-Art action which was identical with the British and American-produced versions.

◄ PLATE 21 This magnificent instrument is a Brinsmead fitted with a dual 65/88-note Angelus action. Designed to play a variety of roll types, including the Wilcox & White 65-note rolls (which play from bottom to top), this universal player installation has a complex spool box with dual drive gears. The five-pneumatic roll drive motor is, unusually, placed on the left. Tracking is manually controlled using a knurled thumbwheel in the spool box. The Angelus action, seen in detail in Plates 32–34, was an early attempt to design a player which would not infringe the Pianola. It was, when designed, novel and reliable, being developed from the organ-playing action devised by its makers, Wilcox & White. The problem was that the action was large and bulky and expensive to service as well as manufacture. In 1921, Angelus went bankrupt and the business was taken over by Simplex who used the name for a while in connection with their reproducing action.

▼ PLATE 22 This top-quality reproducing piano is fitted with the Hupfeld Phonola action, this being the Tri-Phonola. All tubing is in metal. The expression mechanism is to the left of the tracker bar and spool box assembly. To the right at the bottom of the space above the keys is the roll drive motor and above that is the horizontal see-saw tracking pneumatic. The Phonola type of action features an inner transparent cover to the spool box as well as the sliding wood panel in the front fall, seen here in the lifted position. Note the hand controls in front of the key slip and the accent buttons. The main piano lid is seen here on 'half stick'.

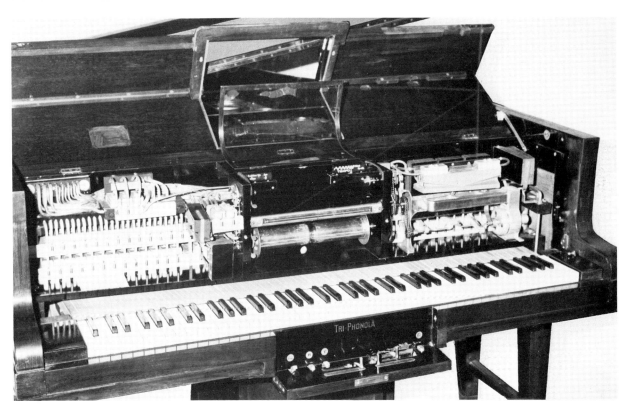

◄ PLATE 23
This is a typical Aeolian action dating from the late 1920s, this example being from a Duo-Art upright. The mounting board above the valve chest or stack mounts, left to right, the terminal block for the themodist and Duo-Art, tracker valve box, tracking motors, spool box, triple wide-bellowed see-saw roll motor.

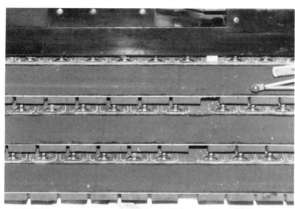

◄ PLATE 24
Removing the front board uncovers the three ranks of valves and pneumatics. Each rank comprises an upper and a lower board, the upper containing the valves, the lower mounting the pneumatic.

PLATE 25 ►
Tearing off a piece of the rubber cloth sealing the gap between the boards reveals the access hole to the valve stem, the pouch board directly above the pneumatic, and the bleed hole.

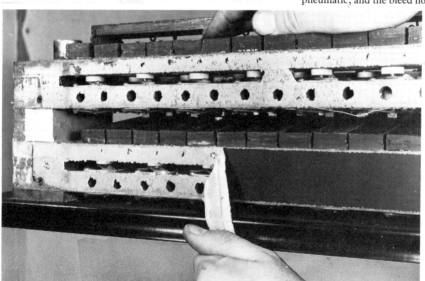

◄ PLATE 26
Opening up an early Aeolian two-deck action starts by tearing off the rubberised cloth sealing the front ends of the chest board. Here the action is upside down. Cleanliness is important in all action repair work as a lump of old hard glue or dust can easily be trapped somewhere where it can later impede the operation of a valve. A vacuum cleaner by the workbench will help to keep dirt and other foreign material out of the action.

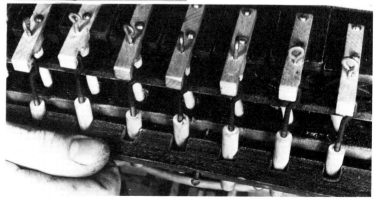

PLATE 27 ►
Before the action can be dismantled any further, the adjustable pitmans which operate the wippens of the piano action must be freed from their guides. Here the locating rail is being taken away leaving the pitmans swinging free on the extension brackets from the bottom board of each pneumatic, to which they are secured by two woodscrews. Note also the eye-ended screw adjuster which regulates the amount of collapse of the pneumatic. The setting up of the restored action will involve using these adjusters to see that each pitman moves exactly the same distance. Each pitman is also threaded onto its bracket wire, so it can be lengthened or shortened. Plate 46 shows how the alignment is set up for reassembly.

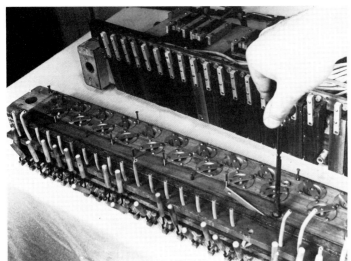

◀ PLATE 28

Separation of the boards is by the undoing of the long screws seen in Plate 40. In the picture, right, the action is once more the right way up and the valve boards are being separated from the pouch boards; watch to see that you keep the screws in the right order as some may be longer than others. The rubber tubing to the lower valves has been cut through to aid dismantling. Subsequently it will be removed, the metal nipples carefully cleaned and sucked through to remove any dust and dirt, and the tubing renewed as the final part of the renovation. The metal valve seats may have corroded where they are in contact with the leather. If this is so, they must all be removed, rubbed clean on a sheet of fine abrasive paper stuck with water onto a sheet of glass, and then painted with a thin coat of polyurethane varnish.

PLATE 29 ▶

Here the valve chest has been opened up and the top board turned back on itself. One complete valve unit has been removed and is seen lying on the pouch board. Visible in the top left is the shaped metal plate which forms the division in the chest which separates treble from bass. In the normal player piano, the suction pressure between the two portions of the stack as separated by this division is varied by the use of control levers. With the Duo-Art, this is regulated from the theme and accompaniment ports in the tracker bar.

◀ PLATE 30

Here is a valve unit removed from the Angelus action in a Brinsmead upright player piano. Whereas in the Aeolian action seen above the valve is centred by a strip of thin metal or red fibre, the Angelus centres its valves in a piece of wood which has a felt-bushed hole in the centre. This particular piano was losing power and notes were not playing. It was found that the alloy dish which forms the valve seat had corroded and a light metal washer keeping the lower portion of the valve straight had also become affected. The remedy was to remove every valve, one at a time, unscrew the leather discs and draw out the valve stem from the polished wood button end – the end which is raised by the pouch. Each metal dish seat was then rubbed smooth and the surface sealed with polyurethane varnish. New leather discs were punched using fully-strained skin backed with hard felt. The job was lengthy and fiddly but the outcome was a totally satisfactory valve operation. Note the delicate springs which Angelus was forced to use to help speed the repetition of this unusual action.

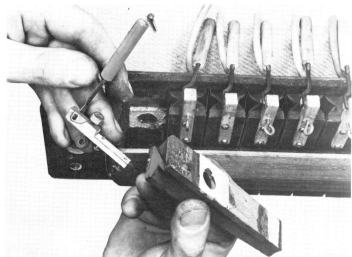

◀ PLATE 31
Here is a pneumatic motor removed from one of the
boards of an Aeolian action. One of the pitman brackets
has been unscrewed to show the adjustment button and
how the wooden pitman is threaded to the wire so that its
length can be adjusted to suit the piano action.

PLATE 32 ▼
From the Brinsmead piano seen in Plate 21 comes this
Angelus diaphragm pneumatic action, below. The almost
square pneumatics with their cranked rods and offset
piano striking linkages are readily seen. Each of these
pneumatics is glued into position in grooves in the pouch
board and this makes removal very difficult with a high
risk of damage. Usually, though, the glue line can be
fractured by carefully loosening the diaphragms.

◀ PLATE 33
The Angelus action, upside down (left),
showing the mass of fabric-covered lead
tubing to the tracker bar (out of view).
The wooden action links have been
disconnected and swung back out of
the way to allow access to some
diaphragm pneumatics, which are not
operating properly. This is done by
unscrewing the leather button nuts
from the cranked action wires seen in
the picture on the right (Plate 32).

PLATE 34 ▶
In the centre of the picture is the defective diaphragm
motor. Clearly seen is a leather patch which some
previous 'restorer' has stuck over the corner of the
leather diaphragm. In reality, if only one or two of
these large motors is damaged, it is acceptable to patch
in this manner but the leather must be very thin brown
tan pouch leather and it should only be glued round
its edges so as not to stiffen the action. The diaphragms
frequently wear and fail at the edges and if this has
happened the whole action must be stripped.

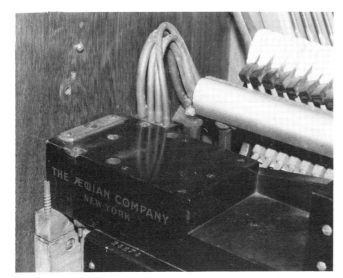

◀ PLATE 35
This early type of Aeolian action shows the terminal block for the themodist and sustaining pedal tubes. When the player action is removed, these tubes are pulled off, remembering, of course, which goes where. Sometimes the tubes are a loose fit and slip off easily. As a rule, if at any time the themodist or bass and treble controls fail, the piano playing loud at all times, the first thing to suspect is that these tubes have fallen off or become damaged. An open-to-atmosphere situation here will apply continuous and unregulated suction at full power. Visible in this picture is the adjusting screw at the front edge of the action board which is used to tip the action to take up any lost motion between pitmans and piano action. This should only be adjusted when the main securing screw, in the centre of the plate, is loose.

PLATE 36 ▶
Rear view of the Pianola action before retubing. The row of pitmans which align with the piano action wippens is clearly seen here. The alignment of these must match the carefully adjusted alignment of the piano action.

◀ PLATE 37
The back view of the Duo-Art Pianola action in close-up showing the Duo-Art switching box in the centre, top. When the Duo-Art function is selected from the normal 88-note full-scale position, the first four notes of the tracker bar scale and the last four are disconnected as playing notes, and the special vertical slits in the tracker bar positioned above these eight note openings are brought into operation. The steel bar running across the centre is to keep the tubing neatly out of the way of the piano hammers. Below this can be seen the pitmans and their adjusters – the pitman guide rail seen in Plate 27 has been removed. The screwdriver blade is indicating one of the link plates which support the decks of pneumatics and valves which together make up the valve chest or stack.

PLATE 38 ▶

This complex array of tubing lies behind the dual tracker bar perforations of a 65/88-note Aeolian Pianola. Note how many of the tubes have developed a 'set' at the nipple ends. This piano had been working perfectly until, after a particularly cold winter, it began missing notes, the hammers striking the strings the moment suction was applied. A strip revealed that these tubes were in many cases perished and broken, allowing unregulated suction direct to the pneumatic action.

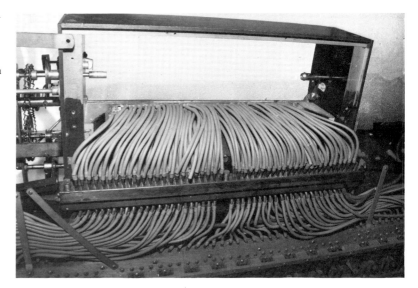

▼ PLATE 39

Close-up of tubes pulled from nipples reveals fractures and sets in the rubber but, more significantly, many of the nipples choked with paper fluff. Several holes were almost entirely filled from years of roll-playing.

▼ PLATE 40

Reassembly of the action should be done before retubing, which should be the last job before alignment and replacement in the piano. Never glue wood faces together. Where a perfect seal has to be achieved, glue leather to one surface and this will make a perfect seal under pressure. At all times follow exactly the same practice as the original builder. Use the same type of material and the same thickness and quality.

▼ PLATE 41

A pianola-restorer's nightmare! This Aeolian action has perished tubing which has partially dissolved into a very nasty and sticky mass. Possibly due to use in a chemical-rich atmosphere, or maybe a faulty batch of rubber, the only way to remove this is to take the action into the open air and scrub it thoroughly with petrol to dissolve off the rubber. Let the action dry thoroughly in air before any further rebuilding. Warning: Do not smoke and no naked lights until the gasolene is fully evaporated.

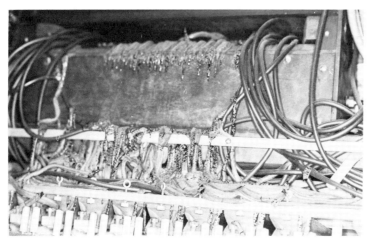

◀ PLATE 42
Detail of the roll-drive mechanism. The gear-shift lever, bottom, is in the 'play' position. The rod which presses against it above its pivot is the brake lever which applies a slight resistance to the top spool chuck so that the music roll is under slight tension while playing.

▲ PLATE 43
Here the gear-shift is in the 'reroll' position and the brake lever has moved to disengage the brake pad from the top spool chuck. Another brake has engaged to put a slight drag on the lower spool chuck during rewind. The gear change is effected by sliding the drive pinion to one side so that it engages with the free chain sprocket driving the top spool chuck.

▲ PLATE 44
Servicing the wind motor consists in removing the guide rails in which the sliding valve boxes move. The seat of each valve must be smooth and highly polished with graphite powder rubbed well into the wood. If there is any roughness in the wood, the whole surface must be sanded to a perfect finish and regraphited.

PLATE 45 ▶
The valve box must also be absolutely smooth and free from any roughness. Similarly the thick air-tight twill cloth covering it must be clean and free from holes. The wooden or metal arms supporting the crankshaft must be free from wear; these are usually bushed with bushing felt and the bushing may need to be renewed.

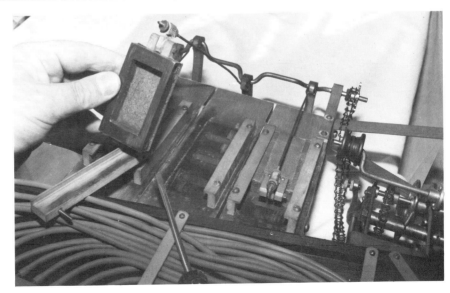

◀ PLATE 46
After rebuilding, the final job is to realign all
the pitmans and this is done by placing a
straight edge along the tops of them with the
action standing the right way up on the
bench. First check the height of the piano
action wippen of the first and the last notes
in the piano. Set the first and last pitmans to
this dimension and then put the straight edge
in position and adjust all the others to this
setting.

▲ PLATE 47
Methods of roll-tracking are many and varied. Aeolian initially used a single-
finger mechanism, above, which was patented by W. J. Jackson-Mellerish
of Aeolian (British Pat. No. 14,725, 1913). This was adjusted to the left edge
of the roll and, during playing, any deviation would open the end of a tube
connected to a single bellows motor which caused the spools to shift.

PLATE 48 ▲
Above, right, is the Aeolian twin lever system developed from the early
Jackson-Mellerish patent. This uses a pair of motors like the unit shown in
Plate 52.

PLATE 49 ▶
A close-up of one of the tracker fingers showing how movement of the finger
uncovers the end of a pneumatic tube, so unbalancing the valve system in
the box seen in Plate 51, shifting the tracking motors to suit. Similar types
of balanced air tracking were used by many makers, a familiar one being a
pair of vertically staggered holes at each end of the tracker bar. The
operation is similar in all cases.

PLATE 50 ▶
A dual 56/88-note player like this
early one by Aeolian used manual
tracking. The large lever to the
right end of the tracker bar moves
a cam to shift the spools. Above
the tracker bar at the same end
can be seen the 88-note spool end
adaptor held in its recess by a
simple turn catch. The large lever
just visible below the left-hand
end of the tracker bar is the 65 to
88 note shifter, while the knurled
wheel seen above it on the end of
the take-up spool is to vary the
width of the spool to suit rolls of
differing widths.

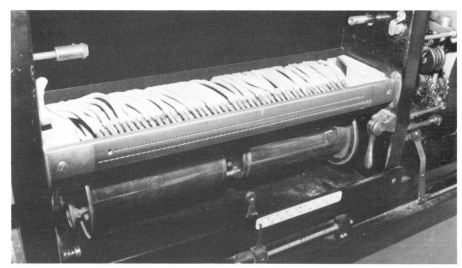

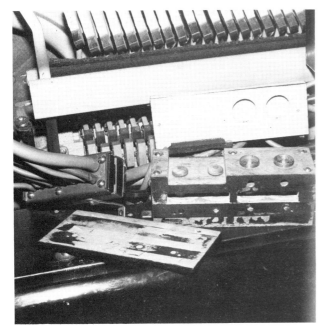

▲ PLATE 51
The tracking system control valves,
above, showing the valve box with the
top and front removed. There is a felt
dust trap in the top of the box.

PLATE 52 ▲
Above, right, the pair of balanced
pneumatics which operate the tracking
adjustment by moving the spool chucks in
the spool box. The sliding gate valves to
the right of it are the themodist and
Duo-Art selectors.

PLATE 53 ▶
This hinged frame was used by Aeolian
to align the aspects of the spool box and
had adjustable ends to suit either 65- or
88-note actions. The slit in the centre
aligned with a tracker bar opening.

◀ PLATE 54

Here are some examples of highly developed player piano actions which need care and attention in restoring. Left is the Hupfeld Phonoliszt-Violina introduced in 1909. Three violins are encompassed by a circular rotating bow and played with the piano from specially encoded piano rolls. Many thousands of these instruments were made but their pneumatic actions required careful maintenance. Today the surviving specimens number fewer than thirty.

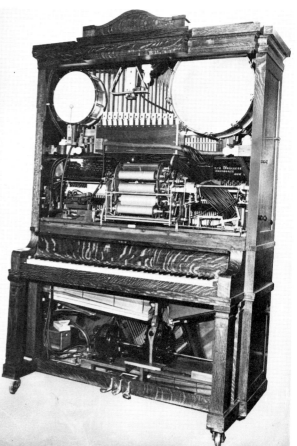

PLATE 55 ▶

The Wurlitzer BX orchestrion was made in 1914 and incorporated percussion instruments as well as a rank of organ pipes. Notable here is the automatic roll-changing mechanism. This is a complex instrument to tackle and the mechanism of the roll-changing system is a restorer's *tour de force*.

◀ PLATE 56

Another player violin is the Mills Violano-Virtuoso, an electrically operated expression piano and violin playing on all four strings. Less refined than the Hupfeld at the top of the page, yet magnificently engineered, this instrument survives in quite large numbers since it was much easier to keep in working order. A novel feature of the electric piano behind the violin is that it is symmetrical in layout with the longest, bass strings in the middle and the treble at each end. This instrument has confounded many a piano-tuner.

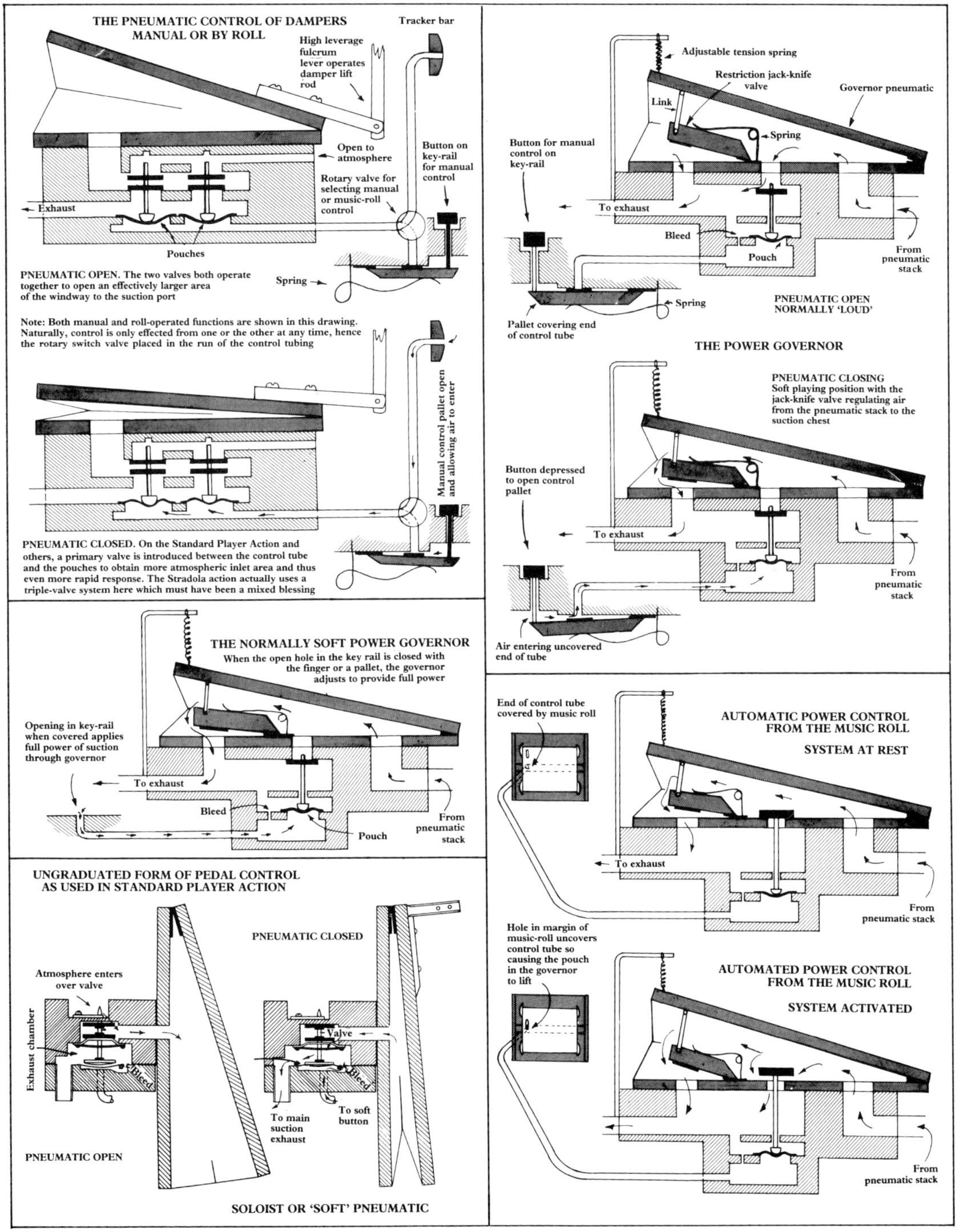

THE PNEUMATIC CONTROL OF DAMPERS
MANUAL OR BY ROLL

Tracker bar

High leverage fulcrum lever operates damper lift rod

Open to atmosphere

Button on key-rail for manual control

Rotary valve for selecting manual or music-roll control

Exhaust

Pouches

Spring

PNEUMATIC OPEN. The two valves both operate together to open an effectively larger area of the windway to the suction port

Note: Both manual and roll-operated functions are shown in this drawing. Naturally, control is only effected from one or the other at any time, hence the rotary switch valve placed in the run of the control tubing

Manual control pallet open and allowing air to enter

PNEUMATIC CLOSED. On the Standard Player Action and others, a primary valve is introduced between the control tube and the pouches to obtain more atmospheric inlet area and thus even more rapid response. The Stradola action actually uses a triple-valve system here which must have been a mixed blessing

THE NORMALLY SOFT POWER GOVERNOR

When the open hole in the key rail is closed with the finger or a pallet, the governor adjusts to provide full power

Opening in key-rail when covered applies full power of suction through governor

To exhaust

Bleed

Pouch

From pneumatic stack

UNGRADUATED FORM OF PEDAL CONTROL
AS USED IN STANDARD PLAYER ACTION

PNEUMATIC CLOSED

Atmosphere enters over valve

Exhaust chamber

Valve

Bleed

To main suction exhaust

To soft button

PNEUMATIC OPEN

SOLOIST OR 'SOFT' PNEUMATIC

Adjustable tension spring

Restriction jack-knife valve

Governor pneumatic

Link

Spring

Button for manual control on key-rail

To exhaust

Bleed

Pouch

From pneumatic stack

Spring

Pallet covering end of control tube

PNEUMATIC OPEN
NORMALLY 'LOUD'

THE POWER GOVERNOR

PNEUMATIC CLOSING
Soft playing position with the jack-knife valve regulating air from the pneumatic stack to the suction chest

Button depressed to open control pallet

To exhaust

From pneumatic stack

Air entering uncovered end of tube

End of control tube covered by music roll

AUTOMATIC POWER CONTROL
FROM THE MUSIC ROLL

SYSTEM AT REST

To exhaust

From pneumatic stack

Hole in margin of music-roll uncovers control tube so causing the pouch in the governor to lift

AUTOMATED POWER CONTROL
FROM THE MUSIC ROLL

SYSTEM ACTIVATED

From pneumatic stack

Figure 20   The various methods of controlling various piano actions pneumatically

apparent complexity appears as insoluble as a Chinese puzzle, replacement of the tubes is not really a difficult task. The tubes run from the first hole in the tracker-bar to the first hole in the action pouch board and thence along to the other end. If each tube is replaced progressively, one at a time, the job is easily done. When automatic pedal controls are fitted, these tubes run from the tracker-bar to a valve block. Wherever possible, cut your new tube using the old one as a pattern. If it is not possible to do this, run the new tube between the two nipples and cut it so as to allow a little slack – there must be no strain on the tube nor must it be either so tight or loose that it can kink.

Over the years, chemical changes take place in rubber and the narrow-gauge rubber tubing used for connecting tracker-bar to chest often perishes. This deterioration manifests itself in one of three ways. First the rubber may remain pliable, but will have developed a permanent 'set' or stretch where it has been pushed on to a nipple. The result is that it will not seal and will readily fall off its connections (see Plates 38 and 39). The next type of deterioration turns the rubber into vulcanite or, in simple terms, makes it brittle rather like macaroni before it is cooked. Tubing in this condition can actually be quite dangerous to break since when it snaps sharp fragments can fly into your face. The third type of deterioration is perhaps the nastiest of the lot, for the rubber changes into a sticky mess rather like an old hot-water bottle (Plate 41).

Removing perished rubber tube can often be quite a job since while it may come away freely in unsupported places it may resist all simple attempts at removal from nipples, revealing all the symptoms of having been bonded on with glue. This is not the case: what has happened is that the nipple has corroded slightly so that rubber and metal have formed a bond.

Careful chipping with a small screwdriver can often help or, if the nipple is accessible, gently squeezing it from two sides with a pair of pliers to crack the rubber. Sometimes, however, as in the case of a tracker-bar where many pieces of rubber have been pushed onto closely spaced nipples, this is hardly possible. The technique I have developed is to use paint-stripper applied liberally to the rubber. This softens the hard rubber after a while and a stiff wire brush can be used to remove the residue. Of course you can only do this with a metal tracker-bar after you have removed it from the piano spool-box as the next step is to wash the whole thing in white spirit to neutralise the stripper, and then thoroughly scrub it in very hot water and strong washing-up liquid. Make sure all traces of rubber and stripper are removed and see that all the ports and tubes are clear – don't poke a wire through them unless necessary to clear an obstruction, but blow down each one.

The task of retubing becomes complicated where large numbers of tubes have to be connected at the tracker-bar and, with certain types of action such as some 65/88 note actions and, particularly, tracker-bars with many extra expression ports such as the Kastner, pushing on the tubing is a job which must be aided by cranked, flat-ended tweezers.

Incidentally, you can lubricate the tubing with water but do not use soap as this can rot the rubber. Chemists sell tubes of surgical rubber lubricant and it is a good plan to rub some of this over the nipples before starting to retube.

Lift the action back into the piano. You should have someone to help you so that a hasty move does not undo all the work you have so far accomplished. The exact method of replacement you will have to find by experiment, but normally you should tip the action so that it leans backwards slightly as it goes into place, so that the lifting pieces of the player action do not foul the wippens. Secure the action into place with the studs and nuts provided and see that they are done up tightly.

Most actions feature an adjustment to the lifting pieces so that they can be brought into the proper position relative to the wippens. With the action at rest, the lifting pieces should just be in contact with the wippens. If all the piano hammers were properly set before replacing the player action, then they should remain all perfectly in alignment with the action in place. Test the action of each note manually from the keyboard, to see that nothing is being fouled.

In lieu of a proper tool, adjustment of the lifting pieces can usually be made using a length of stiff wire with a right-angle bend ⅜ inch long at one end.

With the upper action now restored and installed once more, turn your attention to the bellows system. Examine the exhausters and equaliser(s) for deterioration of the covering, paying close attention to the corners and folds and not forgetting the bottom hinge line. I refer here to equaliser(s) because the early player actions and those of the cabinet-style push-ups used only one large equaliser; the later players often employed one for the bass action and one for the treble, each with a different 'power' as governed by the internal springs.

Bellows cloth can be very deceiving. It must not feel hard, nor must it flake when rubbed. However, even cloth which seems satisfactory may, on test, be shown to be useless. Quite often, rubberised cloth develops thousands of tiny pin-holes through which air can pass, and these holes are only visible when the cloth is held up to the light. If the bellows system will not hold vacuum, i.e. if the equaliser opens fully very quickly after the exhausters have been operated, then it is quite likely that the cloth is porous. When one piece of cloth is found to be porous, it is safe to assume that all are porous and you should re-cover all the moving bellows parts. A serviceable bellows system should maintain its vacuum for between six and eight seconds.

Should it be necessary to open up an equaliser at any time, either to renew the flap valves or to re-cover it, take great care that the internal springs do not fly out and hit you. They are extremely powerful and the haphazard stripping off of the old cloth could lead to a serious accident. It is a good idea to leave a wide strip of the original cloth still in place along the wide top edge of the equaliser so that the spring can be restrained. In re-covering, this strip may be left in place, the new covering passing over it. So long as the new cloth is not glued to the old piece (except at the edges of the equaliser of course) it will not interfere in any way with the operation of the unit. You might resort to a dodge such as holding the boards of the equaliser between rigid floor-braces whilst re-covering but, whatever you do, an appreciation of the vicious bite which an equaliser spring can give is the most important thing.

Notice that the shape of the bellows cloth is very important if a full and strain-free movement of the finished unit is to result. You must cut it evenly about a centre-line representing the whole length of the wrapped-round cloth and this is best done by the use of paper patterns.

Fix the new cloth with hot glue well worked into the weave. On some players the cloth was originally tacked on as well. It is not good practice to have even headed tacks passing directly through the fabric: if you choose to replace using glue and tacks, and provided that there is enough room when the units are assembled, adopt the organ-builders' bellows technique and tack through thin strips of wood about ½ inch by ⅛ inch. Whether you glue only or glue and tack, pay close attention to the forming of the new cloth at the corners to ensure a freely moving close fit.

When restoration is complete, refit the bellows to the piano and seal off the main outlet

51

trunk. Now test the bellows for leaks. After four or five strokes of the exhausters, the foot treadles should offer considerable resistance up to the point of the opening of the relief valve, where fitted.

Final assembly of the player action can now proceed together with the attachment of hand-operated controls. A word about controls, whether in the form of buttons, turn-switches (valves) or levers. These normally pass through slots in the fixed back of the key fall and these slots are lined with bushing cloth or felt. After prolonged use, this material wears away – and attack from moth will destroy it. Always renew these bushings and linings. Where levers are pivoted under the key-bed they are sometimes packed between felt rubbing pads to eliminate squeaks and rattles. Replace these. As for control rods, re-bush the holes through bearing blocks. Rusted control rods make for stiff operation and rapid bearing wear. Clean off all rust with abrasive paper and for a really professional job have the rods nickel-plated (if they are steel); otherwise paint them with clear polyurethane varnish or black enamel. Turn-switches which alter the direction of flow through air valves often corrode solid. Dismantle them, clean all surfaces carefully (do not damage close-tolerance mating surfaces) and if lubrication is needed use a dry graphite lubricant.

Testing, fault-finding and regulation can all be classed under one heading – adjustment. However, assuming that perhaps you have obtained a player in working order I shall include some pointers towards major defects which should already have been taken care of during rebuilding. Although the player piano is at first sight a complex system of piping, motors and valves, this complexity is but an assembly of functional parts and all basically work in a similar manner. Therefore, once we have gained an intimate knowledge of our piano player, common sense will largely dictate what has to be done in the way of adjustment.

First of all, you should test for leaks by sealing off the tracker-bar either by placing a roll of music in position and stopping on the unperforated leader part or by sticking a strip of sellotape across the openings in the bar. Place the tempo lever at the pause position (normally to the far left) and put the re-roll lever to 'play'. Now treadle evenly. If the action and bellows are sound, there should be a mounting resistance felt through the feet. If, however, there is little or no resistance, then there is a leak somewhere which can often be heard as a rushing or whistling. Have a friend treadle while you locate the leak. It may be a hole or split in the bellows, a disconnected air tube or a badly fitting joint somewhere in the action.

Some leaks are very difficult to locate and in these cases you must resort to a process of elimination. First disconnect all the connections to the bellows system, such as the main trunk to the upper action, the motor airway, the supply to the sustaining-pedal pneumatic or hammer-rail motors and so on. Plug these open ends and try treadling again. If there is no great resistance, then you know the defect lies in the bellows system. Check all the woodscrews for security and then examine the cloth of the bellows folds very closely – it is most likely that it will have deteriorated along one of the crease lines (don't forget to check the hinge strip at the root of the bellows as well) or at one or more of the folding corners of the cloth.

Proceed with this elimination method, connecting and testing the various functions one by one. Check the air motor carefully to see that the leak is not being caused by an uneven sliding surface to one of the valves.

Finally, reconnect the upper action and, if this leaks, try tightening all the screws; but beware of overtightening, which will only result in stripping the threads of the screws and making matters worse. (Stripped threads must be plugged with a softwood peg and the screw replaced in the centre of the peg.) If this does not cure the trouble, one can be fairly certain that the primary or secondary valves are not seated properly. If the secondary valves do not make a good seal against the exhaust seats there will be a leak (which may be due to a particle of dust) or the buttons on the other end of the valve stem may be adjusted so that they are touching the pouches, so preventing them from lifting the valves sufficiently. In the case of primary valves, they may not have the proper range of movement or again dust may have lodged beneath the buttons.

There is a good way to short-circuit these tests and that is to move the re-roll lever to the 're-roll' position and hold the motor against turning while treadling. If the treadles offer strong resistance, the indications are that the bellows system is serviceable and that the leak is in the upper action.

After the reassembly of the valve chest in which the valves have been re-covered or re-seated, and even after careful regulation and adjustment, a period of use is often needed before the valves bed down properly on their seats and produce a seal which is effective. This may be found when, after a painstaking rebuilding job, the player action is found to be sluggish with many dumb notes and non-repeating ones.

The remedy is often very simple. In order to bed the valves in, pedal the piano hard and pass your hand up and down the tracker bar twenty or thirty times, covering and uncovering the notes sequentially and to operate the valves. With a power-driven, electric piano, switch on the pump and do the same thing. Alternatively, connect the domestic vacuum cleaner to the stack with a length of rubber tubing and do the same thing: the advantage of this last-mentioned method is that you can perform much of the valve seating with the action out of the piano and on the workbench.

Now comes the test for notes that may not play. The use of the tester roll is called for here and it should be watched closely as it travels over the tracker-bar to see that each note sounds. If any do not, then it may well be that the tube from the tracker-bar to the primary pouch is blocked with dust or fluff from the music rolls. This can be sucked out with the suction pump. If the note does play but will not repeat, the bleed-hole is probably obstructed, or the valves may be sticking, playing once but not repeating. Remove the front board from the valve chest and, using a length of rubber tubing, blow into the suspect hole to check that the valves move. If the primary valve does not move, the tracker tube may be blocked, or the valve held down by some mechanical defect such as corrosion, dampness or dirt. Next try the secondary valves. The action can thus be tested thoroughly by following the path taken by the air in playing. Using a note which plays well as a yardstick, observe how its valves function and compare with the defective ones.

If the bleed-hole is blocked, use a piece of fine wire, bent to suit, and gently insert it into the little hole. This will clear any obstruction. Be careful not to enlarge the bleed; in actions where the bleed is in the form of a small metal cup or celluloid disc with a hole in the centre, take care not to dislodge it.

The bleed-hole is also to be suspected if the action displays slow or sluggish repetition. If a good sucking out from the tracker-bar fails to remedy this, the bleed-holes must be cleaned by carefully probing each one. Now it may be necessary to enlarge a bleed-hole and – whilst this is good for repetition, since it allows rapid equalisation of pressures after a note has been sounded – it adversely affects playing power, since, by the same premise, the air inflating the pouch is being vented faster. Generally speaking, the action should be arranged so that the notes on the test roll repeat well on light pumping at a tempo setting of 80.

If, on test, it is seen that one or more of the hammers are not falling right back to their proper place (assuming the piano action to be in perfect order), this is due to the secondary valve remaining open. The cause may be dirt under the primary valve, causing it to remain open and keeping the pneumatic in a state of collapse.

If the primary valve functions properly but the hammer-action pneumatic remains motionless and inoperative, it may be that the channel between the primary valve and the secondary pouch is blocked. If the secondary pouch works, the trouble must lie in the secondary valve which may be stuck by spread glue or dampness. Satisfactory primary valves coupled with inoperative pneumatics always indicates trouble in the secondary pouch or valve. Valves and pouches can always be checked by blowing them with a rubber tube, holding one end of the tube in the mouth. The pouches should inflate under the merest breath but do not forget that the air is being bled away through the bleed-hole. Secondary pouches, on the other hand, should show a positive resistance when blown, for there is no bleed-hole between the channels. Primaries should, by comparison, offer a slight resistance.

I have mentioned the need to aid newly seated valves to set themselves properly. This fault is not restricted to newly installed valves: sometimes, after an action has been working perfectly, removal and reinstallation may produce inoperative notes for no other reason than that the valves have not seated themselves properly. This can be detected with the test roll and quite often the staccato repetition of the note, as instructed by the test roll, will be sufficient to cause the valve to drop back into place.

The test roll is also of assistance in the reseating of player-action valves after a piano has been moved. Generally speaking, it is harmful to tip a player piano on end but removal men often find it necessary to do just that when shifting an instrument. The result is that the valves become unseated, and, when the instrument is righted, some may not return to their proper place. A few plays with the test roll can often save tears, disappointment and unnecessary work.

When all valves and pneumatics seem to work but the piano will not play certain notes, then the trouble lies in the linkage between the pneumatic and the piano action. This may be a wire, a wooden pitman or, in the case of the Angelus, a complex lever and rod.

Should there be a leak at the exhaust side of the secondary valve, the pneumatic will either not work or, if it does, will work weakly and slowly. If the secondary valve has too much movement, then the movement of the pneumatic would be very weak and the normal playing resistance to the foot treadles would diminish, calling for more rapid pumping. On the other hand, if the secondary valves have too little motion, the pneumatic action will be slow and the player will not sound very loud. Primary valves need not rise more than $1/64$ inch and secondaries between $1/32$ inch and $1/8$ inch, depending on the action. An average is $1/16$ inch and it is imperative that all valve settings, whatever dimension they are, are equal throughout the valve system otherwise there will be a variation in the apparent striking force of each note. The single-valve system should be adjusted to lift between $1/16$ inch and $1/8$ inch, again depending on the action.

On the bellows system, if there is a leak in the flap valve of the exhausters, there will be little resistance to the treadles and little work done for each stroke. If the valve on the inside of the exhauster leaks, there will be normal resistance on the downwards stroke, but an immediate tendency to kick back at the end of the stroke. Also, if one treadle is lightly held fully down and the other pumped, there should be no feedback of motion to the down treadle. If the stroke of one has a counter-effect on the other, however slight, then the inside flap valves are leaking.

Dust and dirt are the enemies of a pneumatic action and the presence of foreign matter between the valves and their seats can cause a whole host of malfunctions: expression-pneumatics operating all the time, notes sounding or not sounding, motors running at high speed even with the tempo control closed, inoperative tracking devices, and so on. Ciphers, the bane of the organ-builder, also affect pianos. A ciphering valve is one which allows a note to be played when there is no note indicated by a corresponding hole in the music roll. The trouble is usually something elementary, such as dirt holding a valve open or a disconnected tracker-bar tube or one with a leak in it. The effect of dirt is best appreciated when you realise that it only takes a few bits of dirt holding a few valves open to cause a pneumatic action to be inoperative, for as fast as air is pumped out air is drawn straight back in again.

Another possible defect is the opposite of a cipher: a note remains silent when it should sound. The pneumatic will not collapse. The cause can be a blocked air passage or a twisted or kinked tube, or the pneumatic may be loose on its seating, deprived of its operating vacuum by an unwanted air inlet.

If the action cut-off is not working properly, then the music will play on rewind. If the cut-off is mechanical, then the trouble should be easy to locate – a broken linkage, a stripped thread or similar. If the cut-off is pneumatic, then the defects which can plague such a system should be investigated – a sticking valve, a blocked or kinked tube, a disconnected tube.

If you find that the pneumatic stack will show no vacuum – in other words there is no operation of the pneumatics when the bellows are operated – the trouble may be the incorrect setting of the primary valves. Or perhaps they have been unseated. This is fairly common when a piano is shifted, as mentioned earlier. If the instrument worked well before, it is necessary only to keep the instrument playing for an hour or so to enable the valves to drop back. However, where this is not the case, the cause may be valve-guide corrosion (where the valves have guide pins), or perhaps the pouches have lost their suppleness. The pouches must be soft and pliable and the valves must seat correctly.

If the action just does not play and no other cause can be found, it is fairly obvious that the action cut-off valve is remaining closed. This may be caused by a detached suction hose, in which case the treadles offer no great resistance. Alternatively, if the valve is closed and the hoses are all present and correct, there will be heavy resistance to the foot treadles.

If the player works well, but the Themodist controls do not work and the piano plays *forte* at all times except when the hand-controls are used, you should suspect that one of the Themodist tubes is leaking or may even have become disconnected. This can happen at the junction block where all function tubes can be intentionally separated to remove the top action from the piano. Early Aeolian actions had quite long lengths of rubber tubing hanging on junction block nipples and with age these could quite easily slip off.

The most sensitive and important feature of the player piano is the air motor. Its smooth operation, flexibility of speed without hesitation and silence in motion is crucial to the perfect performance of the instrument. The ability to control the motor delicately and precisely lies at the core of the individuality of playing a roll and its failure to operate in that manner will thus have a drastic effect on the music played. Music rolls are arranged to agree to certain pre-arranged tempi and these correspond to certain numbers which are indicated on the tempo scale forming part of the motor control, and which are also called up on the music roll. The following table shows first the tempo pointer setting and then the proper distance which the paper should travel over the tracker-bar measured in feet per minute:

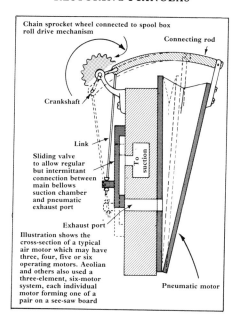

Chain sprocket wheel connected to spool box
roll drive mechanism

Connecting rod

Crankshaft

Link

Sliding valve
to allow regular
but intermittant
connection between
main bellows
suction chamber
and pneumatic
exhaust port

To suction

Exhaust port

Illustration shows the
cross-section of a typical
air motor which may have
three, four, five or six
operating motors. Aeolian
and others also used a
three-element, six-motor
system, each individual
motor forming one of a
pair on a see-saw board

Pneumatic motor

Figure 21   Section through typical wind motor for driving the music roll mechanism

Number	Ft/min.	Number	Ft/min.
10	1	80	8
20	2	90	9
30	3	100	10
40	4	110	11
50	5	120	12
60	6	130	13
70	7		

During manufacture, the air motor was originally calibrated at at least three points in this speed range but for the purpose of repair it is normally adequate to see that the paper travels 7 feet in one minute with the tempo setting at 70. Test rolls are normally intended to be run at 70 but – and watch carefully for this – it is usual for reproducing-piano test rolls, as mentioned in the next chapter, to run at 80.

If the motor runs faster than it should, the spring in the motor governor must be slackened off slightly; if the motor runs too slow, the spring must be tightened. All speed calibrations are best done either with the test roll marked off at 1 foot intervals with a pencil or with any suitable music roll. A watch with a sweep second hand can then be held by the roll whilst playing to check the speed setting.

If the motor runs too fast immediately you start to treadle hard, the motor governor is not closing sufficiently. The adjusting screw for the jack-knife valve should be brought out a fraction until this is cured. Do not alter the spring setting unless the motor also races on normal pumping.

If, as soon as you start to pedal hard, the motor slows down, the governor must be closing too much. Again, the regulation of the jack-knife setting screw is the answer. Screw it in a little so that the governor closes a fraction more. If the motor drags on light pumping, then the spring tension needs to be increased.

Should the motor run irregularly (visibly moving erratically or momentarily stopping, particularly when carrying a heavy load such as at the end of a long roll, and emphasised by a slow tempo setting to begin with), this usually means that the sliders of the motor are not seated correctly. They may be warped or the surfaces may need regraphiting. Where there is a chance that they are warped or roughened, rub down both sliders and their mating surfaces on a sheet of fine glass-paper resting on a dead flat surface, such as a piece of plate glass. After

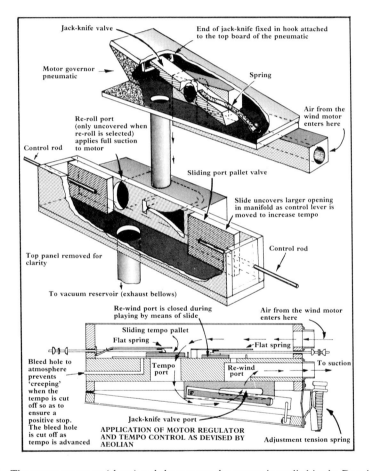

Figure 22   The tempo governor (above) and the manner the system is applied in the Duo-Art governor assembly

sanding, they can be burnished by rubbing hard on the plate glass. To regraphite, gently breathe on the surface to make it very, very slightly damp and then dust on graphite and rub it into the wood with the finger. Continue in this fashion until the whole surface is 'bright' with graphite and the wood grain completely filled. Never use any form of oil, either on its own or mixed with the graphite. The essence of graphite is that it is a perfectly dry lubricant which minimises drag between moving mating components. Some people claim to achieve the same results with talcum powder or french chalk. Admittedly, the initial effects are similar, but talcum and french chalk are basically the same substance and they absorb moisture. A talcum-lubricated motor will work well for a while, but will rapidly slow up and become gummy and erratic. Use only graphite of the type made for locksmiths, although, as a 'running repair' you can rub a very soft pencil, such as a 6B grade, over the surfaces so long as the pencil point does not indent the wood.

Other problems which can lead to irregular running of the motor are badly adjusted or bent connecting-rods, and, of course, leaking pneumatics. Pneumatics are often found to have been strengthened in manufacture by the addition of small corner gussets in the central folds.

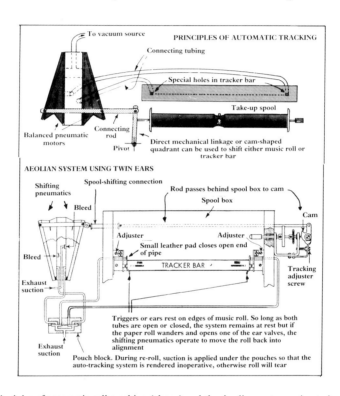

Figure 23 Principles of automatic roll-tracking (above) and the Aeolian system using twin ears to feel the movement of the edge of the music roll

These patches are usually of leather glued to the rubber cloth and they deteriorate rapidly. If you endeavour to replace these patches, you will only serve to increase the friction of the motor and it is far better to re-cover the pneumatics completely with thin rubber cloth. Regarding connecting-rods, it is important that each slider should move the same distance each side of the central position. Most connecting-rods have threaded ends and, by disconnecting one end, the rod can be screwed in or out to make it longer or shorter. Some cheaper pianos had fixed wire links and all you can do with these, if they need adjustment, is to bend them carefully to the desired setting. Other instruments had wooden links and these featured felt bushes in their ends. These harden or disintegrate in time and thus produce the same effect as incorrect lengths. The bushes are made of thin piano felt glued to form a bearing lining in the hole of the link. The link is usually split and secured with a tensioning screw to facilitate both renewal of the bush and also assembly.

Should the motor run fast continuously, the speed valve connected with the rewind device in the tempo box is failing to close or else the tempo valve is not seating properly. If there is a silent control lever or button, this may be operating the speed valve due to a leak in its tube. If the action has an automatic, pneumatic rewind device worked by a hole in the tracker-bar exposed at the end of the roll, look to this for any signs of leakage or broken tubing.

The spooling and unspooling of the music roll can cause trouble. If the motor turns at speed without a roll in place, but will only shift the music slowly when in place, even at top speed, then the small brake-pad which bears on the spool drive to keep the roll under slight tension on rewind may be affording friction during the 'play' mode. It should be disengaged from the brake plate during playing. Again, if the music respools loosely, this is due to this brake not offering enough resistance, and it must be adjusted so that it just bears on the brake plate.

If the action dampers remain in the lifted position (the so-called loud-pedal effect), there may be a leak in the tube from the tracker-bar if it is automatically controlled. Where control

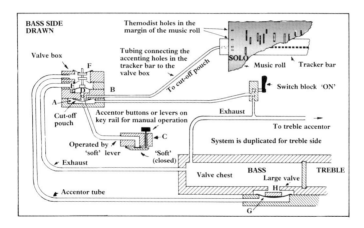

Figure 24   The operation of the Themodist accenting system. Fixed to the bottom of the valve chest is a small panel into which run two rubber tubes and a large exhaust tube. This panel contains the Themodist accenting valve, G. With the Themodist in the 'on' position, the cut-off pouch A is drawn by the exhaust suction clear of the air channels B, thus preparing them for action under the control of the small Themodist perforations in the music roll margins. The two 'soft' levers of the manual expression control are then set to the 'on' or 'soft' position, thereby closing the two small pallets C which shut off open air. The pouch D is thus deflated by the bleed-hole E, and the valve F comes to rest. Air enters over the top of F, inflates the large pouch G and closes the port H. All this is achieved in a fraction of a second. When a marginal roll perforation K admits air down the tube B, pouch D is lifted. The valve F is raised and G is instantly deflated, opening H to full suction power. The illustration shows it in this condition. By cutting marginal holes very slightly ahead of the note to be accented (shown by an arrow), the melody can be picked out very effectively, even individual notes in an arpeggio can be accented. When the Themodist is selected 'off', open air is admitted through the switch block to the pouch A, which is thus drawn against the channels B by the action of the bleed-hole E and the valves F and G can be operated only by the two manual 'soft' levers or buttons. When these manual controls are not in use, they hold pallets C open so that under normal suction power the valve F is raised and the pouch G is lowered

is pneumatic from a key-bed button, look for leaks in that tube. The leak may be in the shut-off lever in the spool box. This lever works a valve block which may be leaking. Occasionally, air can enter under the pallet below the key-bed control button and in this case either a stronger pallet spring is needed or the leather facing has become hard and distorted and must be replaced.

When the damper works slowly you must achieve a compromise between the valve settings. The damper-lifting pneumatic requires a great deal of power so that, if it is adjusted to work quickly, it will use a large amount of the available vacuum power which will be felt on the treadles, and also, possibly, in the music. When adjusted to work slowly, there will be no noticeable side-effects to playing. Adjustment is governed by the pneumatic valves. Given long travel and with a suitable, large bleed-hole, operation will be very quick but with the objectionable side-effects mentioned. Adjusted to give short travel, the damper pneumatic will be slow to move.

Sometimes the piano action will not repeat properly when the soft controls are operated and this is usually found where the pneumatic stack is divided with an expression governor controlling each half from a manual control. Adjustment is made by varying the spring tension on the governors, making it greater if the effect is too soft, less if the result is not soft enough. The same rules apply where the vacuum level in part of the stack is controlled by marginal roll perforations (Themodist type) to the expression governor.

Bellows have been dealt with earlier, but it sometimes happens that minor defects develop in an otherwise satisfactory system. There are several problems which can arise, particularly in very cold or damp weather. Flap valves occasionally leak either because of slack or broken stretcher springs (or perhaps the leather strip itself has become excessively stretched or warped) or because dirt has wedged between the board and the leather. You may find that the leather has curled at the edges in which case it should be replaced, but you can get by for a short while by removing the strip, holding it tight between the hands and rubbing it back and forth, mating surface lowermost, over the edge of a board. Finally, rub chalk well into the soft surface of the leather and refit. If the bellows board is bowed, there is not much that can be done, and, if it is very bad, you must remove it and make a new one from thick plywood. Small cracks can be sealed with hot glue and covered with a strip of pneumatic cloth.

There is one problem which you will occasionally encounter. It is one which is not confined to the player piano and is well known to piano-tuners. Sometimes you will find that one or more of the bass strings – those that are wrapped – produces a decidedly peculiar sound. Whilst this sound may appear as a buzz or tinniness, it can take the form of a 'beat' which defies correction by the tuner. This defect is caused by the copper wire wrapping of the string having become slightly loose along part of its length. If the string is otherwise serviceable, it is not essential for the string to be replaced; all you need to do is slacken the string right off at the wrest-pin until the eye loop formed at the opposite end of the string can be slipped off the peg. Now twist the string half a turn in the direction of the copper winding. This serves to tighten it on itself. Replace the string twisted in this way, make sure it is located through the bridge pins correctly, then retune. Nine times out of ten, you will have cured the fault at the expense of a few moments' work. Stubborn strings may want a full turn of twist, but if this still does not cure the trouble then the winding is so loose that the string must be scrapped.

There is a saying that prevention is better than cure and, to this end, the manufacturers of the modern motor car recommend that after every so many miles it should go to a garage for servicing and overhaul. It can do nothing but good to adopt the same principle of 'preventive

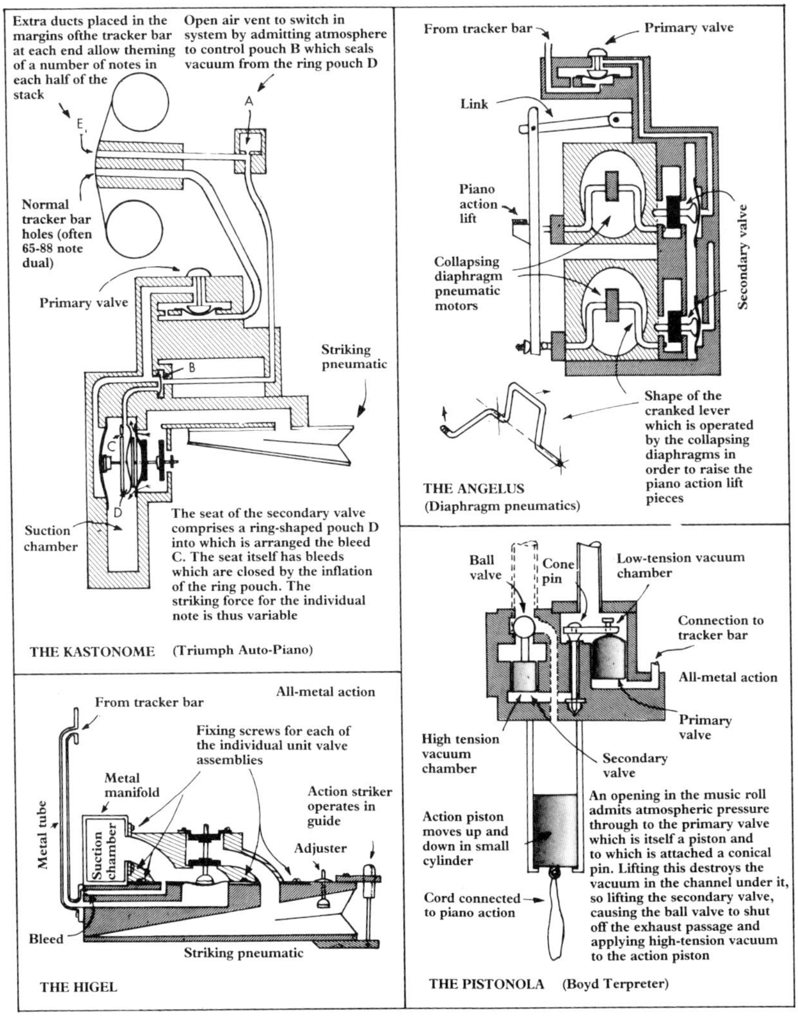
Extra ducts placed in the margins ofthe tracker bar at each end allow theming of a number of notes in each half of the stack
Open air vent to switch in system by admitting atmosphere to control pouch B which seals vacuum from the ring pouch D
A
E
Normal tracker bar holes (often 65-88 note dual)
Primary valve
Striking pneumatic
B
C
D
Suction chamber
The seat of the secondary valve comprises a ring-shaped pouch D into which is arranged the bleed C. The seat itself has bleeds which are closed by the inflation of the ring pouch. The striking force for the individual note is thus variable
THE KASTONOME (Triumph Auto-Piano)
From tracker bar
Primary valve
Link
Piano action lift
Collapsing diaphragm pneumatic motors
Secondary valve
Shape of the cranked lever which is operated by the collapsing diaphragms in order to raise the piano action lift pieces
THE ANGELUS (Diaphragm pneumatics)
From tracker bar
All-metal action
Fixing screws for each of the individual unit valve assemblies
Metal manifold
Action striker operates in guide
Metal tube
Suction chamber
Adjuster
Bleed
Striking pneumatic
THE HIGEL
Ball valve
Cone pin
Low-tension vacuum chamber
Connection to tracker bar
All-metal action
Primary valve
High tension vacuum chamber
Secondary valve
Action piston moves up and down in small cylinder
An opening in the music roll admits atmospheric pressure through to the primary valve which is itself a piston and to which is attached a conical pin. Lifting this destroys the vacuum in the channel under it, so lifting the secondary valve, causing the ball valve to shut off the exhaust passage and applying high-tension vacuum to the action piston
Cord connected to piano action
THE PISTONOLA (Boyd Terpreter)

Figure 25 Four other types of popular player action

maintenance' with the player piano. Depending on the amount of use it has, it should be serviced regularly. Piano-tuning, ideally a thrice-yearly job, is usually considered by piano owners as a once-a-year task. Be this as it may, each time the piano is tuned it is sound policy to go right over the player action, first of all sucking out the tracker with the tracker pump and then systematically going through the whole mechanism looking for defects. Periodic cleaning and dusting inside is also advisable.

Properly cared for, a player piano, whether it be an early model or a late 1930s specimen, will continue to give faultless service for many, many years to come.

CHAPTER 4

Understanding the Reproducing Piano

From the foot-pedalled player piano was developed the electrically pumped piano and, as part of that development, came the expression piano. In this instrument, a certain amount of unregulated modulation between theme and accompaniment was possible in addition to theming melody notes and operating soft and sustaining pedals. The expression piano formed the basis of most of the German and American coin-feed electric instruments for use in public places.

The reproducing piano is a highly developed form of player piano which effectively carries on the technical perfection of music reproduction from where the expression piano leaves off. It is a player piano in which every one of the aspects of human control is automatically performed. It is an instrument which may be switched on and left to play a roll of music with the selfsame certainty of the resulting interpretation as we have today when we turn on the record player. Not that the reproducing piano is in any way a characterless device which denies human participation in making music. With the exception of the keyless 'Red Welte' cabinet player, all of the reproducing pianos made, whilst capable of performing without any manual effort other than putting a music roll in place and switching on, could also be played using manual controls just like a normal player piano, and they could play with ordinary music rolls if required. And, of course, they might also be played by hand as a conventional pianoforte by those skilled in music.

The reproducing piano can do all these things yet, as I stated at the start, it is only a player piano which has been taken a stage further. It has a mechanism which is quite familiar to the owner of a player piano, yet this system is operated by a much more sophisticated device than the comparatively crude hand controls of the normal player piano. So what of its mechanism and its complexities? And, above all, how should one approach its overhaul and adjustment?

Examination of a reproducing piano will indeed show you that it has familiar parts. There is the pneumatic stack, the valve chest, the wind motor, the tempo control, the tempo governor, the cut-off valve – in fact just about everything that we have already detailed in the previous chapter. One large difference is the power section. Where we had foot-operated exhausters and a bellows system in the pedal player, our reproducing piano normally has an electric suction pump. Early models sometimes retained a variation of the familiar system of bellows-type exhausters and drove them with a motor-operated series of cranks and pulley belts. And some models are dual-purpose in that they can be treadled in the ordinary way, or driven electrically: these are called 'pedal electric' pianos and the majority if not all of these are Duo-Arts and are grands. Then there is an upright model which is foot-operated only. In the case of the Duo-Art, these are really only 'half Duo-Arts' since only the treble half of the stack comes under the influence of the Duo-Art system. The Marque Ampico, however, was indeed a full Ampico foot-operated only.

While so many of the actual component parts in the reproducing piano are familiar and although the principles of operation are really quite basic, the manner in which components and principles are united to achieve the coveted reproducibility of a performer's performance is fairly complex. It is extremely sensitive in operation, critical in adjustment and demanding of the highest skills in restoration and servicing.

Unlike the ordinary player piano, where the operator is required not only to put the expression into the music but also to regulate the tempo of the music as necessary, the reproducing-piano music-roll travels at a constant speed.* Where an ordinary roll might have a 'sustain' or pause instruction printed by some notes, the reproducing piano roll will have them perforated to the proper length relative to the speed of the music roll as printed on the leader of the roll and set before the instrument begins to play. Where a silence or rest comes in the music, the ordinary roll will show a 'pause' instruction (probably to save paper), but the reproducing piano roll will continue to travel in blank paper for the length of time chosen by the pianist who recorded the roll. The roll drive speed is thus set at the beginning of the music and left alone. If we can accept that the instrument is basically an ordinary player, all we have now to understand is the mechanism by which it is elevated to the class of the finest type of automatic piano ever put into production. Air remains the motive power, the pressure differential between normal atmospheric pressure and the partial vacuum created within the player mechanism by the exhaust system being used in a more delicately adjusted manner than in the normal floor-operated player piano. Instead of being admitted to the piano functions in full or coarsely regulated part, the power of the partial vacuum created inside the instrument is transferred through monitoring and metering valves which allow varying amounts of suction power to operate the functions. These regulating devices are instructed in the work they must do not by manual lever but by special, additional valves which are in turn given their orders from extra holes in the music roll.

From our knowledge of the pneumatic operation of player pianos (this is detailed in the companion volume to this, *Pianola – the history of the self-playing piano*), we understand how the pedal action (soft and sustaining) can be controlled from the music roll. The accenting of certain notes by themodising is also germane to the concept of the refined player or expression piano. The reproducing piano has to do just the same but – and here is the major difference – it has to be able to interpret the amount of pedal movement and the degree of force used to accentuate a theme or note. As we shall see, all this is done very ingeniously by using components which, in their basic form, we are already familiar with.

Three main types of reproducing piano are most common and most likely to be found by the collector or enthusiast. These, in order of surviving quantity in Britain, are the Aeolian Duo-Art, the American Piano Company's Ampico, and the Welte-Mignon. In the United States, the order reverses the first two and many Weltes were built in New York and thus survive in greater quantities than in Europe. There were quite a few other types, of course, but surviving examples are so few and far between that the chances of finding one now are somewhat slim. The operation is always the same, though; only the details of how to carry out the operation may differ.

---

* A strange feature of the special music rolls made of the test-pieces for the *Daily Express* Duo-Art piano playing contest is that the tempo has to be varied during the playing.

63

Fortunately, reprints of the original servicing and overhaul manuals for these three leading reproducing actions are still available to enthusiasts today. Armed with a piano, a service manual and thorough experience and knowledge of an ordinary 88-note player piano, the average person can restore a reproducing instrument without too much difficulty. What I propose to do in this chapter is to describe the principles of these three makes of action and show you just how they work. But, beforehand, some more of my words of warning! Never attempt to tackle a reproducing piano without first having three special things – first, a proper tester roll for that make of instrument; second, the overhaul manual; and, finally, a vacuum pressure-gauge. Having got these three adjuncts to your work, make sure you use them!

Another word of warning! It is common to find electric pianos fitted with female socket plugs at the piano so that a male mains plug can be fitted in. This means that there has to be a live two-pin plug on the end of a cable which can be accidentally pulled out with obviously dangerous risks. It is vital that you rewire the mains connections to instruments of this type so that the piano has a male plug. Electric pianos were never earthed and so it is a good idea, whilst rewiring the mains lead, to use a three-core cable and connect the earth wire to the case of the motor. In an earlier age, electricity was treated in a surprisingly light-hearted manner and modern thinking on the subject is one of the few manifestations of present-day civilisation which is unquestionably acceptable. Happily, the newspaper headline has not yet appeared which reads 'Collector Killed by Electric Piano', but neglect of the power-supply leads could well precipitate a disastrous happening.

THE AEOLIAN DUO-ART

Most common in the field of reproducing pianos is the Duo-Art made by Aeolian from 1913 onwards. This was made in three main styles beginning with the non-electric, pedal-only model. This was in reality only a 'half Duo-Art' since the reproducing mechanism operated solely on the treble end of the piano, normal techniques using hand controls being used to put expression into the bass. These half Duo-Art models are always upright pianos and can be identified at once by the fact that there is no electric motor or pump and the expression box and accordion pneumatics (explained further on) exist only for the treble end.

The second variant of the Duo-Art is the full reproducing action found in both upright and, more usually, grand pianos. These have no foot treadles or pedals other than the usual soft and sustaining pedals and are fully electrically pumped. The third variety is a style which, in the world of reproducing pianos, is known only to the Duo-Art. This is the Pedal Electric Duo-Art – PEDA for short. Probably only made in grand format and almost always a Weber piano (occasionally a Steck and once in a while a Steinway), this is a full Duo-Art with electric pump. However, by means of foot treadles it can also be pumped like an ordinary player, yet still retaining most of the Duo-Art functions.

The Duo-Art system works by dividing the music into the theme and the accompaniment. Compared with most other reproducing pianos where the music is separated between bass and treble sections, the divided expression system of the Duo-Art operates by two variable vacuum pressures. This division of the valve chest comes between the 43rd and the 44th note on the piano keyboard, and can be seen in Figs 26 and 28. In use the pressure to the left can be vastly different from that on the right. Regulator pneumatics control each at a different fundamental setting so that the theme setting is fractionally stronger than the accompaniment when under identical conditions. This is an acceptable basis, since the theme is usually

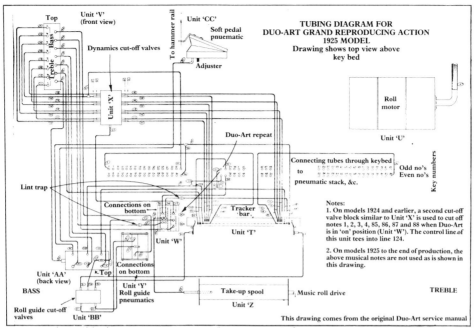

Figure 26   Tubing diagram for the 1926 model Duo-Art grand reproducing action

louder than the accompaniment when both are performed at their softest.

The theme side is normally the treble or right-hand side; the accompaniment side, the bass or left. I say normally, since provision is made for control of either side from the opposite end of the pneumatic stack so that, if called upon so to do, the theme side can operate on the bass half of the stack, the accompaniment on the treble. Alternatively, the entire stack can be governed from either side.

The system operates through four special expression perforations and a theme perforation in each side of the music roll, bass and accompaniment. The ingenious operation of the expression holes will be described in a moment, but before this we will have a look at the special function of the theme control which, like the normal Themodist from which it naturally derives, works from narrow, horizontal openings in the tracker-bar and are the holes immediately preceding and succeeding the music-playing holes. Under normal playing conditions, the loudness level of the whole piano is determined by the accompaniment expression system. When a theme perforation in the paper crosses the tracker-bar, whether it is on the treble or the bass side of the roll, the other side of the pneumatic stack comes under the influence of the theme side of the expression mechanism. This can apply to either bass or to treble, or simultaneously to both sides. By this means, each half of the piano can be controlled by its own tracker-bar theme duct – virtually two separate tracker-bars. However, the moment the duct is opened by a music perforation, the same suction pressure is applied to both halves of the piano. Duo-Art expression holes are always cut ahead of the notes to which they refer to give the action time to respond – usually about ⅜ inch ahead of the notes. Where notes are themodised, the themodising holes are noticeable ahead of the expression openings in the roll. Part of this advance cutting is due to the fact that the Duo-Art openings are above the note openings in the tracker-bar, while Themodist openings are virtually in line with note holes in the tracker-bar.

Expression dynamics are controlled by an expression box which contains so-called zero pneumatics by which the foundation level of the music (with neither expression nor theme modification) is determined. Each zero pneumatic has its own jack-knife valve to cope with the variations of suction pressure which occur in performance (as in an ordinary player piano). These jack-knife valves are controlled by the 'accordion pneumatics', which are so simple in concept yet so perfect in operation. There are two sets of accordion pneumatics, one for each jack-knife valve – one for each side of the piano, bass and treble or, if you prefer it, theme and accompaniment. These comprise four parallel motors each joined to the other, the upper one having a small opening, the next a larger one, and so on until the fourth has the widest opening. The top one is made to collapse only $\frac{1}{16}$ inch, the next one $\frac{1}{8}$ inch, the third $\frac{1}{4}$ inch, and the fourth $\frac{1}{2}$ inch. If all are arranged to collapse together, the jack-knife valve is moved $\frac{15}{16}$ inch. Now, by using these pneumatics in combinations such as numbers 1 and 2, 1 and 4, 2 and 4, and so on, fifteen separate combinations can be achieved (sixteen if we include the zero position), each a shade louder or softer than the other. As there is a set of accordion pneumatics for each half of the keyboard (i.e. each side of the pneumatic stack), one half can be playing *fortissimo* and the other *pianissimo* or any stage between the two.

The accordion pneumatics have numerical values corresponding to the number of sixteenths of an inch which they open, hence they are referred to as numbers 1, 2, 4 and 8. There is another feature of the expression box which we must note and this is the 'spill valve'. Air is continually being drawn out of the expression box by the exhaust system – in reproducing terminology always referred to as the 'pump'. It is being removed from both sides of the pneumatic stack through the pump. To achieve a suitably low vacuum point norm, air is continually bled into the system through what is called the spill valve. This is arranged so that it can be gradually reduced in opening via our old friend the knife-valve, which in turn is worked by the movement of the main knife-valves controlled by the accordion pneumatics. Under normal playing conditions, then, a metered quantity of atmospheric air is fed into the system to reduce the normal vacuum pressure. As the accordion pneumatics begin to collapse, so this amount of vacuum modulation is reduced until a point is reached when accordion pneumatics numbers 2 and 8 have collapsed ($\frac{2}{16}$ plus $\frac{8}{16}$ equalling $\frac{5}{8}$ inch moving either of the knife-valves that amount). When this happens, the spill valve knife-valve closes completely and stays that way during any further increases in movement of the main knife-valves as dictated by the accordion pneumatics. So it is that the vacuum norm can be said to be reached at a position corresponding to an opening of $\frac{5}{8}$ inch on either side of expression box.

Control of the accordion pneumatics is effected through four openings in each side of the tracker-bar which are placed above the first four and the last four musical note openings (see Fig. 27). The openings appear as large, vertical slots and, when operating with Duo-Art rolls, the four music note holes beneath, at each end, are disconnected. To play ordinary 88-note rolls, a lever in the roll box is moved which changes over a valve block, cuts out the Duo-Art expression openings and reconnects the musical note holes. In the Duo-Art mode, 80 piano notes are played.

The collective operation of the above-mentioned parts can be better understood from the following description of the functioning of the system as a whole. Starting with the accompaniment side, if neither the accompaniment nor the theme hole in the tracker-bar is uncovered, the air from each side of the pneumatic stack enters the expression box, passes through the flap valves and passes out through the opening to the accompaniment passage-

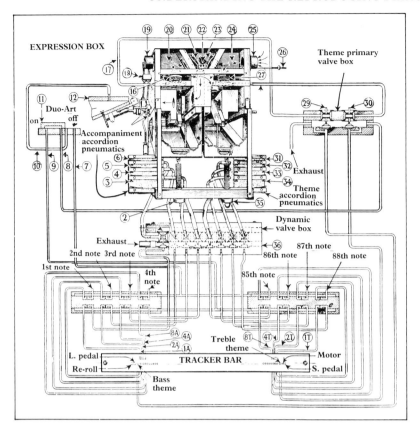

Figure 27
The Duo-Art expression box

way, past the accompaniment regulator knife-valve and so on to the pump where it is exhausted to atmosphere. The speed of the air from the pneumatic stack to the pump depends on the position of the knife-valve, which can be modified by the accordion pneumatics on that side. As we have already seen, there are sixteen different amounts of regulation which the accordions can apply to the knife-valve. Assuming that neither of the theme openings in the tracker-bar is uncovered, this accompaniment regulation will control the whole keyboard.

Now, if the bass theme hole remains closed, but a perforation in the music roll opens the theme hole in the treble, atmospheric air enters and shifts the treble theme primary valve and closes the corresponding secondary valve in the expression box. Air entering the expression box from the treble side of the pneumatic stack is thus made to pass out over the top of the closed secondary valve and thus to the theme-regulator passageway past the knife-valve. The exact position of this valve will now be under the influence of either setting of the accordion pneumatics on the theme side.

If the treble theme opening stays closed, air flow from the treble side passes through the accompaniment side of the expression box and if, at the same moment, the bass theme opening in the tracker-bar is uncovered the bass air flows through the theme regulator.

For manual application of expression on ordinary music rolls, hand controls are fitted together with a device called the 'temponamic' lever, which has a large, circular knurled handle to it. When moved bodily from side to side, this is used to adjust the tempo both in

67

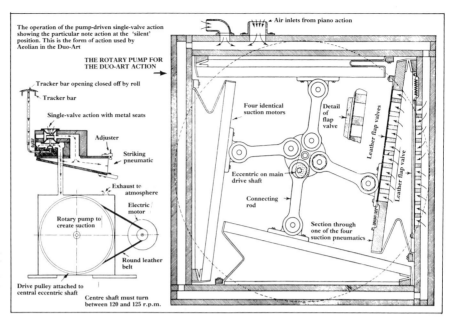

Figure 28
The Aeolian
Duo-Art player
action, left, and
details of the
rotary suction
pump

Duo-Art and manual playing. If the knob is pulled outwards, it is also used to apply manual expression to the accompaniment of ordinary rolls by twisting the knob in a clockwise direction. This serves to regulate the accompaniment knife-valve directly.

Duo-Art pianos were made with two types of pump (excluding early models which used electrically operated belt-driven exhausters). The great majority of models used a four-lobe exhauster pump fitted in a box and a pulley driven from a motor. As the pump rotated, so a crankshaft inside alternately opened and closed each of four bellows motors applied to the main suction trunk. This is shown in Fig. 29. Much later, low-cost upright models were made using a self-contained cylindrical pump. Although far neater and lighter than the lobe pump, it tended to be noisier and more liable to overheat. Hung from a hook within the

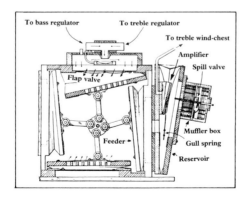

Figure 29   The Duo-Art pump showing its reservoir or equaliser, crash-valve or amplifier, spill valve and regulator box assembly

underside of the piano case, the fully enclosed aluminium housing contained the electric motor and a suction fan. Frequent lubrication of the grease-bearing pads at each end of the motor shaft is necessary with this type of pump. Generally, however, it cannot produce anywhere near as much vacuum as is needed for much serious music.

The application of the Duo-Art system to the grand piano called for the expression box to be constructed along different lines because of the intrinsic differences between the two instruments – grand and upright. The basic principles remain the same but the grand box incorporates a crash valve which functions when the accordion pneumatics reach power

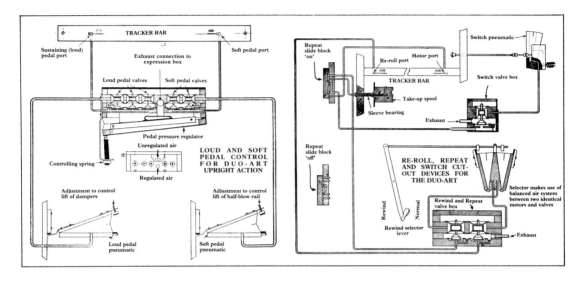

Figure 30   Functions and features of the Duo-Art system

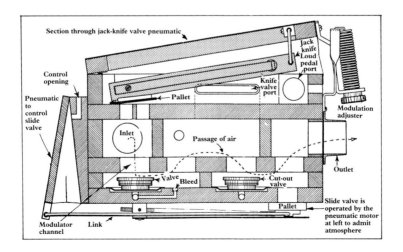

Figure 31   The Duo-Art modulator system

number 15 on the theme side as called for by the music roll.

In operation, it connects the channel from the pneumatic action directly to the pump, bypassing the theme knife-valve so that very quick, loud accents can be obtained.

Another feature, special to the grand installation, is the modulator pneumatic. This provides a means whereby the normal Duo-Art may be modified or softened, without losing any of the dynamic gradations provided by the accordion pneumatics. It also serves as a supply regulator for the sustaining pedal and accordion pneumatics and it is equipped with a cut-out valve for the pneumatic action on re-roll.

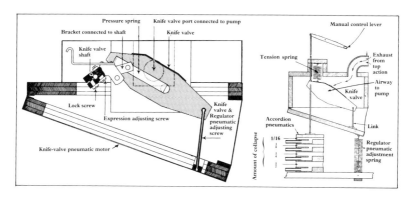

Figure 32   The knife-valve and its operation in the accordion dynamics

The third special control is the keyboard shifter. As already noted, there is normally no rest rail in a grand action (controlled by the soft pedal) but the grand action couples the soft pedal to a cam which shifts the keyboard laterally so that the hammers only strike two of the trichord strings. The keyframe shifting in the Duo-Art is effected by the use of a pneumatic acting on a lever as shown in Fig. 33. On some grands which are fitted with 'half-blow' rails, this is, of course, not used.

The regulation and adjustment of the Duo-Art mechanism is generally well covered in the service manual relating to the action and so will not be repeated here. However, a few general points are worth making at this juncture. Some of the points I shall make here relate not just to the Duo-Art but also to other makes of instrument. This is particularly the case as regards the test-roll.

The test-roll for a reproducing piano is something of a curate's egg – it is only good in parts. Now there can be no doubt that an action can be set up to perform the test-roll perfectly. However, this is absolutely no guarantee that it will perform a favourite music roll adequately. Those who have set actions solely to the test-roll have invariably suffered first disappointment and then confusion. After all, it can be argued, what is the test-roll for if it is not to regulate the action by? Satisfactory performance from a reproducing action is largely a compromise between the ideal of the test-roll and the reality of the individuality of the reproducing action and nowhere is this more apparent than with the Duo-Art which, certainly as regards British-made models, was always set up to suit one particular piano and was thus as individual as a fingerprint.

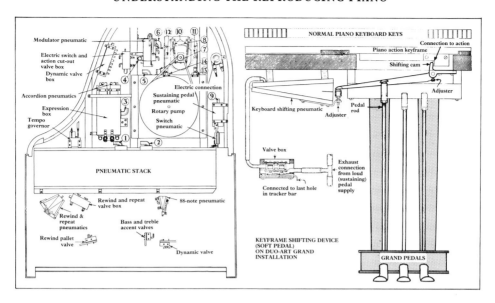

Figure 33   Duo-Art grand installation and soft-pedal keyboard shifting system

The right procedure is to begin by setting up the action to the test-roll – indeed it is absolutely indispensable to use a test-roll otherwise the proper establishment of the grades is too problematical. Once the piano will play the test-roll properly, then proceed with playing a dozen or more different proper music rolls and make whatever tiny extra adjustments are needed to bring out the shades and nuances of each. That dreaded word 'compromise' must rule!

There is probably no more vexing a subject amongst Duo-Art restorers and collectors than the matter of setting the zero expression. Because the Duo-Art system builds up on the zero setting, this setting is of paramount importance. The problem is that when the instruments were first made they were factory-set and no instructions were ever published as to how to attain that level. Matters are not made easy by the provision of a test-roll which is really not very much help at establishing this position. The instrument can be set up to play the tester perfectly, yet when one has a favourite roll with, say, a pianissimo chord or rapidly repeated series of soft notes, these often will not play.

Now, as you will understand, every part of the player action of any instrument is subject to a set of working conditions which cannot, in the way of things, be considered in any way constant. Every individual piano action, however carefully set, will require a very slightly different force to operate, and every pneumatic action for every note is subject to slightly different degrees of valve setting, pneumatic resistance and even suction pressure across the stack.

On top of this, the knife-valve regulators in the Duo-Art are not true pressure regulators since they operate as vacuum throttles aided by the spring-loaded bellows chamber. In fact, there is a throttle valve whose action is theoretically being balanced by the spring-loaded bellows, the whole under the variable influence of the accordion pneumatics.

Now there is something to be said for leaving well alone other than using the test-roll and

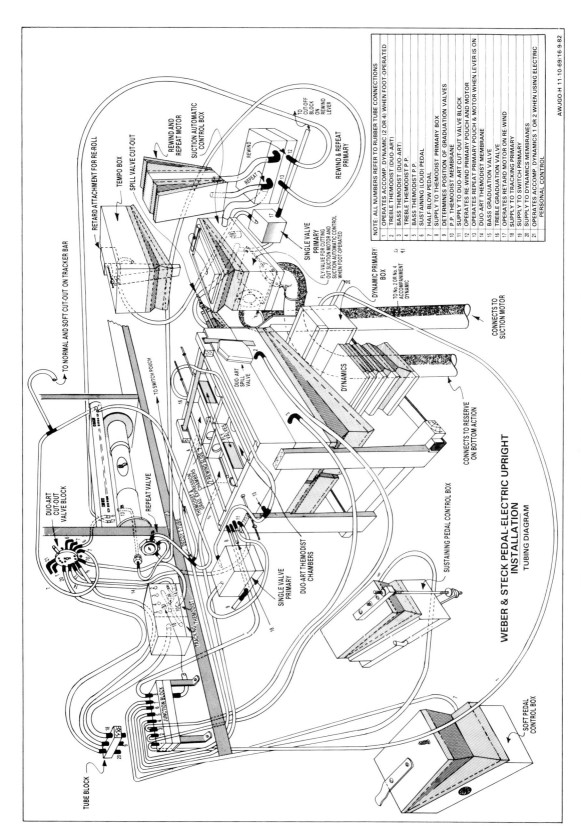

TUBE BLOCK

TO NORMAL AND SOFT CUT-OUT ON TRACKER BAR

DUO-ART CUT-OUT VALVE BLOCK

REPEAT VALVE

TRACKING THEMODIST

DUO-ART THEMODIST CHAMBERS

SINGLE VALVE PRIMARY

THEMODIST TENSION GRAD. EXCHANGERS

REWIND SLIDES

VALVES

JUNCTION BLOCK

DESOT TUBE

RETARD ATTACHMENT FOR RE-ROLL

TEMPO BOX

SPILL VALVE CUT-OUT

REWIND AND REPEAT MOTOR

SUCTION AUTOMATIC CONTROL BOX

REWIND

REPEAT

TO CUT OFF BLOCK ON REWIND LEVER

REWIND & REPEAT PRIMARY

SINGLE VALVE PRIMARY

FLY VALVE FOR CUTTING OUT SUCTION MOTOR AND SUCTION AUTOMATIC CONTROL WHEN FOOT-OPERATED

DUO-ART SPILL VALVE

DYNAMICS

DYNAMIC PRIMARY BOX

To No. 2 OR No. 4 ACCOMPANIMENT DYNAMIC

CONNECTS TO SUCTION MOTOR

CONNECTS TO RESERVE ON BOTTOM ACTION

TO SWITCH POUCH

SUSTAINING PEDAL CONTROL BOX

WEBER & STECK PEDAL-ELECTRIC UPRIGHT
INSTALLATION
TUBING DIAGRAM

SOFT PEDAL CONTROL BOX

NOTE: ALL NUMBERS REFER TO RUBBER TUBE CONNECTIONS	
1	OPERATES ACCOMP. DYNAMIC (2 OR 4) WHEN FOOT-OPERATED
2	TREBLE THEMODIST (DUO-ART)
3	BASS THEMODIST (DUO-ART)
4	TREBLE THEMODIST P.P.
5	BASS THEMODIST P.P.
6	SUSTAINING (LOUD) PEDAL
7	HALF-BLOW PEDAL
8	SUPPLY TO THEMODIST PRIMARY BOX
9	DETERMINES POSITION OF GRADUATION VALVES
10	P.P. THEMODIST MEMBRANE
11	SUPPLY TO DUO-ART CUT-OUT VALVE BLOCK
12	OPERATES RE-WIND PRIMARY POUCH AND MOTOR
13	OPERATES REPEAT PRIMARY POUCH & MOTOR WHEN LEVER IS ON
14	DUO ART THEMODIST MEMBRANE
15	BASS GRADUATION VALVE
16	TREBLE GRADUATION VALVE
17	OPERATES RETARD MOTOR ON RE-WIND
18	SUPPLY TO TRACKING PRIMARY
19	SUPPLY TO SWITCH PRIMARY
20	SUPPLY TO DYNAMICS MEMBRANES
21	OPERATES ACCOMP. DYNAMICS 1 OR 2 WHEN USING ELECTRIC PERSONAL CONTROL

AWJGO-H 11-10-69/16-9-82

Figure 34 Weber and Steck pedal-electric upright installation diagram

your favourite roll and making them both play acceptably. Some of the problem was recognised originally by the roll editors who varied the expression setting for softly played single notes and for chords.

Of course, there is yet another problem and that is the thoroughness of your restoration workmanship. The slightest leaks can be crucial to these low settings and a pianissimo passage which theoretically should play as intended may be reduced to the odd note sounding by the presence of stiffness in the individual actions (either piano action or player action), lost motion in the setting of the player action with the piano action, or leaks which may be either in one note action or across the stack as a whole.

The critical setting of the Duo-Art centres on the accordion pneumatics, not so much to ensure perfectly even and regular stepped opening and closing, but to ensure that the increments of opening are correct for the loudness function of the piano called for at that setting.

The most important thing to remember is that the setting of the accordion pneumatics at $1/16$ in., $1/8$ in. and so on should only be taken as a guide and must be regulated individually to suit the particular instrument. When setting up for the first time, set them in the stated steps, but do not shun adjustment to these dimensions during regulating to the test-roll.

Zero setting is a lengthy job involving arranging all the individual actions to operate evenly on zero intensity. In practice the thing to do is to adjust until *all* the notes just sound. Check that you have reached this point by adjusting a small amount further, whereupon you should find that some of the notes start to miss.

Adjustment for repetition involves careful attention to the bleed-holes. In some cases where pouches are themselves slightly porous, it is possible to close up the bleed altogether and still get perfect repetition. This indicates that the pouch is acting as its own bleed and, provided that the porosity is right, not excessive, and that the leather is otherwise sound, there is no reason why you cannot leave this alone, closing off the bleed with a small patch of stiff paper or leather glued on with Evostik Resin W (white glue). Of course, if the pouch is too bad it must be replaced or resealed with a little egg-white.

Soft pedals on the grand piano usually operate the keyboard shift but, because this invariably requires the use of a large and hence somewhat sluggish pneumatic motor to shift the keyboard, almost all makers later adopted to the use of the half-blow rail which partially raised all the hammers closer to the strings for all but their top-class models. However, the abandonment of the keyboard shift and its replacement by the half-blow is not altogether faithful to the music and its interpretation. One member of the Player Piano Group has overcome this by letting into the key-bed of his piano a row of bronze studs which match with steel rubbing plates let into the underside of the keyframe, so providing reduced friction points. Alternatively, the rubbing points can be dry-lubricated with powdered graphite rubbed into the timber (*not* graphite grease or anything in any way oily).

THE AMERICAN PIANO COMPANY AMPICO

The Ampico reproducing action, introduced prior to 1913, is a more complex system and was produced in three distinct types. The first of these was the early Stoddart Ampico. The Model A action was produced for both grand and upright actions, the expression unit and other detail components being re-engineered in 1920 from double- to single-valve systems. In 1929, the action was completely redesigned, there being very little resemblance between the

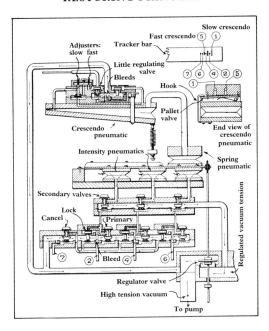

Figure 35   Dynamic mechanism of the Ampico Model A reproducing piano

earlier model and the new one. With the introduction of the Model B, the production of upright actions was dropped, so, whilst all Ampico uprights were Model A, Ampico grands were made as Models A and B. There was also a pedal-only upright version known as the Marque Ampico.

The tracker-bar of the Ampico system has a total of 98 openings comprising 83 ordinary note holes, 7 expression openings at the left end, and 8 at the right. Automatic tracking is achieved by a pair of 'ears' recessed into each end of the tracker-bar.

Operating on an entirely different system from the Duo-Art, the essence of the Ampico expression system is the delicate balancing of a regulating valve between two sets of pneumatics. The dynamics of the Ampico system are measured in the terminology of fast and slow crescendo valves, intensity pneumatics, and lock and cancel valves.

Ampico designers claimed that they found by experimentation that the ear could distinguish about six different degrees of accents when the playing was soft, and naturally less as the playing became louder. It was also found experimentally that no number of steps produced a smooth crescendo effect; to say nothing of expression shades. When the Ampico first appeared, it had sixteen steps to work with, to produce dynamic effects, but these were soon found to be entirely inadequate to give smooth crescendo or expression effects. The mechanism was, therefore, redesigned to enable it to produce these effects. Subsequently it was found that sixteen steps of loudness were unnecessary to produce accents.

The Ampico system of dynamic control, subsequently developed, provided just seven steps of loudness. By means of side perforations in the music roll, the intensity of the playing can be set to any of these seven steps and remains so set until a subsequent perforation, or combination of perforations, sets it to another step. The change in intensity takes place

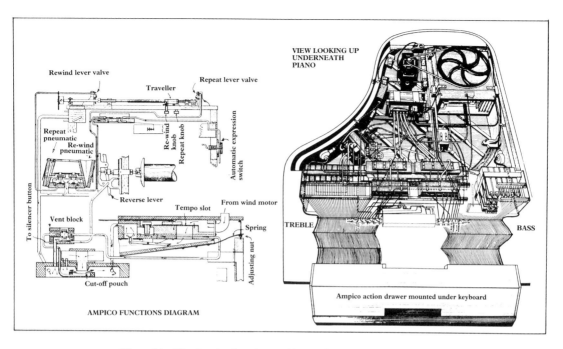

Figure 36   The Ampico functions and layout for the Model A installation

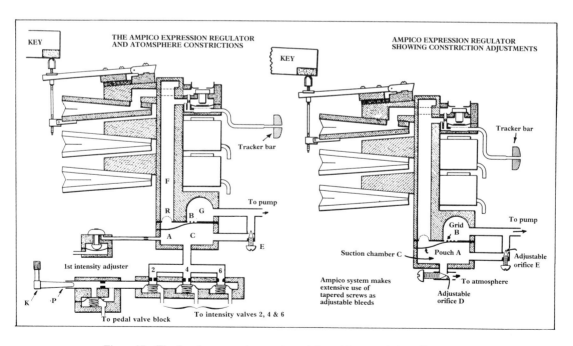

Figure 37   The Ampico expression regulator, left, and its constriction adjustments

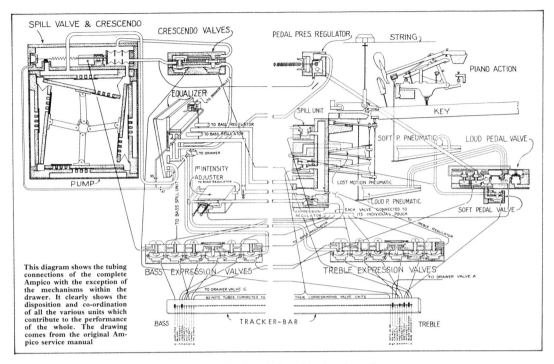

Figure 38   The installation of the Ampico action

practically instantaneously. By quick changes in intensity settings, melody notes or accented notes can be brought out without affecting the loudness of the surrounding notes. Using the steps and the crescendo at the same time made it possible for acceptably smooth crescendos to be played at the same time as clearly defined accents being given.

The function of the dynamic mechanism is to control the loudness of the playing. The system of dynamic control makes it possible to get sudden changes of loudness or gradual fluctuations, crescendos or diminuendos.

The seven degrees or intensities of loudness are used to produce accent and sudden stepping-up effects, while the spring pneumatic mechanism makes it possible to increase smoothly the power of the playing from the softest to the loudest at any speed required. Both of these mechanisms can work simultaneously and produce accent or step effects during a crescendo.

The regulator valve is secured to the regulator valve stem which is in turn fastened to the lever arm. Three little 'intensity pneumatics', attached to the underside of the lever arm, are fed by vacuum pressure; so are the striking pneumatics. The spring pneumatic, which is fastened to the upper side of the lever arm, is fed with air from a regulator pneumatic controlling the softest intensity. This pneumatic functions during crescendo effects and is therefore conveniently called the crescendo pneumatic. The crescendo pneumatic in turn gets its supply, through a constricted channel, from a little regulating valve. The rubber tube leading from the top of the little regulating valve is a muffler tube.

The intensity pneumatics pull down on the lever arm and tend to close the regulator valve, while the spring pneumatic pulls up and tends to open it. When there is no crescendo taking

76

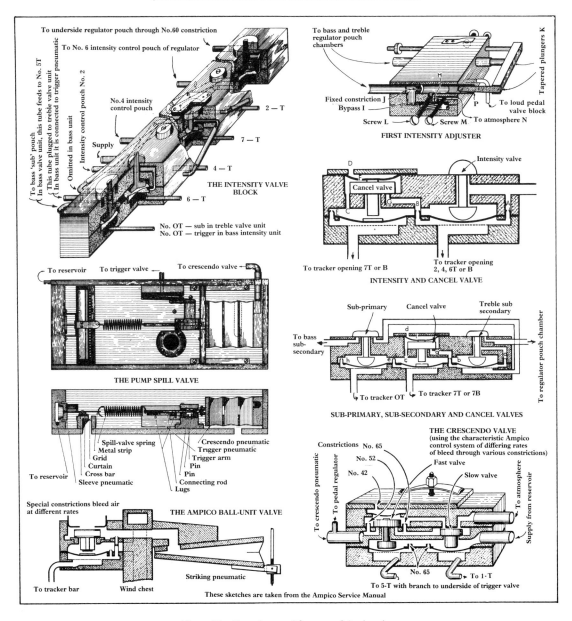

Figure 39   Functions and features of the Ampico

place, the up-pull of the spring pneumatic is constant and even. When a crescendo is taking place, the up-pull of this pneumatic gradually increases.

The dynamic mechanism not only controls changes in the loudness of the playing but it has the very important function of maintaining an even pressure of vacuum, regardless of how many notes are being played.

If no notes are being played, the regulator supplies just enough air to make up for leakage.

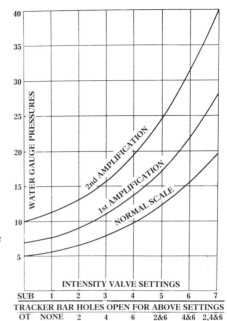

Figure 40   The Ampico intensity scale

When a note is played it causes the vacuum tension in the wind chest to drop slightly and, as it is this same air which supplies the three intensity pneumatics, their down-pull on the regulator valve is lessened and the valve opens slightly, thereby letting more air pass through it, but only enough to increase the down-pull of the intensity pneumatics to a point where it just equals the up-pull of the spring pneumatic. The regulator is so sensitive that it will correct a drop in the tension which is imperceptible in the playing and barely noticeable on a water gauge.

If atmosphere is admitted to one of the intensity pneumatics, the down-pull on the valve is lessened and it rises until the pressure is great enough to make it possible for the down-pull of the remaining two pneumatics to equal the up-pull of the spring pneumatic. You will appreciate that the different steps are obtained by admitting atmospheric air to the different intensity pneumatics singly or in combination. Quick accents are produced by stepping the pressure up just as the note to be accented is played, and instantly stepping back again.

The operation of the step mechanism is as follows:

Regulated air is admitted to the three intensity pneumatics through three valves, which are located on a wind chest supplied with the same vacuum pressure as is supplied to the striker pneumatics. These three secondary valves, as they are called, are in turn controlled by three primary valves located in a high-vacuum wind chest exhausted direct from the pump.

It can readily be seen that decreasing the down-pull on the regulator valve is equivalent to increasing the up-pull. To produce a quick step change, the down-pull of one or more of the intensity pneumatics is suddenly released by admitting atmospheric air to it.

The function of the intensity pneumatics is an interesting application of the lever. By arranging the pneumatic motors under a lever so that one is near the fulcrum, another is in the centre and the third at the greatest distance from the fulcrum, the pull of each one upon that lever is different. The intensity pneumatics thus exert different pulling powers on the regulator valve, due to their different locations on the lever arm. The one nearest the valve stem has the greatest effect while the one nearest the fulcrum has the least.

The valve nearest the fulcrum is called the No. 1 intensity valve and is controlled by the No. 2 hole in the tracker (counting from the treble end for the treble regulator and from the bass end for the bass regulator). With no intensity valves raised, the loudness of the playing is called No. 1 intensity. The following table shows the settings for the various intensities of playing:

Intensity of playing	Intensity valves open	Holes in tracker open
No. 1	None	None
No. 2	No. 1	No. 2
No. 3	No. 2	No. 4
No. 4	No. 3	No. 6
No. 4	No. 1, No. 2*	No. 2, No. 4
No. 5	No. 1, No. 3	No. 2, No. 6
No. 6	No. 2, No. 3	No. 4, No. 6
No. 7	No. 1, No. 2, No. 3	No. 2, No. 4, No. 6

* (Alternative setting)

In order that the sides of the music roll will not be weakened by long chains of expression or intensity perforations, a lock valve is provided for each primary valve, and a single cancel valve controls all the lock valves. Each primary valve is supplied with a bleed but this bleed is not placed directly between the wind chest and the tracker duct, as is the case with the bleeds of the primary valves of the striker pneumatics. A channel from the primary valve leads to the lock valve and thence to the bleed. When the primary valve is closed, suction is admitted to the underside of its pouch through the bleed, but when the valve rises atmospheric air passes over the lock valve and through the bleed to the pouch, thus locking the valve open. When the lock valve is raised, it shuts off the channel from the primary valve and connects the bleed with the wind chest, thereby neutralising the pouch and allowing the valve to come back to its seat.

The cancel valve acts as the primary valve for all three lock valves and, when it is operated from the No. 7 hole in the tracker, all three lock valves are raised, and any primary valve which is up will drop back. If, however, a primary valve tracker hole is open simultaneously with the lock valve, the primary valve will remain up because more air is admitted to the pouch than can be withdrawn through the bleed. If the cancel valve hole in the tracker is closed before the primary valve hole, the lock valves will drop, and the primary valve which was open will remain locked in the open position.

This is accomplished by having the primary valve perforation in the music roll a little longer than the lock valve perforation. For instance, if the alternative setting of No. 4 intensity is on, No. 1 and No. 2 valves will be open. Now if we wish to drop back to No. 3 intensity, the cancel valve hole No. 7 will be open at the same time as the No. 4 hole, but the No. 4 hole in the music roll will be extended a little beyond the No. 7, so that the No. 2 valve will be held open not only while the No. 7 hole cancels the No. 1 valve, but long enough to let the lock valves return to their lower seats, when the No. 2 valve will then keep itself locked open. This system of setting is frequently employed in the Ampico music roll.

The loudness of the No. 1 intensity is adjustable as will be explained further on, but the other steps are not adjustable in their relative loudness to the No. 1.

The functioning of the spring pneumatic mechanism works in the following manner. The three intensity pneumatics tend to close the regulator valve, while the spring pneumatic pulls up and tends to open it. By admitting atmospheric air to any of the intensity pneumatics, an instant decreasing in the down-pull on the regulator valve takes place, and therefore an instant change in the loudness of the playing is achieved.

Now, as we have seen, increasing the up-pull on the valve produces exactly the same effect as decreasing the down-pull and it is by gradually increasing the up-pull that crescendo effects in the playing are obtained. The fact that step effects or accents are caused by changing the down-pull on the regulator valve while crescendo effects are caused by changing the up-pull on it makes it possible to produce both these effects at the same time.

The spring pneumatic is connected by a rubber tube to the crescendo bellows. This crescendo bellows is in turn connected to a regulating valve by means of a small tube. After entering the valve board, the channel passes into the metal speed-regulating block which contains two small, pointed adjusting screws, which are for the purpose of timing the slow and fast movements of the crescendo bellows.

The air passes first through the slow adjustment, then through the fast adjustment, then to the regulating valve. The pouch of this valve is connected by means of a channel to a pallet valve which is operated by a hook connected to the movable board of the crescendo bellows. There is an ordinary bleed connecting the pouch channel with the high-tension wind chest. The hook is of such a length that it engages the pallet valve just before the crescendo pneumatic becomes fully distended. The crescendo bellows is pulled open by a spring which is adjustable. This adjustment is for the purpose of setting the No. 1 intensity to the right loudness.

Now let us go back to the channel leading from the crescendo bellows to the regulating valve. As already stated, this channel passes through the slow adjustment, but there is a bypass around this adjustment which is controlled by a bypass valve consisting merely of a pouch, which normally has atmospheric air under it so that it is distended against the bypass channel, thereby keeping it closed. Normally all the air flowing to the crescendo bellows must pass the slow adjustment, which is so set that it takes the bellows eleven seconds to close. Likewise it takes about the same time to open.

When the crescendo bellows is open nearly to its full extent, the hook engages the pallet valve and opens it, thereby admitting atmosphere to the regulating valve pouch and raising the valve. As soon as the crescendo bellows begins to close due to the regulating valve being raised, the hook allows the pallet valve to close and the valve again seats itself. The regulating valve actually floats between its upper and lower seats, mixing just enough atmosphere from above it with suction from below to produce the right degree of reduced pressure on the air in the crescendo bellows to counteract the spring.

The bypass valve around the 'slow' adjustment is controlled by an inside working primary valve, which in turn is controlled by the same pallet valve that controls the slow crescendo valve. If there is a sudden demand for exhaust, caused, for instance, by the playing of a heavy chord, there will be a perceptible movement of the regulating valve and likewise the spring pneumatic will close a little and the crescendo bellows open slightly, thereby lifting the pallet valve away from its seat further than normal. The channel from the inside working primary valve is located nearer the fulcrum of the pallet valve, so that it does not open effectively until after the other hole is wide open. When this sudden demand takes place, not only is the latter hole opened wide enough to cause the regulating valve to go up against its upper seat, but the primary valve hole is also opened and this causes the primary valve to open, thereby admitting suction to the pouch of the bypass valve, which allows the air to flow through the bypass around the slow adjustment. The flow of this air is then only constricted by the fast adjustment, which allows the crescendo bellows to close much faster. This faster motion brings the movable board of the crescendo back to its normal position very quickly, so that normal conditions are almost instantly restored.

Crescendo effects are obtained in the following way. From the two ducts controlled by the pallet valve there are two branches. The one leading from the regulating valve duct connects with the No. 1 hole in the tracker, while the one leading from the inside primary valve duct connects with the No. 5 tracker hole.

The vacuum pressure of the air in the spring pneumatic is of course the same as that in the crescendo bellows, and as the setting of the spring determines the vacuum in the crescendo bellows and spring pneumatic it likewise determines the loudness of the playing. When everything is normal, the pallet valve controls the position of the crescendo bellows, but, when the No. 1 hole in the tracker is opened, atmosphere is admitted to the regulating-valve pouch faster than the bleed can exhaust it, and the valve is raised so that suction, without any mixture of atmosphere, is admitted through the fast and slow adjustments to the crescendo bellows, which is slowly collapsed. If the No. 5 hole in the tracker is opened at the same time as the No. 1, the crescendo bellows will collapse much faster.

As the bellows closes, it stretches the spring, thereby causing it to pull harder. This spring is designed so that its pull, when the crescendo bellows is almost completely closed, is just sufficient to produce tension enough on the air within the crescendo bellows and spring pneumatic to pull up on the main regulator valve enough to raise the loudness of the playing to the level of the No. 7 intensity, which is the loudest.

As the crescendo bellows closes gradually the pull of the spring likewise gradually increases and thus is produced a gradual rise in the loudness of the playing – a crescendo.

Under these conditions the regulating valve ceases to perform its function as a regulator and becomes the controlling valve of the slow crescendo. It is therefore generally called the slow crescendo valve, while the inside primary valve when operated from the tracker becomes the fast crescendo valve, and is usually so called.

To produce a slow crescendo the No. 1 hole in the tracker is uncovered. When the hole is then closed a slow decrescendo takes place. To produce a full speed crescendo the No. 1 and No. 5 holes in the tracker are opened. If both holes are then closed a slow decrescendo takes place, but, if only the No. 1 hole is closed and the No. 5 kept open, a full speed decrescendo takes place. If the No. 1 hole in the tracker is opened by a series of perforations 2 inches long separated by about 1 inch, a half-speed slow crescendo is produced, for the crescendo is on for 2 inches of the music roll and off for 1 inch, then on again for 2, etc. If an unbroken slow crescendo perforation is in the music roll, and with it are a series of short fast crescendo perforations, the effect will be a crescendo the speed of which is intermediate between the slow and fast. By varying the intervals between the short fast crescendo perforations, different intermediate speeds are obtained.

Connected to each side of the wind chest is a small pneumatic with a long spring. Inside this pneumatic is a small bumper spring. This pneumatic is a regulated tension reservoir and is for the purpose of taking some of the work of regulating off the regulating valve, when various numbers of notes are being played at low intensities. It keeps the regulator from 'jumping' and operates very much as does the equaliser in an ordinary player piano.

81

The Model B Ampico, introduced in 1929, represented a complete rethinking of the reproducing action. The salient points of difference are as follows.

The expression regulator is constructed along quite different lines and contains only one moving part – a rubber diaphragm. The elimination of moving parts from the expression regulating apparatus makes for a more rapid, silent action.

The crescendo apparatus is incorporated in the pump assembly and controls both the bass and treble sections of the action simultaneously. Two steps of pump amplification are employed – the second one providing for louder fortissimo effects than possible with the earlier model. Both steps of pump amplification and the crescendo are produced by the same mechanism, which itself is part of the pump assembly.

The intensity valve system, controlling the expression regulator, is greatly simplified by the elimination of the intensity lock valves. This elimination does not involve any change in the function of the intensity valves themselves. They serve exactly the same purpose as before but are cancelled by a less complicated mechanism. A pedal regulator is employed, which at all times supplies the pedal-actuating apparatus with constant power, irrespective of the vacuum pressure generated by the pump.

The unit valves which control the striker pneumatics are modified so as to eliminate the primary valve system, whilst at the same time preserving the precision and speed of valve action obtained by the double-valve system (this followed suit with Aeolian's engineering of the Duo-Art which reverted to being a single-valve system). Each striker pneumatic was adjusted in manufacture, so that its power was exactly suited to the individual piano-action element which it operated. This adjustment was accomplished by varying the normal opening of the pneumatic, so achieving a far greater evenness of playing under pianissimo conditions.

An additional intensity valve, known as the 'sub-valve', is added for the control of the expression regulator in both the bass and treble sections of the action. This, together with the striker pneumatic adjustment, provides pianissimo effects which were not possible with the Model A. A small hand lever, situated under the piano, adjusts the first intensity within limits to suit the room in which the piano is being played.

The wind motor of the Model A is replaced by a specially designed electric motor which drives the music roll through a centrifugal governor. The control of the governor is far more precise than can be obtained with an air-motor governor. Ample power for driving the roll under all conditions is provided by the electric motor, and tempo registration and alteration is instantly achieved and maintained within very fine limits. Added to all this, facilities are provided for large-diameter music rolls to be used which can play for thirty minutes.

Now let us examine the detailed parts of this action and see how they work.

The expression regulator is illustrated in Fig. 37 and consists of a perforated partition or grid (B) forming a seat for the rubber cloth pouch (A) which controls the flow of air from the wind chest (F) to the chamber (G), and thence to the pump.

The chamber (C) under the pouch, is connected to pump suction through the adjustable opening (E) and to atmosphere through the variable opening (D). If (E) were open and (D) tightly closed, pump suction through (E) would pull the pouch completely away from the grid and full pump suction would be admitted to the wind chest (F). If these adjustments were reversed, with (E) tightly closed and (D) open, pump suction in chamber (G) would cause the pouch (A) to seal the holes in the grid and no suction would be developed in the wind chest (F).

Without changing the pump pressures, adjusting the openings (E) and (D) between these extremes will produce a suction in the chamber (C), which is a fractional part of that developed by the pump, and this fractional suction will peel the pouch away from the grid, until there is developed in the wind chest the same degree of suction that exists in chamber (C). The pouch will then be in balance and any change of suction in the chest (F), due to the playing of notes, etc., will be instantly rectified by a movement of the pouch (A). Any increase in pump suction will give a corresponding fractional increase in suction in the chamber (C). This is used in producing amplification and crescendo effects.

The opening (E) is adjusted at the time of manufacture to fit the scale of intensities to the particular piano into which the Ampico is installed. The opening (E) can also be adjusted to even up the No. 1 intensity pressures, bass and treble.

The size of opening (D) is variable and is automatically controlled from the music roll. The opening is actually made up of four different sizes, 0, 2, 4, and 6 (Fig. 37), which may be opened or closed, either singly or in combination, from the music roll. Three of these openings are arranged longitudinally along the bottom of chamber (C) and one connects into the side of this chamber.

For the purpose of making this figure perfectly clear, all parts are shown in transverse section, except the openings and valves which are diagrammatic and are shown in longitudinal section. The three openings and pouch valves are actually built into the bottom board of the regulator and not isolated as shown.

Disregarding for the moment the parts of the apparatus at (H) and (I) of the first intensity adjuster (see under 'loud pedal valve block'), atmosphere enters tube (P) around the tapered pin (K), flows through (J) and then through 2, 4 and 6, any or all, into chamber (C). With 2, 4 and 6 open and 0 closed, the suction maintained in chamber (C) produces the first intensity. The closing of 2, 4 and 6 singly, or in combination, reduces the atmosphere influx to chamber (C) and produces different degrees of suction in it. These different degrees of suction cause the regulator (A) to open different amounts and produce the same suctions in the wind chest (F). This gives the different steps in the intensity scale.

With 2, 4 and 6 and 0 open, the suction, maintained in chamber (C), produces an intensity which is lower than the No. 1 intensity. This is called the 'sub' intensity and is used to obtain extreme pianissimo effects. The pouches controlling 2, 4 and 6, as well as the opening 0, are operated by valves in the expression valve block. All of these openings, 0, 2, 4 and 6, are of fixed size, each having its proper and constant effect upon the intensity scale. They are manufactured to accurate limits and must never be altered.

Two regulators as described above are used – one for the bass, and one for the treble. The entire regulation is accomplished by the balance of pressures established on both sides of the regulator pouch, by means of the relationship between the respective fixed orifices. There are no mechanical parts to be moved during the process of regulation, when action suction must be accurately maintained, or instantly changed. All of this is accomplished by the slight movement of a thin rubber cloth pouch, the weight of which is only a few thousandths of the weight of the moving parts of the other regulating systems.

The first intensity adjuster, shown in Fig. 39, is shown in detail in Fig. 41. It serves to provide a method whereby the owner of the piano can vary the soft intensity to compensate for climatic conditions, the size of the room and so on.

The opening at (P) is controlled by a tapered plunger (K), inserted into the open end of a tube leading from the chamber (C) through a fixed constriction (J) to atmosphere. Movement

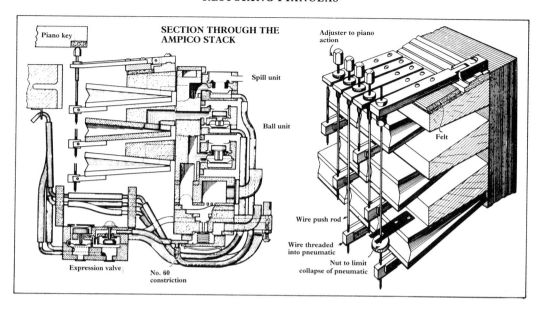

Figure 41   Section through the Ampico chest or stack and detail of the adjustments

of this plunger increases or decreases the atmosphere admitted through 2, 4 and 6 to the chamber (C) and provides a ready means of adjusting the first intensity. It does not affect the higher intensities. The bass and treble plungers are mounted together and are provided with a handle which projects slightly through the hiding curtain just behind the action stack. Pulling the handle out admits more atmosphere to the chamber (C), and further reduces the lower intensities; pushing the handle in reduces the atmosphere influx to the chamber (C) and raises the lower intensities.

The handle should be set as far out as possible, so that the softest notes, which are played with the 'sub' intensity and the soft pedal, will just barely speak. This block also contains the loud pedal compensating device described further on.

The expression valves are built in three blocks – bass intensity valves, treble intensity valves, and crescendo valves. The bass and treble intensity valves are in two separate blocks and are located on the bottom side of the action stack just in front of the expression regulators. They are interposed between the tracker-bar and the expression regulators, and are used to obtain sudden changes in loudness of playing.

In the treble-intensity valve block, Fig. 39, there are six valves: the sub-primary valve 0T, three intensity valves 2T, 4T, 6T, the cancel valve 7T, and the treble sub-secondary valve. The bass-intensity valve block is interchangeable with the treble block and all valves, but one, function the same.

The valve which is used in the treble block as the sub-primary is used in the bass block to control the amplifier trigger. The three intensity valves in each valve block lock themselves open when sprung by a short hole in the note sheet. The sub-secondary valve locks itself open when sprung by the sub-primary valve 0T. These four valves are unlocked by the same cancel valve. This locking and cancelling is best understood by referring to Fig. 39, which shows diagrammatically one intensity valve and the cancel valve.

Normally, suction is communicated to the underside of the intensity valve pouch through

84

a small bleed (A), thereby allowing the pouch and valve to rest in the 'down' position. When the intensity hole in the tracker-bar is opened, the valve rises and atmosphere is admitted from the upper seat to the pouch through the small bleed (A). When the tracker-bar hole is closed, this atmosphere, through the small bleed (A), holds the intensity valve locked up. With this valve locked in the 'up' position, atmosphere is admitted to its corresponding regulator pouch valve, which allows the spring to raise it and close its constriction to the chamber (C), Fig. 39.

When the cancel hole in the tracker-bar is opened, the cancel valve raises and admits suction through the large bleed (B) to the underside of the intensity valve pouch. This suction overcomes the effect of atmosphere coming through the small bleed (A), and the intensity valve returns to its 'down' position. When the intensity valve resumes its 'down' position, suction is admitted to the underside of the regulator pouch valve, which lowers to its normal or 'down' position. In this position, atmosphere is admitted through the constriction to the regulator pouch chamber.

The cancel valve is provided with a bleed (E), to return it to its seat after the tracker-bar hole is closed. This valve is held firmly against its lower seat by a small pouch (F) above it, which receives its suction through a small hole (C) leading to the suction chamber of the valve block. The upper side of this pouch is always in communication with atmosphere through a small hole (D). The cancel valve has four holes under its head, instead of the one (G) as shown.

These four holes communicate through large bleeds to the four valve pouches which the cancel valve controls. They are the three intensity valve pouches, 2, 4 and 6, and the sub-secondary valve pouch. A diagram of the sub-primary, sub-secondary and cancel valve connections is shown in Fig. 39. The sub-secondary valve operates in the same manner as the intensity valve, except that it is sprung from a hole under the head of the sub-primary valve instead of directly from the tracker-bar. The bass sub-secondary valve is sprung from a second hole under the head of the sub-primary valve. When the 'sub' hole 0T in the tracker-bar is open, it springs the sub-primary valve which, through the two holes under its head, springs the bass and treble sub-secondary valves. They both lock up and have their corresponding effect on the regulator pouches. Either one of these valves may be cancelled at will by the use of its own cancel valve.

The valve, which in the treble-intensity valve block is used as the sub-primary, is used in the bass block to operate the amplifier trigger. The actual arrangement of these valves in their block is shown in Fig. 39.

By using a series of valves controlled by one cancel valve it is possible to control the entire expression mechanism with very few tracker-bar holes, and so dispense with a great many extended perforations in the music roll. Furthermore, the design of the intensity valves ensures quietness of operation. The chambers of all pouches operated from the tracker-bar are equipped with strainers which keep dirt, coming in through the tracker-bar, from obstructing the bleeds. The intensity valve blocks are held together by means of springs which ensure tightness under all climatic conditions.

The pump spill-valve mechanism determines the degree of suction generated by the pump. It is located directly on the pump and consists of three major parts: (a) the governor, which holds the suction at any predetermined degree; (b) the crescendo pneumatic, which can gradually increase the pump suction as desired; (c) the amplifier trigger, which can lock the spill-valve spring in either of its two amplified positions.

Fig. 39 shows a plan and elevation view of the mechanism. A lead from the pump terminates in a chamber covered by a grid (C), the amount of opening of which is controlled by a curtain valve (D). This curtain valve is a strip of rubber cloth a little longer than the grid, one edge of which is secured to the face of the grid. It is doubled back on itself and the other edge is fastened to a light crossbar (E). The crossbar is pulled by the spill-valve spring (A) in the direction which rolls the curtain valve over the grid. It is pulled in the opposite direction by a sleeve-type pneumatic (F) which unrolls the curtain off the grid. The sleeve pneumatic is connected to pump suction by a tube (G) from the high-pressure reservoir. This tube contains a small constriction.

With the pump in operation, pump suction increases until the pull of the sleeve pneumatic, as it uncovers the grid, is the same as the opposing pull of the spill-valve spring. The point at which they balance is the regulating point. If the pump suction increases, the sleeve pneumatic (F) opens the curtain valve (D), and spills more atmosphere into the pump, and so reduces the suction to the valve determined by the spring (A). If the pump suction drops, the sleeve pneumatic is weakened and the spring rolls the curtain valve over the grid holes. This reduces the atmosphere spill into the pump and brings the pump pressure back to where the spring and sleeve pneumatic are again in balance.

During re-roll it is desirable to increase slightly the pump suction. This is accomplished by spilling a small amount of atmosphere into the sleeve pneumatic, which reduces the tension of the air therein. This makes it necessary for the pump to generate a slightly higher vacuum so that the pull of the sleeve pneumatic will balance the pull of the spill-valve spring.

The tube connecting the cut-out primary to the action cut-out pouch is linked, through a constriction, into the tube leading from the high-pressure reservoir to the sleeve pneumatic. This connection is made between the sleeve and the small constriction. When the cut-out primary valve is raised, atmosphere is spilled into the sleeve pneumatic, through the constriction, and thus causes the pump pressure to be increased. Due to the fact that a sleeve pneumatic has practically a constant pull throughout its travel, and to the extreme lightness of the moving parts, its action is instantaneous and the pump suction is maintained uniform. Instead of outside atmosphere being spilled directly through the grid, an opening is provided, connecting the pump-housing chamber with the sealed pump spill box, whereby most of the atmosphere exhausted from the mechanisms is again used for spilling purposes. This reduces air noise.

The crescendo pneumatic (H) is connected to the spring (A) by means of a connecting rod (M). When the pneumatic (H) is gradually collapsed, the pull of the spring on the curtain (D) will gradually increase and produce a corresponding increase in pump suction, which is communicated to the regulator pouch.

As this pump suction gradually increases, it raises the suction in the chamber (C) and produces a gradual raise or crescendo in the scale of intensities.

There are two speeds of crescendo: the slow crescendo, in which the pneumatic takes about four seconds to collapse; and the fast crescendo, in which it takes about half a second. As with the Model A, by combining the two many different speeds of crescendo can be obtained.

The slow crescendo is operated by a valve controlled from the 1T hole in the tracker-bar, and the fast crescendo is operated by a valve controlled from the 5T hole in the tracker-bar.

The No. 1B hole, in the bass end of the tracker-bar of the Model B Ampico, is not used. The No. 5B hole is used in conjunction with the shut-off mechanism, which stops the motor when the music roll has been rewound and if the 'Repeat' switch is not set to bypass it and play the roll again.

The amplifying mechanism makes use of the crescendo pneumatic and its connecting rod (M) to the curtain valve, a trigger (J) and a trigger pneumatic (I). The trigger pneumatic is normally held collapsed by suction from its operating valve, which as previously explained, is located in the bass intensity-valve block.

When the amplifier hole 0B in the tracker-bar is opened, atmosphere is admitted to the trigger pneumatic which is opened by its spring. This brings the pin (K) on the trigger arm in line with the lug (N) on the connecting rod (M). When the crescendo hole 1T is opened simultaneously with the amplifier hole 0B, the lug (N) will strike the pin (K), thus allowing only a partial collapsing of the crescendo pneumatic. When the holes 0B and 1T are closed, the trigger bar is pulled back before the crescendo pneumatic opens and the pin (L) on the trigger arm (J) is drawn in, behind the lug (N), and this holds the spill-valve spring stretched to its mid-position. This holds the pump pressure at what is called the 'first amplification'.

To raise the pump pressure from first amplification to second amplification 0B and 1T holes are opened simultaneously. This allows the trigger arm to move forward, until the pin (K) rests against the fin connecting the two lugs. In this position pin (L) is out of the path of lug (0) and the crescendo pneumatic pulls lug (0) beyond the pin (L). On closing 0B and 1T holes, the trigger pneumatic pulls pin (L) against the pin beyond lug (0) and, as the crescendo pneumatic releases, the pin is caught behind the lug and the spring is locked in the second amplification position, or highest pump pressure.

To bring the spring back to the first amplification position, the 0B tracker-bar hole is opened by a short perforation in the music roll. This moves the pin (L) out from behind the lug (0) for just an instant, and gets it back behind the lug (N) before it passes, thereby stopping the travel of the connecting rod at the first amplification position. A somewhat longer perforation in the music roll is required to bring the spring from the second amplification position back to normal. A hole under the head of the trigger valve is joined into the fast-crescendo tracker tube 5T. This causes the crescendo pneumatic to operate quickly whenever the amplifier hole 0B is opened simultaneously with the slow crescendo hole 1T.

It will be seen from the foregoing that pump suction regulation, crescendos, and the two degrees of amplification are obtained by one piece of mechanism whose moving parts are very light and frictionless.

The intensity scales are illustrated in Fig. 40, which demonstrates the three intensity scales of 'normal', 'first amplification' and 'second amplification'. The lines represent the approximate pressures of the various valve settings when the normal No. 1 intensity is 5·6 inches and the normal pump pressure is 20 inches. The normal No. 1 intensity may be set slightly higher or lower than 5·6 inches, according to the heaviness of the particular piano action used, or climatic conditions.

Each of the eight valve settings gives three gauge pressures, i.e. the normal pressure; a higher pressure when the first amplification is set; and a still higher pressure when the second amplification is set. Thus by the use of the expression valves alone twenty-four different gauge pressures may be obtained. In addition to these twenty-four fixed pressures, the crescendo mechanism makes it possible to obtain any intermediate pressure desired.

The Ampico normal scale is not an arbitrary succession of steps, but is based on the different degrees of loudness that are perceptible to the ear. These different, perceptible degrees of loudness are called 'audibility steps'. The factory setting of the pump pressure is marked on the pump spill box. The only way to alter the pump setting is to modify the spring.

In reading gauge pressures on the Model B Ampico, always connect at the tap-plate under the centre of the piano.

The crescendo valves are used to control the pneumatic which produces gradual increases and decreases in loudness of playing. The slow- and fast-crescendo valves are mounted in one block, which also contains the constrictions which govern the speed of operation of the crescendo pneumatic.

In Fig. 39 there is drawn a section of the crescendo valve block. The 'fast' valve is equipped with an auxiliary pouch to return it to its seat. This pouch connects to atmosphere at all times by a small inlet. Slow crescendo is produced by opening 1T hole in the tracker-bar. The crescendo will continue as long as this hole is open, or until the pump suction reaches its maximum value.

Opening the 1T hole raises the slow-crescendo valve, thereby shutting off atmosphere, and exhausting the crescendo pneumatic at a low speed through the No. 52 bleed, over the top of the fast valve and through the No. 65 bleed. When the 1T hole is closed a slow decrescendo takes place, but the slow decrescendo is a little faster than the slow crescendo, because the atmosphere comes in across the top of the slow valve, across the top of the fast valve and thence through the No. 52 bleed. During slow crescendo, the air passes through two constrictions. During the slow decrescendo it only passes through one constriction.

For a fast crescendo, tracker-bar holes 1T and 5T are opened simultaneously. Both valves are thereby raised, permitting the crescendo pneumatic to be exhausted, without passing the air through either the No. 52 or the No. 65 constrictions. When the tracker-bar hole 1T is closed and the 5T is left open, a fast decrescendo is produced.

A tube from the pedal-regulator, containing a No. 70 constriction, is connected to the tube leading to the crescendo pneumatic. Through it is supplied a minute amount of pedal suction to the crescendo pneumatic at all times so that when it is in the open position its fabric is held taut. By having no slack in its cloth, the pneumatic responds instantly when the 1T hole in the tracker-bar is opened.

The crescendo valves, by controlling the pump spill-valve, automatically produce crescendos or decrescendos in both the bass and the treble side of the action simultaneously. This lends itself to reproducing the artist's interpretation as shown by the method of Ampico recording.

Although the expression system of the Model B is different from that of the Model A, the ability to accent notes during crescendos by means of the intensity valves is retained.

The action stack comprises the wind chest, two expression regulators, three decks of action pneumatics, lost-motion action adjusters, the tracker or poppet wires, two action spill-valves, two intensity valve blocks and the so-called ball-unit valves.

All these parts are manufactured in one complex (see Fig. 41) and the components are closely spaced.

The wind chest is built of a solid piece of maple and is extremely rigid. It features a main windway along the bottom edge and a supplementary windway along the top. These two windways are connected by a series of vertical holes, from which are led the supply channels to the ball-unit valves. The high-pressure chests, with their grids, are glued to the wind chest and form an integral part of it.

Atmosphere is drawn from the main windway directly into the expression regulators, through a series of round holes, each protected by a sieve. These sieves prevent any particles of dirt from reaching the grids of the expression regulators. Each high-pressure chest, bass and treble, is exhausted through two ⅝ inch tubes which run direct to the high-pressure reservoir. The ball-unit valves are accurately located by guides and studs so that their holes will register exactly with those in the chest.

The decks are made of maple and are secured to the wind chest by heavy springs, to reduce chances of leakage at the joints.

The poppet wires, shown in Fig. 41, are threaded top and bottom: the top thread provides adjustment for the hexagon head A to take up lost motion which comes from the packing of the felt pads under the keys. It is taken up in two ways: first, to remove general lost motion, the whole action can be raised by screwing 'in' on the hanger screws. These screws are located in the action bracket at each end of the stack. Second, after the general lost motion has been taken up, individual adjustment to the poppets can be made with the hexagon nuts A on the tops of the poppet wires B. To make the adjustment, remove the piano action from the piano and place it on a table. With a gauge, measure the height from the bottom of the keyframe to the bottom of the depression made in the pad under the key. With this distance obtained, check the height of the poppets from the key-bed to the top of the hexagon nut. Any lost motion is taken up by screwing the hexagon nut upward. Hold the poppet wire above the head with pliers and turn the hexagon nut with a spanner. The bottom thread on the poppet wire passes through the pneumatic tip C and provides for the adjustment of the striker pneumatic opening.

Differences in the piano action, due to the different weights of hammers, varying frictions at pin joints and rubbing points, may make the soft playing uneven. In rectifying this, advantage is taken of the varying power of pneumatics at different openings, bearing in mind that a wide-open pneumatic gives more power than one half closed.

Making the opening of the striker pneumatic greater when more friction is encountered in the action, and reducing the opening when there is little friction, compensates these differences and so effects an evenness of soft playing. This is adjusted in manufacture and should not need to be changed until after it is found necessary to regulate and voice the piano action.

Once the piano action has been regulated and voiced, it may be found that some of the pneumatic openings have to be readjusted, to even out the soft playing. The use of the tester roll will show up any such deficiencies and also serve to show when adjustments have been properly made.

The action pneumatics are controlled by the ball-unit valves. Their construction is shown in Fig. 39. Each unit consists of an 'inside' valve with a very small fixed bleed connecting from under its pouch to the suction chamber, and an additional larger bleed provided with a ball check valve, connecting from under the pouch to the valve chamber.

When the tracker-bar hole is open, atmosphere enters under the pouch and works with maximum efficiency to raise the valve, because at the outset air can leave the pouch chamber only through the No. 70 bleed. As the valve approaches its top seat, suction in the valve chamber increases until air flows from the pouch chamber upwards through the ball check valve, as well as from the open No. 70 bleed. As the upward travel of the valve nears completion, both bleeds are open and the valve reaches its outside seat, not suddenly but slowly and with no perceptible noise.

When the tracker hole is again closed, the valve starts downwards. Its stem is in contact with the pouch, and during the first portion of the valve's downward travel air may escape from the pouch through two paths. One of these is the No. 70 bleed, which is always open; the other is the ball check bleed, which is open when the valve starts downward. As the valve proceeds towards its inside seat, atmosphere enters the valve chamber, and, before the valve completes its travel, atmospheric pressure and gravity seat the ball, closing the No. 60 bleed. Thereafter, air can escape from the pouch through the No. 70 bleed only, and the valve is retarded in its downward travel, so that it reaches its inside seat while travelling at a relatively slow speed, and thus, again, produces no noise.

This bleed system was claimed by Ampico engineers to be the most effective and efficient method of venting a pouch. During most of the upward travel of the valve, the smallest bleed consistent with efficiency is open. Therefore the maximum amount of energy admitted by the tracker-bar is used for lifting the valve promptly. As the valve completes its upward travel, the venting of the pouch is augmented greatly by the opening of the ball check bleed, whereby the speed of the valve is reduced at the last end of its stroke, and it comes to rest, noiselessly, against its seat.

Similarly, during the reverse of this operation, the maximum venting is available through the two open bleeds during the start of the downward travel of the valve, and, toward the end of its motion, the venting is again changed and reduced to the point where the valve cannot make undue noise when it contacts with its inside seat. The advantages of the double valve control of the striking pneumatic are all embodied in this single-unit valve.

Because screens (R) are placed in the pouch chamber of the units to protect the bleeds from dirt, it is never necessary to clean them out. Besides the intensity regulator, this valve is one of the most highly developed pieces of apparatus in the Ampico.

For a more detailed account of the operation of the Ampico together with servicing instructions, you are referred to reprints of the original manuals which are available.

THE 'ORIGINAL' WELTE-MIGNON

The Welte reproducing action comprises two distinct types – the so-called 'Original' Welte-Mignon, which plays only special music-rolls 13½ inches wide, and the Welte-Mignon (Licensee), which was produced in America by the Auto Pneumatic Action Company, to Welte patents. This latter action used standard-width music rolls. Original Welte-Mignon actions comprise three basic types – the cabinet reproducing player which is a 'push-up' instrument made up until the 1930s, the grand action which was always made to fit above the keyboard in the upper portion of the piano (as compared to the underneath installation of the Duo-Art★ and Ampico pianos), and the action used in upright instruments. The principles of the three variants are to all intents and purposes identical. All Original Welte-Mignon actions are powered by an electric motor driving exhausters and the power installation is always characterised by sound, solid engineering and, in the upright and cabinet players, by the use of flat drive belting instead of the round leather or V-rope drive favoured by other makers. American-built Welte-Mignons used standard-type sliding-pallet roll motors while German-built models all used the trefoil, conical in-line motor.

Welte tracker-bars have 99 openings comprising 81 playing notes, 8 expression holes to the left and 10 to the right. In addition, there are two pairs of staggered holes for the 'balanced leak' type of roll-tracking system.

★ The Pedal Electric Duo-Art and some other later grands used above-keyboard actions which, although a neat, compact installation, did not have the power of the larger, under-keyed action with its graded pneumatics.

THE
WELTE
CABINET
PLAYER

THIS Instrument is attachable to, and removable from, any piano in a few seconds, and achieves the same perfect reproduction as the combined models.

Height	-	3 ft. 4 ins.
Width	-	4 ft. 1 in.
Depth	-	1 ft. 9 ins.
Nett Weight	-	354 lbs.
Packed Weight	-	548 lbs.
Measurement	-	41 cub. ft.

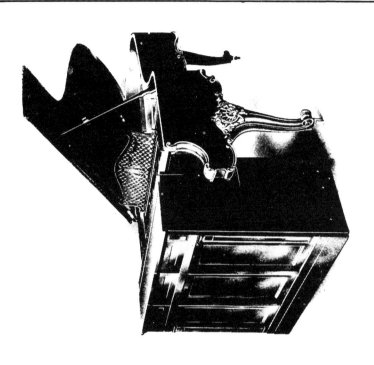

Figure 42   The Welte cabinet player or 'vorsetzer'

Dealing first with the Original action, the amount of available playing power can be pre-set by adjustment to a spring governing a spill valve. The essence of the Welte expression system is a system of mechanical locks controlling the expression pneumatics. These locks – one is shown in Fig. 43 – comprise a plate attached to the moving board of a pneumatic motor, which can engage in a hook attached to the moving board of another, smaller motor mounted

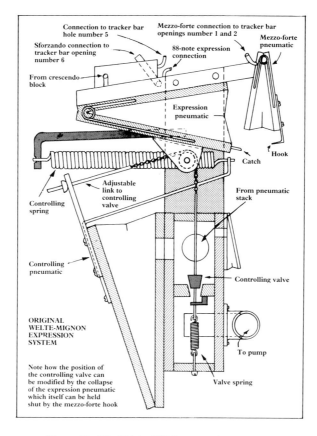

Figure 43   The Original Welte expression system

at right angles to it. As the motor controlling the expression function collapses, the lock motor is also made to collapse, so trapping the plate beneath its hook. To cancel the function, the suction is bled from the lock pneumatic, allowing it to open, thereby releasing the expression pneumatic. This avoids the need to apply continual suction to the expression pneumatic, which would call for impossibly long perforations in the music roll. It is interesting to note that this system of mechanical locks had already been extensively used by Welte. The Welte pipe orchestrion organs had employed a similar method for the selection and cancelling of organ stops.

Eighteen expression holes are used in pairs, the left side using the odd numbers to set an expression operation, and the even numbered holes to cancel, whilst the right side uses the even numbers to set the operation and the odd to cancel. The two sides of the piano are divided and self-contained and each operates a conical valve which controls the level of suction for that side. The valve is lifted by a controlling pneumatic, the equilibrium of the valve being maintained by a tension spring fixed beneath it. A mezzo-forte pneumatic – in fact the hooked locking pneumatic – is arranged so that, if the expression pneumatic is only partly collapsed, this may also collapse and hold the expression pneumatic from further movement (Fig. 43). It can also be employed to reduce overall volume by preventing the full movement of the controlling pneumatic, which would result in the loudest playing level. These functions are set in operation by the tracker-bar perforations.

The controlling pneumatic serves to balance and maintain a level of suction, regardless of the number of functions which are taking suction power to operate, and it does this by regulating the suction by means of the conical valve. The expression pneumatic has the ability to move suddenly to produce a sforzando or slowly to produce a crescendo and it does this by pulling on the conical valve. The expression pneumatic is normally open, allowing the conical valve to be maintained at its lowest position. Under these conditions, the playing power is normally at its minimum and almost all degrees of playing call for the opening up of the passageway restricted by the valve. The inlets into the expression pneumatic comprise one small and one large inlet for the rapid or slow movement of the motor.

To govern the position of the main expression pneumatic, four functions are used from four tracker-bar openings. These are crescendo on, crescendo off, sforzando on and sforzando off.

An unusual feature of the Original action is that, unlike the other reproducing actions described, it contains no definite steps of volume increase. As we have seen, the normal playing intensity is with the conical valves governing each half of the piano at their minimum setting. All volume is built on the movement of pneumatics to add more power to that minimum setting. Now, this is all very well for a mechanical datum, but, for the practical playing of the piano, it was found too nebulous to rely on building everything except the most pianissimo of tones on a low suction pressure. For this reason, a further point was established by which the operation of the expression system could continually be checked and regulated. This point is provided by the mezzo-forte pneumatic with its locking hook. By allowing this to interact with the controlling pneumatic, as dictated by the normal musical expression, the level of sound could be monitored and the controlling pneumatic kept in its proper range of movement. Because in the normal playing of a piece of music the piano plays for much of the time at something like medium volume, this mezzo-forte pneumatic may operate at frequent intervals, and there is no perceptible sense of the instrument 'hunting' in volume.

THE WELTE-MIGNON (LICENSEE)

When the Welte-Mignon (Licensee) action was re-engineered by the Auto Pneumatic Action Company in New York, the major visible alteration was the substitution of music rolls made of ordinary paper and cut 11¼ inches wide. The unusual 3-pneumatic conical roll-drive motor, characteristic of all Welte instruments, appears in both variants but was later replaced in American models by the familiar flat slide-valve motor and crankshaft. The divided pneumatic stack remains and this is controlled by a 'pressure regulator', which serves as the governor pneumatic in the Original action, an 'expression regulator' and a 'stop pneumatic' – all parts which show a strong similarity – compare Fig. 43 and Fig. 44. The conical valve is replaced by a spring-balanced knife-valve, which is a far better method of regulating suction when you consider the analogy of endeavouring to close off the waste-pipe of a bath full of water by slowly lowering the bath plug – the closer it gets to the hole the greater the pull, until finally it goes home with a jerk.

In the grand installation, control of the crescendo expression system is fundamentally the same but, instead of the fast and slow crescendo relying purely on the tension spring to the valve under the overall direction of the expression pneumatic, this spring tension is continuously varied under the guidance of a 'modulator pneumatic'. The working pressure of the action is maintained at whatever level may be required by the 'governor pneumatic', and this is continuously under the guidance of the 'expression pneumatic'. We will examine the functioning of this in detail.

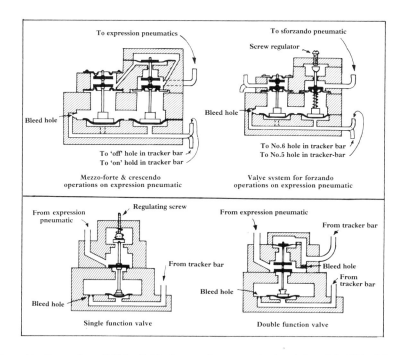

Figure 44   Comparison of Welte Original expression system (top) and that of the Welte Licensee

The Welte-Mignon (Licensee) action makes use of two identical expression units. One is used to control the bass, and the other the treble. The first may be considered as representing the left hand of the pianist and the second as the right hand.

Each expression unit comprises three units: the governor pneumatic (marked A in Fig. 46), the expression pneumatic (B), and the stop pneumatic (C). The governor pneumatic is connected directly to the suction by the tube marked (D) and to the pneumatic action through the tube (E). The purpose of the governor is to maintain an even flow of air from the pneumatic action, so that the 'touch' is the same regardless of how many notes are being struck at any one time.

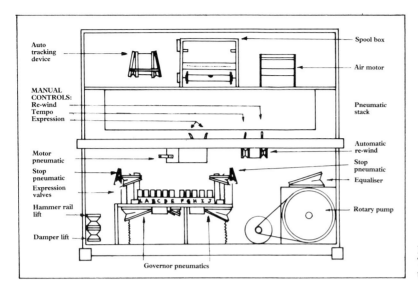

Figure 45
The Welte Licensee
upright installation

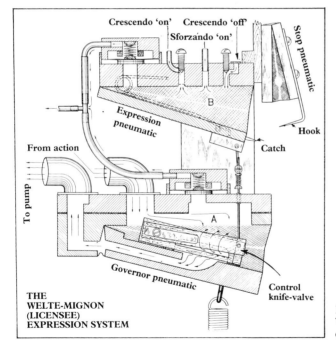

Figure 46
Welte Licensee
expression system

The even flow of air is maintained by the control valve, which covers the opening of the channel (F) leading to the suction, through the moving board of the pneumatic. This special knife-valve, when in normal position as shown in the illustration, allows the piano to play pianissimo and to produce the softest hammer blow at which the notes will repeat.

The expression pneumatic is the smaller motor placed directly above the governor. Its moving board, which is kept normally open by a spring (G), is connected with the control valve by the connecting rod (H). The expression pneumatic serves to control the flow of air from the top pneumatic action.

The differences between the expression system of the Original and (Licensee) actions are now fully apparent. The difficult control of the conical valve of the former is overcome by the smooth and easy operation of a jack-knife valve.

The governor (marked A in Fig. 46) maintains the flow of air at a given point. The expression pneumatic regulates or controls the flow of air to a desired point. The flow of air is, of course, adjusted by the opening or closing of the expression pneumatic and its incumbent knife-valve. Side perforations in the music roll are employed to move the expression pneumatic in several ways, separately or in concert, to produce a wide range of expression. The pneumatic may be closed slowly by allowing suction through the small opening marked (I), which has the effect of causing the action gradually to play louder – the crescendo effect. Alternatively, the pneumatic may be closed very quickly by allowing suction through the large opening (J), which has the effect of causing the hammers to strike a quick, sharp blow. This is called sforzando. A combination of the two may be employed so that, while the pneumatic is gradually closing under the suction of opening (I), a momentary opening of the suction (J) will produce a subtle fractional accent as in the original playing of the artist.

Control of diminuendo, achieved by the reverse procedure, can likewise be varied, all combining to enable the action to play the very lightest to the very heaviest blow almost instantaneously, or to build up to fortissimo or decrease to pianissimo as slowly as may be required.

From this it can be seen that the level of the piano is infinitely variable and without fixed steps in graduation. Here we have basically the same characteristics as with the Original action, but both improved and simplified.

In the Original action, we had the so-called mezzo-forte pneumatic. The same feature applies with this action except that it is termed the 'stop pneumatic'. This motor, with its engaging hook, can be used to stop the opening or the closing of the expression pneumatic beyond a certain point, so limiting the maximum volume or minimum pianissimo if required.

The connections for the operation of the expression system are easily related by referring to the tracker-bar diagram for this action shown in Figs 47 and 48.

The sforzando system comprises the sforzando valve unit through which the expression pneumatic is emptied rapidly. This is illustrated in Fig. 46. The reverse of this operation is provided through a similar valve which is under the control of the sforzando – off duct in the tracker-bar. The sforzando valves are single-function valves.

To enable the action to be controlled manually, when using ordinary rolls, a valve block is placed between tracker-bar and pneumatics into which connect pipes leading to the hand controls. Changeover from manual to automatic expression is achieved in the normal way by the use of a switch valve.

The tracker-bar has the same hole pattern as the Original and the expression valves are of two basic types – single-function and double-function (see Fig. 44), and they are arranged on the valve board as follows: L, A, B, C, D, E, F, G, H, I, and J. The single-function valves are A, B, I, and J. C, D, E, F, and G are double-function valves, and H, L and E together operate the sustaining-pedal pneumatic motor. This combination is necessary because the sustaining-pedal tracker hole is No. 3 in the bass end for Welte (Licensee) rolls, and No. 8 in the treble end for the other rolls. Tracing the pipelines from the tracker-bar to the valves, we find the following:

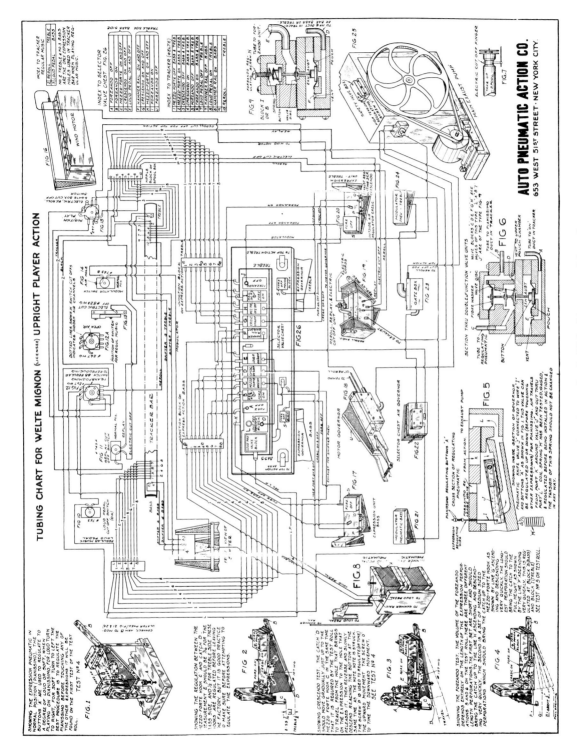

Figure 47   Installation diagram for the Welte Licensee upright action

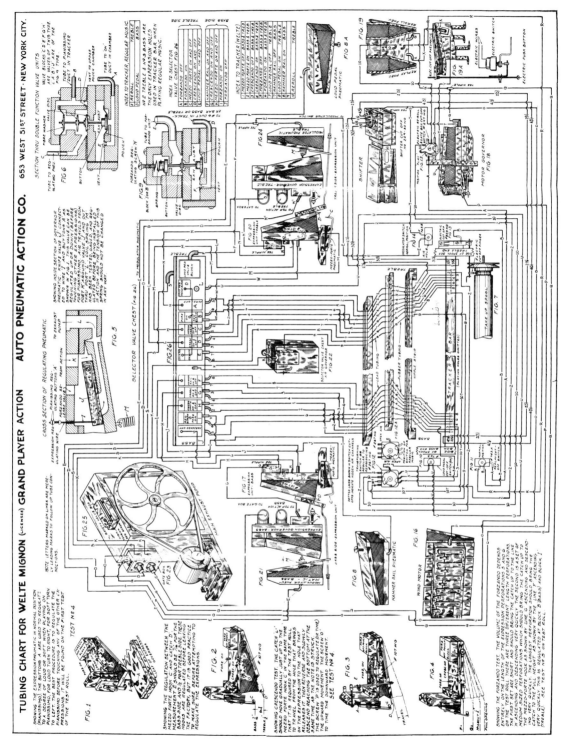

Figure 48   Installation diagram for the Welte Licensee grand action

On the bass side, tubes 1 and 2 lead to C; 3 and 4 lead to D; 5 leads to A; 6 leads to B; and 7 and 8 lead to F. On the treble side, tubes 1 and 2 lead to H; 3 and 4 lead to G; 5 leads to J; 6 leads to I; and 7 and 8 lead to E.

Once you understand how the single- and double-function valves work, the operation of the instrument should be fairly obvious. To delve further would be to repeat much that has already been said.

What I have attempted to do here is to outline how these instruments work. With service manuals readily available through the enthusiastic endeavours of Harvey Roehl, whose New York business – The Vestal Press – is entirely devoted to mechanical music and its literature, the owner of one of these instruments has the fullest available information to draw upon to aid its restoration.

OTHER TYPES OF REPRODUCING ACTION

In concluding this chapter, brief mention should be made of the best of the other reproducing actions. The Solo Carola was a foot-treadled reproducing instrument, which made particular point of its ability to strike solo and accompaniment notes simultaneously or independently throughout the entire length of the keyboard and with any degree of power required.

Each opening in the tracker-bar was matched with a narrow slot coinciding exactly with it and just above the note holes (not to be confused with the Aeolian theme slots found on some instruments and placed over the central notes). These slots were connected to a small bellows which could independently select the position of each hammer relative to the strings, before the striking pneumatic was brought into operation. Unfortunately, the Solo Carola was not to catch on to any great extent, and specimens are very rare even in America.

Wilcox & White, who produced the Angelus players and player pianos as well as the Symphony player organ, made the Angelus Artrio reproducing piano. This was an interesting instrument in that almost the entire action was mounted in a drawer under the keyboard (it was made mainly for grand pianos). Unlike the Ampico, the drawer contained, in addition to the transmission, music-roll box and controls, the complete pneumatic stack and expression system. The action depended on 13 expression openings in the tracker-bar – 5 for the controlling governor, 4 for the treble governor, and 4 controlling the bass governor. Melody and accompaniment playing-levels could be controlled by the main governor, or by either the bass or treble governors.

The Angelus action was made by the Hallet & Davis Company, of New York, until the late 1920s. Even so, it is still rarely come across today.

The Artecho was produced by the Amphion Piano Player Company, a subsidiary of the American Piano Company. It used a divided chest and a system of intensity valves, lock and cancel valves and in some respects resembled the Ampico early action made by the parent company. The Artecho was also known as the Celco and the Apollo.

The Aria Divina was another contender for the market for a reproducing instrument.

European contributions to the reproducing piano market included the Hupfeld Duophonola and Triphonola actions, and the Carola action made by Blüthner in London. The latter was dropped as being too costly compared with the competition, and the Hupfeld was certainly a success even if only on a limited scale in Europe.

My earlier words in this chapter may justly be repeated here. The chances of finding an instrument of one of the less known makes are now extremely slim – that is why I have concentrated on the 'big three'. However, acquisition of one of the others need not present unsuperable problems thanks to the endeavours of a few collectors both in England and in America, who have preserved rare literature on these pianos. The British Piano Museum is a first-class starting-position for any inquiries.

REPRODUCING PIANOS – TRACKER-BAR TUBING GUIDE

Duo-Art, 94 tracker openings

1	Rewind	88	Theme level 4
2	Sustaining pedal	89	Theme level 3
3	Bass theme	90	Theme level 2
4	Accompaniment level 1	91	Theme level 1
5	Accompaniment level 2	92	Treble theme
6	Accompaniment level 3	93	Shut-off/replay
7	Accompaniment level 4	94	Soft pedal (hammer rail or
8 to 87	80 playing notes, C$\sharp$ to G$\sharp$		keyboard shift)

Note: when playing normal, non-Duo-Art full-scale rolls, the action of selecting Duo-Art off couples holes 4 to 7 and 88 to 91 as playing notes.

Ampico Model A, 98 tracker openings

1	Slow bass crescendo	91	Rewind
	(decrescendo when released)	92	Cancel treble intensities
2	Bass intensity 1	93	Treble intensity 3
3	Sustaining pedal	94	Fast treble crescendo/decrescendo
4	Bass intensity 2	95	Treble intensity 2
5	Fast bass crescendo/decrescendo	96	Hammer rail
6	Bass intensity 3	97	Treble intensity 1
7	Cancel bass intensities	98	Slow treble crescendo
8 to 90	83 playing notes, B to A		(decrescendo when released)

Ampico Model B, 100 tracker openings

0	Amplifier	91	Rewind
1	Blank	92	Cancel treble intensities
2	Bass intensity 1	93	Treble intensity 3
3	Sustaining pedal	94	Fast crescendo/decrescendo
4	Bass intensity 2	95	Treble intensity 2
5	Blank	96	Hammer rail
6	Bass intensity 3	97	Treble intensity 1
7	Cancel bass intensities	98	Slow crescendo
8 to 90	83 playing notes, B to A		(decrescendo when released)
		00	Sub intensity

Note: Openings 2 to 93 and 95, 96 and 97 perform the same functions as in the Ampico Model A. Opening 00 gives an intensity level lower (softer) than normal for *ppp* playing. Openings 0 and 98 are dual-function holes which control three levels of vacuum tension – normal, 1st amplification and 2nd amplification. The Model B single crescendo system covers both bass and treble. The terminology used here and the method of numbering the holes conforms to the system used in the Ampico servicing manuals.

Welte-Mignon ('Red Welte' with 12⅞ in. wide music rolls), 100 tracker openings

1	Bass mezzoforte off	5	Bass sforzando off
2	Bass mezzoforte on	6	Bass sforzando on
3	Bass crescendo off	7	Hammer rail down
4	Bass crescendo on	8	Hammer rail up

9	Motor resistance valve off (slower)	95	Treble sforzando on
10	Motor resistance valve on (faster)	96	Treble sforzando off
11 to 90	80 playing notes, C to G	97	Treble crescendo on
91	Rewind	98	Treble crescendo off
92	Blank	99	Treble mezzoforte on
93	Sustaining pedal on	100	Treble mezzoforte off
94	Sustaining pedal off		

Welte-Mignon (Licensee) (11¼ in. wide music rolls), 98 tracker openings★

1	Bass mezzoforte off	89	Rewind
2	Bass mezzoforte on	90	Shutoff (sometimes blank)
3	Bass crescendo off	91	Sustaining pedal on
4	Bass crescendo on	92	Sustaining pedal off
5	Bass sforzando off	93	Treble sforzando on
6	Bass sforzando on	94	Treble sforzando off
7	Hammer rail down	95	Treble crescendo on
8	Hammer rail up	96	Treble crescendo off
9 to 88	80 playing notes, C to G	97	Treble mezzoforte on
		98	Treble mezzoforte off

★Note: the replay opening in the tracker bar is situated between openings 1 and 2.

Welte ('Green') 98 tracker openings

1	Bass sforzando off	94	Treble sforzando on
2	Bass mezzoforte	95	Treble crescendo
3	Sustaining pedal	96	Hammer rail
4	Bass crescendo	97	Treble mezzoforte
5	Bass sforzando on	98	Treble sforzando off
6 to 93	88 playing notes (full player compass)		

Note: the 'Green' Welte action dispenses with the lock-and-cancel valve principle used in the Original ('Red') and Licensee systems, using conventional chain perforations in the music roll to keep functions operational. The only function to operate with the characteristic Welte pneumatic locking hooks is the bass and treble mezzoforte, but again engagement is dependent on the length of roll perforation rather than a lock/cancel valve sequence.

The restorer of reproducing pianos and expression pianos who seeks additional information on scales is referred to Art Reblitz's valuable list of tracker-bar information contained in *Treasures of Mechanical Music* (see Bibliography).

CHAPTER 5

Player Organs and Their Overhaul

It may at first seem strange to include reference to organs in a book on pianos, but there is some justification for this since the player varieties of both pianos and organs use similar systems whereby a series of perforations in a paper roll is transformed into music by pneumatic means. Furthermore, there are many player-piano collectors who also have in their collections player organs, and so, although there is an obvious difference, there are equally obvious similarities.

This will only be a short guide through the more common types of player organ since much of the foregoing material in this book can be applied to the player organ with ease by the practical enthusiast. I shall not delve deeply into the history and derivation of the various types of instrument, even though some of that history has inevitably been recounted already as the background to the development of the player piano. By the same premise, I shall not go to great lengths to tell you how to dismantle and resurrect a player organ, but will rather concentrate on working principles and broad methods of overhaul and give a guide to the restoration process.

Let me begin by detailing the points of similarity between the player piano and the player organ. Both have keyboards and can be played by hand as well as by paper roll. Both rely for their operation on the creation of a difference between the air pressure inside the instrument and the pressure of the surrounding atmosphere, which means that both have foot-operated treadles or power-operated pump units. Both instruments have a pneumatic system comprising valve chests and a visible tracker-bar and spool-box assembly. Both are decidedly heavy to shift.

There were quite a few makers of pneumatic player organs but first let me explain that I am talking about the reed organ in general. Player pipe organs made by Welte, Aeolian, Estey and Wurlitzer are more akin to the conventional pipe organ and are referred to in my book *Barrel Organ*. Makers of the player reed organ were in the main those with experience in the making of player pianos, reed organs and harmoniums – there was virtually no entrepreneurial maker largely because of the considerable skills and manufacturing plant needed to make these pieces.

In terms of popularity and hence numbers made, the leader had to be Aeolian's Orchestrelle, produced both in America and, by process of knock-down component assembly, at Aeolian's English factory at Hayes in Middlesex.

This marque appeared in at least 16 styles and sizes between the close of the last century and about 1920. From the Orchestrelle was developed a player pipe organ with Duo-Art-type mechanism as well as models with detached console. Next came Wilcox & White of Meriden,

Connecticut. This company, a true pioneer in player pianos with its refreshingly different Angelus player, designed and built an instrument called the Symphony. This was an early instrument which first appeared in the late 1880s and which was to remain in production until the very early years of this century. An unusual mutant was the Angelus Symphony, a version of the Angelus piano player with which was incorporated several ranks of reeds. With this instrument, the operator could perform on either reed organ or piano or on both together just by selecting the stops on the player. It is important that organ and piano remain perfectly in tune. These were at one time very popular and there are still a few to be found.

The Maxfield organ, stemming from the basis of McTammany's patents and the Munrow Organ Reed Co., was a British contribution patented in 1896, and models cost up to £25. The Maxfield was the product of one of London's numerous manufacturers of reed organs, harmoniums and piano players. It used music rolls which were narrow by comparison with others – they were a mere 5½ inches wide – and was altogether a small instrument, having only 31 of its 61-note manual playable from the roll. Both the Orchestrelle and Symphony, by comparison, played a full 58 notes from the roll.

There were several other makers but products of these companies are seldom encountered today. This is a pity because the later models which tried so unsuccessfully to capture the market dominated by American products were, generally, of a superior quality. Produced in Paris by the Mustel company was the Mustel Concertal, one of the finest of all player reed organs and judged so for a number of reasons. First, it featured a tonal basis which was far more colourfully and artistically established than that of the single-manual Orchestrelles. Second, the keyboard was truly divided between left-hand and right-hand stops (unlike the Orchestrelle's, which is purely divided in half with two draw-stops to operate on each full rank of reeds). And third was the highly developed Mustel system of control, using locking knee swells almost as sforzando pedals, and combining the 'prolongement' stop for the bass notes and the foundation setting of the organ into two small treadle cheeks which could be operated by the twist of the foot while pedalling.

Another maker was Estey, a maker of very high-quality reed organs of the American-organ genus. This company made fullest use of the tonal possibilities of reeds and Helmholtz chambers to produce its instruments.

Wurlitzer and Hammond made varieties of their organs which could be roll-operated and many of the Wurlitzer orchestrions were more organ than piano. The Hammond was an interesting instrument, few of which were made and even fewer of which survive. In this the electric organ was made to work by a pneumatic player action built into it.

To begin with, let us take a quick look at how these conventional reed organs work and how the player action must function.

In an earlier chapter on pneumatic pianos, I show how air at pressure either greater or less than that of the atmosphere can be made to perform certain duties while equalising itself with atmospheric pressure. In the player organ, there are two separate air systems – one to operate valves and pneumatic motors to instruct a certain note to speak, and another to provide that note with the necessary body of air. In the latter system, the air must be used to 'blow' the reed in one of the manners described below. Both these pneumatic systems rely on foot treadles like those of the player piano to provide the pressure differential.

103

A reed can be sounded only by allowing air to pass through it,* but there are two distinct methods of passing air through a reed. One is by creating a suction on one side of the reed so that when a valve is opened atmospheric pressure rushes in, sounding the reed in passing; the other is to create a pressure on one side of the reed so that when a valve is opened the air at pressure rushes out to atmosphere, making the reed sound on its way.

This is the basic difference between the harmonium, which blows air through its reeds, and the so-called American organ, which has a more strident and prompt tone because it sucks in air through its reeds. The harmonium relies on the inflation of pressure bellows beneath the reed pan. However, the term 'American organ' may cause confusion since both the Aeolian Grand model and the Wilcox & White Symphony were suction models. Later models were produced with reeds which were blown.

The suction models of these instruments are relatively simple and some of the smaller specimens of this type (the Maxfield, the Tonsyreno, and the Aeolian Grand) are far from complex to overhaul once you have embraced the principles of, say, the player piano and the simple organette.

In the suction model, air is exhausted constantly from the inside of the instrument by means of large exhausters similar to those used in the player piano. However, because the volume of air at atmospheric pressure which is admitted to the inside of the organ during playing, particularly when playing a sustained chord on full organ (with all the stops open), is very large, the player organ has exhausters and a suction reservoir or equaliser much bigger than those of the piano. Whereas the piano has two exhausters and an equaliser of about the same size, the player organ has two exhausters and a vacuum storage reservoir which is generally as big as can be accommodated inside the lower part of the instrument.

Another point to remember is that the pneumatic system which forms part of the automatic playing of the organ is also a vital part of the organ when it is used for manual playing. There is still need to treadle when playing by hand so that there is an air pressure differential inside the instrument to allow the reeds to speak. From this we can readily see that there must be some form of shut-off or bypass valve, which cuts out the keyboard for automatic playing, yet may readily bring it back into function whilst at the same time shutting off the mechanical part of the action – that is, essentially, the tracker-bar and roll-winding air motor.

This dual function is achieved in a relatively simple manner. In suction models of the Aeolian – these were initially known as the Aeolian Grand but after about 1900 all models, both pressure and suction, were styled Aeolian Orchestrelles – the changeover from roll to manual playing is mechanical and is achieved by pulling out a special stop-knob. This shifts a leather-covered bar, normally stowed in the spool box, which automatically slides out and covers the tracker bar openings. As this comes out, a set of small spring-loaded pallet valves is raised *en bloc* to touch the bottom of the keys in the keybed under the keyboard. In this mode, when a key is pressed a corresponding pallet in the system is raised, opening a small piston and plunger in an airway. This allows air to enter a narrow passage and inflate a pouch on the pouch-board. For manual playing, then, this piston and its attendant pallet is controlled by the key in this way. When played automatically from the roll, the piston and its pallet is moved away from the influence of the key, the tracker-bar sealing strip is moved, and the

---

* I am discounting here the highly effective and interesting 'percussion' stop fitted in French harmoniums which employs piano-type hammers to strike the reed, and which is also a feature of one tone-rank in certain two-manual-playing Aeolian Orchestrelles as well as the Mustel organs mentioned above.

pouches in the pouch-board come under the control of the openings in the music roll exactly as in the player piano. On the Wilcox & White Symphony player organ, the tracker-bar sealing is effected for manual playing by lifting up a leather-covered bar hinged to the tracker-bar at the same time as drawing a stop to lift up a similar pallet box beneath the keys.

The principle of operation of the suction model Orchestrelle is illustrated in Fig. 49.

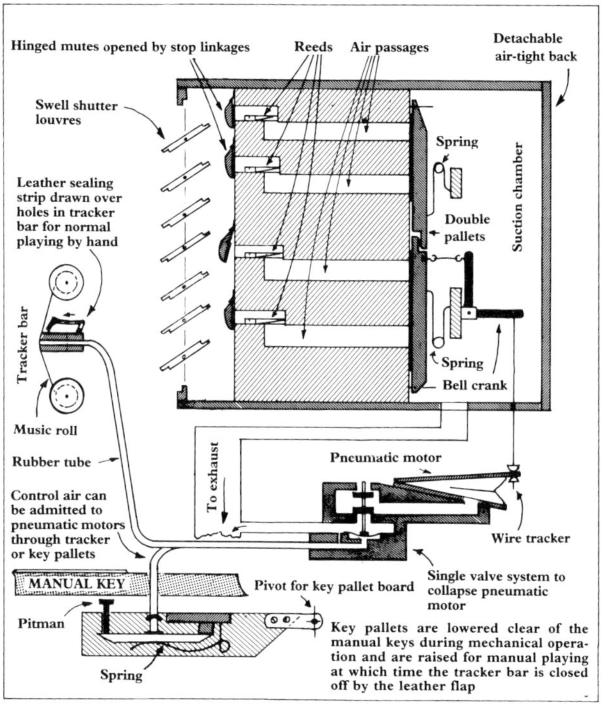

Figure 49   The Aeolian Grand suction action for player reed organs

Both the suction or Aeolian Grand and the pressure Orchestrelle work on the principle of utilising air at a pressure other than normal atmospheric. However, whereas so far we have been talking about instruments where that pressure is negative, i.e. a partial vacuum, the Orchestrelle works on a positive pressure, i.e. air at a pressure greater than that of the atmosphere. Instead of suction, then, inside the Orchestrelle we have air at pressure created by foot pedals which operate pressure bellows instead of exhausters. In the Aeolian Grand, the foot pedals operated player-piano-type exhausters which draw air out of the reservoir which is normally kept open against heavy springs. The Orchestrelle's bellows compresses air into a reservoir which is held normally closed by springs attached externally. Added to this, the air motor for driving the roll mechanism must be driven from the suction side of the bellows. This means that in order to cater for the varying air pressures encountered during playing and to maintain an even motor speed the motor must be driven through both a knife-valve (regulating supply and demand) and its own equaliser to work that valve according to the motor speed setting. This equaliser on the pressure Orchestrelle is a long, slender pneumatic motor normally held open by Y-springs and controlling a valve from an adjustable wire and pallet-valve in the centre of its moving board.

A further problem with the pressure models is that there is no suction to operate the primary pneumatics. Since they cannot be operated by normal atmospheric pressure, the difficulty is overcome by operating the pouches which control the valves by air at pressure greater than atmospheric. This means that the tracker-bar and music roll must be contained in an airtight box, into which air is pumped from the pressure system. Access to the roll is thus achieved by a sliding glass door in this roll box and the instrument will not play with this door in the open position. The pressure supply to the roll box is also equipped with a cut-off valve so that, for rewinding and for manual playing, a sliding valve can be made to seal the windway. Again, to prevent there being a 'buffer' of air in the tracker-bar and also because manual playing uses separate valves in the windway from tracker-bar to pouch, the tracker-bar air supply is sealed by a leather flap valve in the spool box for manual operation.

The larger model Orchestrelles which play from two-manual roll arrangements and have 116-note tracker-bars work using two steps of air pressure. Besides the normal pressure used to operate the instrument, there is a high-pressure wind system which feeds the spool box itself with its very small apertures, and also to the key touch-box. This is to ensure that there is enough wind to operate the pouches and to ensure adequate repetition under the roll-playing mode. This extra pressure comes from a secondary bellows inside the main bellows and reservoir.

From previous chapters I hope you will have gleaned some knowledge of how keyboard pneumatics and primary/secondary valves systems operate. For this reason, I shall now confine my comments to describing those details which are placed above the pneumatic stack and which relate only to the player organ.

Since the Aeolian Orchestrelle is the most common of the player organs, and since the basic principles can be applied to the other styles and makes, we will have a general look at the two types of such an instrument – the suction type and the pressure type.

THE AEOLIAN GRAND

The suction model comprises a large vertical chest which is divided into narrow, vertical compartments, 58 in number (one for each note of the keyboard), and running from front to back. Along the front of all these vertical compartments is arranged a number of rows of reeds, each reed mounted individually in a wooden cross member and each corresponding with one of the vertical passages. There may be 4, 6, 7 or 8 of these rows of reeds and the reeds in each row are of a slightly different form or shape, so as to produce a sound of different characteristic. The chambers in the wooden cross-members, in which the reeds are mounted, are also of a different shape in each row, so as to impart different tonal characteristics to the reeds inside. In this way, subtle variations in tonality can be engineered so that one row of reeds sounds entirely different from another, for example french horn, oboe and trumpet. Each row of reeds is provided with a hinged, tight-fitting flap which seals off all the reeds and which is connected to a stop-knob on the keyboard fascia. When a certain rank of reeds is required to speak, the performer draws the respective stop which opens this hinged flap. Air can now be drawn in through the reeds when a signal for a note to sound comes from tracker-bar or key.

The back of each of the 58 compartments in the vertical chest is sealed by a pallet. In fact, because the vertical passage is so long – about 12 inches from top to bottom – the pallet is made in two halves, put together so that both operate as one. The opening and closing of these pallets is controlled from small pneumatic motors or bellows provided, as in the piano, on a windway controlled by pouches and valves. The difference is that these pouches and motors can be controlled both by the holes in the tracker-bar and also by the keyboard. Between the pallets and the motors run wire pull-downs or, sometimes, cranked rods. All the pallets and, in fact, the entire back of the vertical chest is enclosed in an airtight casing and the operating rods or pull-downs pass out of this through felt seals on their way to the pneumatic stack. Air is continually exhausted from this enclosed chest. When a note is required to sound and the respective motor collapses, it opens one of the pallets, via the pull-down, inside the chest, which contains air at a pressure less than that of the atmosphere. If one of the reed-carrying members on the front of the chest now has its hinged flap opened (by drawing the stop on the keyboard fascia), then air will immediately be sucked into the vertical compartment through the reed. If more than one row of reeds is opened, then air will rush in through several reeds, producing the same note from several reeds of different tonalities.

This chest is supported by, and fixed to, a horizontal platform which is built just below the keyboard level of the organ. Consider, if you like, that this is a table. Beneath the table are fitted the treadle-operated air exhausters and the exhaust reservoir. Above the table is mounted the chest. The airway into the exhaust reservoir is matched by a slot in the table which also matches a slot in the chest, so that the air pressure differential in one is directly united with the other. Part of the air inlet system holds the air motor, which provides rotary motion to the mechanism for transporting the music roll, and this is controlled and governed in exactly the same way as in the player piano.

THE AEOLIAN ORCHESTRELLE

We will now turn our attention to the pressure-operated instruments, and perhaps the best start is to forget all that we have learned about suction systems and exhausters, for here we are dealing with air at pressure. The action of treadling operates feeders instead of exhausters – feeders which are continually pumping air into a reservoir, which supplies a large quantity of wind to circulate inside the chambers of the instrument, and by means of which the many reeds can be blown adequately.

The pressure Orchestrelle consists of a table upon which the mechanics of the organ may be located, such as wind motor to drive the music roll, stop linkages, pneumatic valves, and so on. This table also contains the windways for the keyboard operation of the instrument and thus ends with a double, staggered row of pouches along the back edge. Beneath the table is the centreboard, having upon one side the wind reservoir and on the other the two treadle-operated feeders. Wind from the reservoir is taken to two vertical trunkings of wood, which run from each end of the table to the top of the instrument. The inside faces of these trunkings have certain openings between which fit first of all the pneumatic stack above the pouch board, and then successive narrow boxes, one on top of the other, each containing one stop of reeds: in Aeolian terminology these are called 'tone ranks' and they are wider in planform at the bass end than at the treble. Air at pressure is thus admitted to the inside of the tone ranks from both ends at the same time. Similarly, air is admitted to the pneumatic stack from both sides.

The passage of air from the vertical trunking into a tone rank is controlled by a large pallet

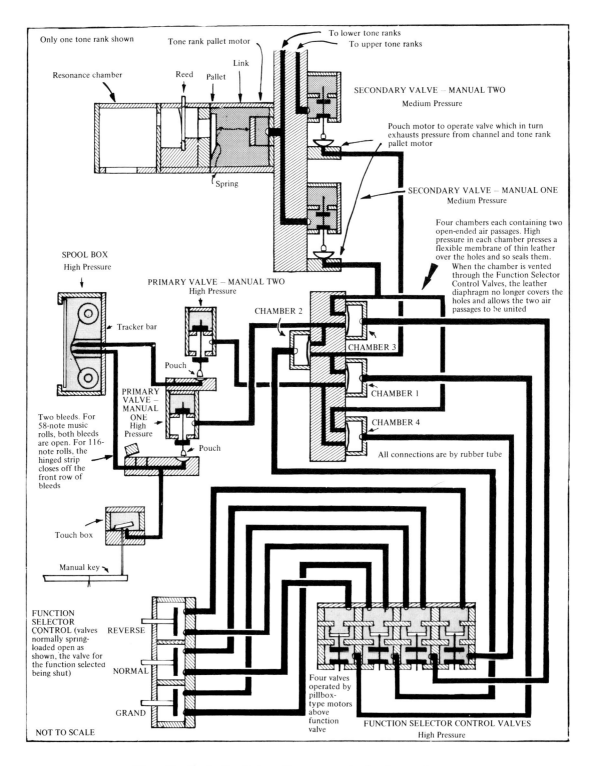

Figure 50   The Aeolian Orchestrelle pressure action for player reed organs

valve which in turn is controlled by a linkage to the stop-knob on the keyboard fascia. As a precaution against excess air pressure in a tone rank causing the momentary sounding of a reed in that box after the stop has been shut off, the stop linkage is also connected to a felted hinged flap, rather like that which we have already seen on the suction models, to cover the air exit from the reeds.

To summarise, the actual speaking part of the organ consists of two vertical wind chests, between which are fixed ranks of reeds, each rank voiced in a different way. Air is passed into the tone ranks from both ends, and may be shut off by master pallets which close the respective air passage in the chests. So long as the feeders are being treadled, air pressure exists in these two vertical chests.

The speaking part of the organ – the means by which notes are made to sound, is rather more complex. Each rank of reeds, as well as being fixed to the side chests, is fitted to the back of the organ and this back is made up of panels of timber containing vertical passages. Each reed in each rank is matched by an opening in the back of the tone rank which matches an opening in the backboard of the organ. At the bottom of the backboard the vertical passages end with another opening, which lines up with openings in the pneumatic valve stack. Air is under pressure in the passages in the backboard all the time the instrument is being operated. When a note is to be played, a valve in the pneumatic stack is pushed up by the pouch in the pouch-board, so closing off the air-pressure inlet to that valve, and opening the backboard passage to atmosphere, so bleeding out its air pressure.

We now have two functions explained – air pressure in the tone rank and the exhausting of a column of air relative to every reed, in all the tone ranks, which represents one predetermined note.

Inside the tone rank there are two sections. The first is a section common to all the reeds (actually this is not entirely true as we shall explain further on, but it will suffice to accept this for now), and the other is made up of small compartments, one for each reed, along the back of the tone rank. These compartments are in communication with the windways in the backboard. The compartments are separated from the main portion of the chest by a soft leather diaphragm, into which is cemented a small bearing block carrying a wire hook. Each reed, fixed into the front edge (the common passage) of the tone rank, is covered by an inwards-opening pallet and the wire hook is connected to the pallet by a link of thread-covered soft wire. Movement of the leather diaphragm therefore causes the reed pallet to open and shut.

Now we can see how the system works. So long as air exists at an equal pressure inside the tone rank and also inside the backboard windways, the reed pallets are kept closed by a light spring. The moment the pressure is exhausted from one backboard windway, all the diaphragms connected to that windway will collapse under the pressure of the air in the tone rank, so opening the respective pallet in each tone rank corresponding to the note to be sounded. The air pressure can now escape through the reed, making it speak.

The apparent complexities of this system are best explained by Fig. 50. For clarity, this functional drawing shows one particular note (one hole in the tracker-bar) and only one of the tone ranks. In practice, a number of tone ranks are connected to the backboard airways.

Referring now to the drawing, air chambers (5) and (3) are subjected to air pressure at all times while the machine is being operated, i.e. while the feeders are being treadled or the electric blower is in operation. When a stop is drawn, the respective tone rank (1) is also subjected to pressure. Chambers (5), (3) and (1) are common to the whole keyboard compass.

Airways (a) and (h) are relative only to one keyboard key or one note in the keyboard scale, and each hole in the tracker-bar is connected, via its own airway (a), to its own pouch (c), thereby controlling its own valve assembly (g). This in turn regulates air to an individual passage (h) and operates separate diaphragms (i) and pallets (k).

When the instrument is at rest, i.e. when it is not making any sound, the roll box (6), the valve chest (3), the backboard (2) and the tone rank (1) contain air at pressure from the bellows. In this state, the lower of the two valves (g) seals the vent (f) to atmosphere, and at the same time pallet spring (l) seals pallet (k) from the reed.

When air is admitted to a pouch (c) through the tracker-bar (a), the pitman (d) is raised, the upper of the two valves (g) closes off pressure airway (e) and exhausts air from the airway (h) through the vent (f). This causes the pouch (i) to contract, thereby drawing open the pallet (k) against the spring (l) via the link (j). In this condition the reed (7) will speak.

To ensure prompt return of the action to a silent condition the moment the tracker-bar airway (a) is once more closed, air in the tracker-bar passage is allowed to escape quickly via the bleed-hole (b), thereby allowing the pouch (c) to contract under pressure of air from airway (e) on to the upper of the two valves (g). The moment the exhaust vent (f) is once more closed, air is immediately admitted into airway (h), pouch (i) is extended, and pallet (k) closes. Because the pressure in the tone rank is equal to the pressure in the backboard, pouch (i) is free to take up a position on its own, equal to the closed position of pallet (k).

If the action becomes sluggish and cannot produce a rapid staccato, the travel of the valve assembly (g) may be too great, the clearance between (d) and (c) too small, or the bleed-hole (b) too small. Because air is admitted at constant pressure through (a) when a note is speaking, bleed-hole (b) can be slightly larger than optimum, but, of course, this again may delay speech by making the operation of the valve assembly (g) too slow.

Variation of tonal colour is achieved by the various ingenious methods of mounting the reed (7) in its box (1). A typical installation is shown in the illustration. In this a hinged flap (n) covers the major sound passage. When the reed speaks normally, the sound is allowed to pass into a comparatively large chamber, the only exit from which is a small hole (m). The shape and size of the chamber, the size and positioning of the hole (m) and the relative position of the reed (7) assist materially in providing tonal variation. If the hinged panel (n) is opened, the reed speaks more or less freely to atmosphere through a large chamber, thereby producing a completely different tone.

It will be seen that, regardless of which stops are drawn, the operation of the pouch (i) via the airway (h) continues all the time the instrument is being played. Only when air is admitted into the tone rank (1) will the system speak. The main entry into the tone rank (1) is via a hinged pallet at the sides of the vertical wind chests. It is these pallets which are controlled directly by the stops.

In dismantling the pressure Orchestrelle, the first point, having removed the upper half of the case, is to take off the backboard. This comprises a number of sections which fit next to each other. Each section is dowelled with small wooden pegs to the table and is then screwed with a large number of woodscrews to each of the tone ranks, the pneumatic valve chest and the pouch board. The bass end boards are also screwed to the organ table from below over the area of the sub-bass reed box assembly, which itself can be removed as a separate unit. When removing and replacing the backboard sections, be careful since they are a very tight fit and you should try not to break off the locating dowels, although it is not too important if the odd one snaps off. Take off the end boards first as these can be reached from the front of the organ with a length of 1-inch square timber with which you can tap them free of their dowels with a mallet. Have somebody behind to steady the boards and remember that they are laminated into windways and are thus not as robust as they appear: do not use excessive force in their removal. The boards are all numbered, but it is as well to make your own chalk marks to aid reassembly. Each of the screws has a washer and a small spring under the head – keep these separate from other screws from the organ.

With all the backboard sections off, unscrew the side panels from the vertical side chests. This allows access to the screws which secure each end of each tone rank to the chests. Some of these reed boxes are very heavy – you will see that they are asymmetric in shape and each one differs in shape and proportions. Have someone support the weight of the boxes one at a time, starting from the top, as you unscrew and remove each of them. Note that there is a soft leather seal between the ends of the boxes and the mating portion of each chest. If this sealing gasket is broken it must be replaced, using soft white skin available from an organ-builder. So long as the gasket is not too hard, you can reconstitute it by brushing with a stiff wire brush to restore the knap to the leather. The same treatment should be applied to all pallets which are disturbed or which look as if they are not able to seal properly. The ideal is to replace all leather pallet faces but this is not always essential. When all the tone ranks have been removed, the last item to be removed is the pneumatic valve stack and this needs to be handled carefully, as otherwise it may puncture the pouches or bend the valve stems, unless lifted straight out once the screws have been removed.

The sequence of reassembly is the reverse of dismantling and the first item to be replaced is the pneumatic valve stack.

The adjustment of the primary valves tends to be critical. Assuming that the leather of the pouches is in good condition and supple enough, and also that the small, circular pressure pad, cemented into the centre of each pouch is present, the clearance between the bottom of the valve stem and the top of the pad must be about $1/32$ inch and certainly no more than about $3/64$ inch. Since the valve stems are threaded in the actual valves, it is possible to screw the valves down to this clearance, extremely precise though it may sound. In this position of rest, the bottom of the two valves on the stem must seat evenly on the vent hole of the valve chest. The top valve must be open between $1/16$ inch and $3/32$ inch, for proper operation. These valve adjustments must be made with the pneumatic stack properly fixed in its final position, between the vertical side chests. Since there are two distinct pneumatic systems in the organ – the keyboard and the mechanical – the operation of these valves can be checked before the backboard is replaced and, if the organ has been fully dismantled, before the tone ranks are fitted. All you must do is make sure all the other air vents in the vertical chests are closed and then have someone select 'manual' on the stops and depress each note on the keyboard by hand, whilst pumping the feeders. You can now watch the functioning of the pouches and valves from the back, making any necessary adjustments as you go. Ensure also that all the bleed-holes are clear of dirt or other obstruction, and see that the valves move freely in their guide rails.

Having completed the adjustments of the valves, proceed with replacing the tone ranks from the bottom upwards, again having somebody to take their weight until the side screws are in place. Once all the boxes are refitted, you can turn your attention to the pieces which form the backboard. See that all the circular leather or fibre washers, which are placed around each opening, are present and in good order. Tease up their surfaces with the wire

111

brush. If one is missing, before replacing it make sure that it has not stuck to the matching hole in the reed box (tone rank).

Position the centre section of the backboard first and replace all the woodscrews loosely. Now position both the end sections and again put back the screws finger-tight. The remaining boards are next put back; spring them carefully into place if necessary. Only when all the screws are already in position loosely should you start to tighten them up. You will find that each tone rank has two rows of screws, one along the top of the back edge and one along the bottom of the back edge. Tighten the screws for each box alternately, one top, one bottom, one top, and so on all the way along in a zigzag fashion. When all the boxes are secured in this manner, tighten the intermediate screws. Make sure all are firmly home. The remainder of stripping, servicing and reassembly is straightforward.

Earlier I said that the tone ranks received air through both ends via the vertical wind chests. This is correct but the reed boxes are, in fact, divided into two unequal portions by a thin plate of steel, which is placed between the twenty-first and the twenty-second note up from the bass end of the keyboard – the A below middle C being the first of the upper division and the immediately preceding G being the last of the lower division. This break in each rank of reeds enables the performer to make subtle use of his controls to play music with a 'heavy' bass accompaniment on several stops, whilst at the same time playing the melodic tenor and treble theme on a 'solo' stop. The converse of the technique is also possible, bringing out the melody on several stops whilst sketching in a soft bass on different stops.

The break in each bank of reeds is therefore used to achieve two stops from tone rank. To explain this, one rank may be divided so that the upper portion is controlled by a stop marked 'Oboe', whilst the lower is controlled by a stop marked 'Bassoon'. This represents a fairly logical tonality between these two instruments of the orchestra. Another rank will be divided into 'French Horn' at the upper part and 'Gemshorn' at the bass, whilst another may be 'Cremona' and 'Melodian'. The performer may choose to have all three upper parts of the tone ranks playing, whilst he may select only 'Gemshorn' out of the bass portions to bring in a bass which may not drown the music. This characteristic, of breaking the rank of reeds into two separate stop controls, is also found on the suction models but, of course, there the reeds are all mounted together into the vertical common chest and only the cover strips need to be divided.

Operation of the tone rank controls (the draw-stop knobs on the keyboard fascia) and the other functions of the Orchestrelle were achieved in two ways. The early Grands and Orchestrelles used mechanical controls where drawing a stop moved a roller bar through suitable linkages so that it pulled a wire and opened the windway pallet in the vertical side chests. Later models moved to an entirely pneumatic system of control which was both lighter in touch and quieter to work. With pneumatic controls, the key is the accurate setting of the small primary valves mounted adjacent to the vertical chest pallets and connected to the stop fascia via rubber tube. A properly adjusted valve will instantly move and give very precise selection. However, these little valves create more problems than any other in the organ in my experience. The setting must be no more than $3/64$ inch and the valve seals must make a proper air seal otherwise they will 'float' and operate very sluggishly.

The player organ has several other features such as a 'Vox Humana' stop, which controls a small air turbine which can be set to revolve in the upper portion of the reed boxes adjacent to the reed openings of one rank of pipes. This turbine turns a paddle which breaks up the sound and produces a wavering effect on each note. Another feature is the 'Swell', which consists of a number of closely spaced louvres or venetian blind shutters which close off the entire front of the organ inside the case. When these shutters are closed, the organ speaks quietly or muffled. By opening the shutters, the volume of sound can be made to increase. The swell is controlled by a knee-board worked by the right knee of the performer. A further feature is the 'Full Organ' or 'Great Organ'. This is worked by a knee-board for the left knee and as it is moved it takes control of all the stop linkages and gradually opens up each stop. So long as this board is held over by the knee whilst treadling, all the stops are open and free to speak, regardless of the stop knobs which are drawn. As the board is released, so the stops close, leaving once more only those for which the knobs are drawn.

Armed with this explanation of the operation of the player-organ mechanism, the repairer should have a fair idea as to how he should set about repair and restoration. As a guide, here are the principle snags which you are most likely to find, together with the correct action to take:

FAULTS AND THEIR DIAGNOSIS

When played manually, one or more notes sound continuously. This can be due to one of three things: (a) the key sticking in the down position; (b) the pallet beneath the keyboard, which operates for manual use, has a loose or broken spring, (c) there is a hole in the leather sealing strip over the tracker-bar or it is just not seating properly. It can also be due to a perforated rubber tube or a missing tube.

When played from the roll, one or more notes do not speak at all, even when sustained. This means that either there is a broken tube connection, the tracker hole is blocked (it should be sucked out with a pump), or the valve clearance is incorrect. It could also be due to a perforated pouch.

When played from the roll, one or more notes are slow to speak. This means that the bleed-holes are too large or the valve clearance is too great.

When played from the roll, one or more notes are prompt in speech but will not repeat staccato, producing one long note instead of a number of short notes. This means that the valve clearance is too little or the bleed-holes too small.

When one note speaks, an adjacent one 'whimpers'. This means that air from one windway in the backboard is getting through to another windway, and may be due to the board not being tightly screwed to the tone ranks, dirt trapped between backboard and tone ranks so preventing it from being tightened properly, or the small leather washer between tone rank hole and backboard hole being torn or missing.

The organ will not play at all mechanically. This means that the keyboard manual-playing stop-knob is disconnected from the keyboard manual-pallet rail underneath, so leaving open both the mechanical airways in the tracker-bar and the key pallets.

When played manually, certain notes suddenly begin to screech. This means that a pallet is not closing in a stop. A common feature amongst suction organs, this can be rectified by locating the reed, and then removing the controlling pallet at the back of the vertical chest and either re-leathering the sealing face or teasing it up with a fine wire brush.

The air motor to driving the music roll is sluggish, erratic or inoperative. This can be due to damp affecting the sliding seals, a disconnected airway, or the control valve being disconnected.

On pressure models, the rewind for the roll is very slow and requires heavy treadling. This is due to the shut-off valve, which cuts air pressure from the roll-box, not closing properly. With the roll-box open, the rewind will speed up, but air is still being wasted. If you can hear and feel air at pressure coming from the windway into the roll-box during rewind, remove the cover of the box (it is attached with simple hooks along top and both sides and is located by pegs at the bottom) and check the operation of the valve when the 'rewind' stop-knob is drawn. If it does not close fully, then adjust the linkage until it closes and makes a proper seal.

The organ plays on rewind. This is exactly the same as on the player piano and the same valve selector adjustment should be carried out.

A reed suddenly produces a muffled, flat tone. This indicates either that a piece of dirt has got on to the reed or that it has fractured through age. Draw out the reed with a reed hook (use this tool carefully and engage it only in the recess provided, otherwise the reed tongue will be damaged) and examine it. Holding the reed up to the light, you should be able to see an equal amount of light between the tongue and the plate all the way round. Use a soft brush to clean away any dust and dirt. If the reed still sounds flat, then it is probably cracked. Some cracks are almost impossible to see, even with a magnifying glass. A cracked reed must be replaced. Most large piano-sundries houses also carry reeds and, if they cannot match it with an entirely new reed, they can fit a new tongue and revoice the old one for you, if you send them also the reed an octave above and an octave below the damaged one.

It goes without saying that loose, cracked or otherwise damaged rubber tubing will have a serious effect on the performance of the instrument. Similarly, the feeders, equalisers and exhausters and pressure reservoirs must be in good order and free from cracks and leaks. The main reservoir is covered with a rubberised cloth, considerably thicker than that used in the player piano, and, if you have to re-cover, use material of the same thickness and quality, matched from the piano-sundries house. Never use thinner material – it just will not last.

With this résumé of the works of the player organ, the amateur should be able to solve his overhaul problems, once he understands the principles of the pneumatic player action common to both piano and organ.

Finally a word on a subject which, I know, causes much confusion, misunderstanding and speculation. The novice to the organ may be perplexed by some of the terminology used to describe the organ stops as written on the stop-knob faces. He will probably see 'Bourdon 16 ft', 'Trumpet 8 ft', 'Flute 4 ft' and, on some of the larger instruments, 'Piccolo 2 ft'. He may deduce that these dimensions refer in some way to the reeds or to the reed boxes. In truth, he has no need to concern himself with this part at all. What significance the dimensions have will become apparent when he begins to play his newly restored instrument. Suppose you start by drawing 'French Horn 8 ft', in the upper part of the organ, and matching it with 'Gemshorn 8 ft', in the lower. If you now play manually, you will find you have a complete scale. You can now select two more stops, again marked '8 ft', and you will find that this second rank of reeds produces a unison sound – in other words, sound at the same pitch although of a different character. Now pull one of the bass stops marked '16 ft' and you will find that the bass notes are suddenly reinforced with notes sounding an octave below the others: in other words you are playing two notes, an octave apart, from one key.

On the treble register, you draw a stop marked '4 ft' and find that you are now playing two notes from one key: this time the '4 ft' stop is producing a note an octave above the normal. If you draw a '2 ft' stop, you are an octave above that again, or two octaves above the first note you played with that same one key.

Thus the dimension is related to the pitch of the note. The larger number of stops are marked '8 ft', so the organ is said to have 'a basis of eight-foot pitch'. If you double the number, i.e. 8 to 16 ft., then you decrease an octave from the normal. If instead of doubling the 8 you halve it to 4 ft, you have moved an octave higher; halve again to 2 ft and you are two octaves higher.

This characteristic, based on the physical dimensions of a proper organ pipe, and the terminology of a real pipe organ, allows subtle tones in the performance of a music roll. You can, for example, accentuate the melodic line of a tune by playing it in 'octave unison' in this manner. Likewise, you can accentuate the bass by bolstering up a nominal 8 ft with a 16 ft stop.

The middle C on an 8 ft organ stop is equal to the middle C of the piano, and for this reason a piano is said to be of 8 ft pitch.

The art of playing the player organ is perhaps more aesthetically satisfying than that of the player piano. The skills needed are just as involved if you are to produce a perfect performance. The novice may scoff at the thought that there can be any skill needed to get an interpretation from a roll of music on such an instrument. Give him ten minutes with one, though, and he will be a wiser man, if no more technically competent. But the art, for art there is in playing both piano and organ from roll music, is a true art with its own fair share of fundamentals, mechanicals, abstracts and sympathies, and to attempt to do justice to it would require an altogether separate, lengthy work. To some, I am certain, the art will need no interpretation, for the mere possession and fulfilment of such an instrument will cultivate an understanding tantamount to the art spontaneously. To others, it may forever remain a murky mystery.

APPENDIX A

Music Roll Makers and Brand Names

There were very many different manufacturers of music rolls throughout the world and inevitably it is impossible to trace them all. Equally, there were very many brand names of piano roll. The following list provides the names and addresses of the majority of recorded music roll makers together with the more common roll names and trade-marks which were used in their retailing. There were, however, many thousands of different names used on piano rolls and once again such a listing is unlikely ever to be complete. Even so, this may prove of value to the collector who seeks to try to own a roll by each of the many makers, so forming a 'one-of-a-kind' roll collection.

A.B. CONSUMERS MUSIC CO.   Station C, Buffalo, New York, USA. Makers of cheap music rolls.

ACCENTIST   Music rolls made by Impérial Entoilé, Paris.

AEOLIAN CO., THE   24, av. del Conde de Penalver, Madrid, Spain. Makers of piano rolls.

AEOLIAN CO., THE   46 Gran Via, Bilbao, Spain. Director: E. Izaguirre. Spanish branch of the Aeolian Company. Maker of music rolls.

ALTOONA MUSIC ROLL CO.   Altoona, Pennsylvania, USA. Also factory at Lansdale, Pa. Founded in 1919, manufacturer of Victory instrumental piano rolls, Superba word rolls and a series of quality word rolls called Master.

ANGELUS-ARTRIO – *See* ARTRIO-ANGELUS.

ANGLO-AMERICAN PLAYER ROLL COMPANY   Melbourne, Australia. Founded by one-time conductor and arranger for the Majestic Theatre Orchestra in Melbourne Len Luscombe who made the first piano rolls in Australia – out of brown paper. Later produced commercially under the label Broadway. Imported much new American roll-perforating machinery into Australia which, on the takeover by MASTERTOUCH (q.v.) in 1957, formed the nucleus of that company's expansion in business.

ANIMATIC   Quality piano rolls made by Hupfeld for the Phonola. Rolls have the word 'Phonola' as watermark at regular intervals plus the initials H & E (see HOFFMANN & ENGELMANN) and the year of manufacture. Rolls with the legend ANIMATIC-T are for the Triphonola reproducing piano.

ARTISTYLE   Name used by Universal Music Co., London.

ARTISTYLE MUSIC ROLL CO.   15 Prince of Wales Crescent, London NW1. Makers of music rolls.

ARTONA MUSIC ROLLS LTD   22–4 Westcliff Road, Ramsgate, Kent. This company was founded by Mr Gordon Iles, who at one time worked for the Aeolian Company at Hayes, Middlesex. Strictly a one-man business, Mr Iles produces player-piano rolls, both newly recorded ones made by himself and copies of existing rolls, under the trade name 'Artona'. His roll-punching machinery was acquired when the old Aeolian Co. went into liquidation. He also makes copies of Duo-Art music-rolls.

ARTISTS' MUSIC ROLLS   Marketed by M. Sinclair, 16 Orchard St, London W, *fl.* 1914.

'D'ARTISTS'   Brand name of piano rolls made by René Seybold, Paris.

ARTRIO-ANGELUS   Reproducing piano rolls made by Wilcox & White, Meriden, Connecticut.

ATLAS PLAYER ROLL CO.   35–7 Fifth Street, Newark, New Jersey, USA. Makers of Atlas player piano rolls and A-R rolls. 'Popular word rolls: Foreign word rolls' it advertised.

AUDIOGRAPHIC   Name used by Universal Music Co., London, for series of costly annotated rolls edited by Percy Scholes.

AUTOMATIC MUSIC ROLL COMPANY   1510 Dayton Street, Chicago, Illinois, USA. Music roll manufacturers owned by J. P. Seeburg Company.

AUTOMUSIC PERFORATING COMPANY   53 Broadway, New York, USA. President James O'Connor. Makers of piano rolls who advertised: 'We arrange and cut Perforated Music Sheets for automatically operated musical instruments.'

AUTOPLAYER   Name used by Universal Music Co., London.

BACHMANN & WERNER   1–2 Herlossohnstr. Leipzig, N.22. Maker of player pianos and also music rolls, fl. 1930.

BACIGALUPO, GIOVANNI   71a Schonhauser Allee, Berlin, Germany. Renowned maker of street organs and pianos who also produced player piano rolls under the name 'Excelsior'. Bacigalupo died on 10 July 1978 aged 88.

BENNETT & WHITE, INC.   67–71 Gable Street, Newark, New Jersey, USA. Established 1913. Makers of the Artempo Word Rolls. 'Music as actually played'.

BENRATH & FRANK   Düren-Mariaweiler, Germany. Makers of player rolls, fl. 1930.

BERLINER NOTENROLLEN-FABRIK 'EOLAND' OTTO P. F. HANKE   12, Wöhlerstrasse, Berlin, N.4. Makers of music rolls, fl. 1912.

BILLINGS PLAYER ROLL COMPANY   Enterprise Building, Milwaukee, Wisconsin, USA. A subsidiary of piano accessory manufacturer Billings Spring Brass Flange Co., this company introduced the Staffnote music roll which featured the music written in regular music notation along the edge of the paper. Company was founded in 1921 by Fred C. Billings.

BLANCAFORT, JUAN BTA   La Garriga, Barcelona, Spain. Makers of piano rolls.

BLOHUT, MEISSNER & CO   Moltkestr. 80, Leipzig H, Germany. Established in 1907 as makers of piano rolls. Specialised in the making of artistic rolls under the name 'Original-Kunstler-Notenrollen'.

BLOHUT, JOSEF   11 Naumburger Str., Leipzig, Germany. Maker of piano rolls, fl. 1930.

BOL, JOSEPH   61 rue d'Angleterre, Brussels, Belgium. Maker of piano rolls, fl. 1930.

BRAITERMAN FEDDER COMPANY   Brafco Building, Baltimore, Maryland, USA. Makers of the Mel-O-Art piano roll.

BROADWAY   Label owned by The Anglo-American Player Roll Company of Melbourne, Australia, taken over by Mastertouch in 1957.

CAPITOL MUSIC ROLL CO   721 North Kedzie Avenue, Chicago, Illinois, USA. Makers of music rolls. Labels bear initials 'N.O.S.'

CAPITOL ROLL & RECORD CO   721 North Kedzie Avenue, Chicago, Illinois, USA. Makers of piano rolls bearing the initials CMC arranged to form a circle inside a triple row garland.

CHASE & BAKER CO.   Buffalo, New York, USA. Chase & Baker music rolls were identical with those produced under the name of the MELOGRAPHIC ROLL COMPANY (q.v.). All rolls were stamped with a circular motif showing the company name between concentric circles surrounding a triangle containing the words 'Lint Paper'.

CLARK ORCHESTRA ROLL CO.   De Kalb, Illinois, USA. Makers of Orchestra brand multi-tune music rolls for 65-note electric pianos. President of company was Ernest G. Clark, brother of player pioneer Melville Clark. The company was founded in 1920 and quickly became leader in its field.

COLUMBIA MUSIC ROLL COMPANY   22 South Peoria Street, Chicago, Illinois, USA. Advertised as 'the only *truly synchronised* word roll, having the words printed exactly opposite their corresponding notes'.

CONNORIZED PLAYER ROLL CO.   817–21 East 144th Street, New York, USA. Established before 1908, this company became one of the largest suppliers of rolls in the United States and expanded continually both as regards production capacity and catalogue. The name came from a patented paper process which was said to ensure that the paper would not shrink or swell in any climate.

DELUXE REPRODUCING ROLL CORPORATION   Branch of the Auto-Pneumatic Action Co. (q.v.) which produced the Welte-Mignon (Licensee) reproducing action. Both companies were located in the same New York building.

DENTON, WM S.   4 Park Street West, Newark, New Jersey, USA. Maker of music rolls, *fl.*1909.

DRESDEN SACHS PAPIEROLLEN FABRIK.   Manufacturers of special paper for piano rolls, *fl.*1912.

L'ÉDITION MUSICALE PERFORÉE   64 rue La Boëtie, Paris 8e, France. Makers of player piano rolls marked 'L'E.M.P.' and including associated names as 'L'Édition Musicale Salabert' and 'Francis-Day'. Made in France, these were good quality rolls and in 1930 the company advertised that its catalogue included 4,500 titles.

EDITORIAL EUTERPE   Box 3144, Valparaiso, Chile. Makers of player piano rolls, *fl.*1930.

ELLIOTT'S   78 Finsbury Pavement, London, EC. Makers of the Acme piano roll which used an 'Imperial Linenised' label, had a blue cartridge paper apron, and was probably named 'Acme' after the roll-perforating machinery of that name.

EMPECO   Hand-played music rolls made by Michael Preuss & Co. GmbH, 12, Warschauerstr, Berlin O.34. *fl.*1930.

ESPANA MUSICAL, S.A.   c. Pizarro, Zaragoza, Spain. Maker of piano rolls, *fl.*1930.

EXCELSIOR NOTENROLLEN-FABRIK   The piano-roll-making arm of the business of street organ builder GIOVANNI BACIGALUPO. Was in business before 1912 at Finnländische Strasse 13, Berlin N.113, and, later, at 71a, Schonhauser Allee.

F.I.R.S.T.   *See* FABBRICANTE ITALIANO RULLI SONORI TRAFORATI.

FABBRICANTE ITALIANO RULLI SONORI TRAFORATI   Better known by the initials F.I.R.S.T. (and always spelled with the full points between), an Italian maker of piano rolls which manufactured under licence from G. Ricordi & Co., the music publishers which appear to have owned the company.

FILMUSIC COMPANY   6701–15 Santa Monica Boulevard, Hollywood, California, USA. Makers of special rolls for 88-note organs offering '100 per cent more melody and action out of your 88-note organ than if played by hand'. The music, obviously for theatre-player use, was 'recorded monthly for your show' and the company offered '10 Picturolls for $10' along with a library of some 1,000 'excellent organ rolls'.

FISCHER A.-G, A.E.   Postfach 2, Bremen, Germany. Makers of piano rolls, *fl.*1930.

FLUESS, LOUIS   65, rue de la Hache, Borgerhiut-Anvers, Belgium. Maker of rolls for pianos and orchestrions, *fl.*1930.

GENERAL MUSIC SUPPLY CO.   524–8 West 57th Street, New York, USA. 'Manufacturers of perforated music rolls for all standard player pianos', *fl.*1908.

GLOBE CO. THE   154 North 11th Street, Philadelphia, Pennsylvania, USA. Makers of Globe Music Rolls, established in 1919. Became absorbed into the STANDARD MUSIC ROLL CORPORATION of Orange, New Jersey (q.v.), which then used the Globe name for its less expensive line of rolls.

GRIESHABER, JOSEF   3, Blumenshalstr., Leipzig, Germany. Maker of piano rolls, *fl.*1930.

GULBRANSEN MUSIC ROLL CORP.   599 Eleventh Avenue, New York City, and 3232 West Chicago Avenuc, Chicago, Illinois, USA. Incorporated in 1926 to produce 'new and improved music rolls true to hand playing minus mechanical effects'.

HAND PLAYED MUSIC ROLL CO. LTD   1 Hanover Yard, Hanover Street, London. Makers of piano rolls, *fl.*1930.

HERBERT COMPANY, THE   Newark, New Jersey, USA. Makers of 'square-cut' (*sic*) piano solo rolls.

HIGEL LTD   149 Albion Road, Stoke Newington, London. Makers of piano rolls, *fl.*1930.

HOFFMANN & ENGELMANN   Neustadt a.d. Haardt, Germany. Makers of special paper for piano rolls. Always identifiable by the watermark 'H & E' together with the year of manufacture occurring throughout length. Makers for Hupfeld and later taken over by that company.

HUBERT, JOSEF   210 Mallinckrodstr., Dortmund, Germany. Maker of piano rolls, *fl.*1930.

118

IMPERIAL   Player-piano rolls were manufactured under this name by the PERFORATED MUSIC CO. (q.v.). These 65- and 88-note music-rolls were made in a patented one-piece box and the start of the roll was reinforced with glazed linen, hence the term 'linenised'. Also used a steel spool and a D-shaped tag to the roll end.

IMPÉRIAL ENTOILÉ   25 Boulevard des Italiens, Paris. Makers of 65- and 88-note music rolls under the brand name Accentist, *fl.*1920.

IMPERIAL MUSIC CO.   27 Queen Victoria Street, London, EC. Makers of piano rolls.

IMPERIAL PLAYER ROLL CO.   Chicago, Illinois, USA. Founded around 1915 for the manufacture of piano rolls. Roehl relates that one of its officers, Thomas E. Kavanaugh, later became general manager of the National Music Roll Manufacturers' Association of Chicago. Imperial was controlled by the Cable Company and manufactured, as sole licensed manufacturer, the Solo Carola Record rolls. Also made Imperial Hand Played Records and Imperial Songrecords.

INDIVIDUAL PLAYER ROLL COMPANY   Jersey City, New Jersey, USA. Makers of piano rolls for branded outlets. Manager Anthony Galasso (quoted in Roehl) described his business as 'recording player rolls for song writers, composers, and dealers under their own special labels'.

INTERNATIONAL PLAYER ROLL CO.   66 Water Street, Brooklyn, New York, and 125 North Ninth Street, Philadelphia, Pennsylvania, USA. Established in 1919. Manufactured 'word rolls for expression reproducing pianos'. Also made the 'International Concert Series' in which were featured 'all of the better class of operatic, medleys, and classical numbers'. The company was later in business at 142 Berkeley Street in Brooklyn and at 30 Main Street in Boston until it finally became absorbed into the Q.R.S. business (q.v.).

I.X.L. COMPANY   Philadelphia, Pennsylvania, USA. A small maker of piano rolls, apparently short-lived.

KEYNOTE   Song rolls made by MUSICNOTE ROLL COMPANY (q.v.).

KIBBEY MANUFACTURING COMPANY   Marine Building, 136 West Lake Street, Chicago, Illinois, USA. Makers of the Klean-Kut music roll. Advertised music rolls 'for nearly all electric pianos, orchestrions, and photo-players'.

KLEAN-KUT   *See* KIBBEY.

KRAUS, PAUL   19, Wissmannstr., Leipzig-Neushonefeld, Germany. Maker of spools for piano rolls, *fl.*1930.

LAMBERT-BRONZE, M.   Rue Clemenceau, Ans, Belgium. Maker of piano rolls, *fl.*1930.

LEABARJAN MANUFACTURING CO.   521 Hanover Street, Ohio, USA. The Leabarjan Manufacturing Co. was incorporated on 10 October 1911 with a capital of $100,000 to manufacture a home roll perforator. Designer was John C. Lease and other company members were Carl Bartels along with a financial backer called Janzen. From each man came three letters in the company name. Bartels was president until ultimately his son Leo F. Bartels assumed ownership until 1928. Several models were made, ranging from hand-operated devices up to electrically-operated multiple-sheet punches. Total production is thought to have been fewer than 1,000 with the most popular model, the number 5, selling for $75 (David L. Junchen, in Q. D. Bowers, *Encyclopedia of Automatic Musical Instruments*).

LEIPZIGER PIANOFORTE- U. PHONOLAFABRIKEN HUPFELD-GEBR. ZIMMERMANN A.-G.   4, Peterstr, Leipzig, Germany. Makers of player pianos and piano rolls. This was the name used by Hupfeld after the business had been taken over by Zimmermann the piano-builders, *fl.*1930.

LOCKWOODS   76 & 78 City Road, London, EC. Musical instrument dealers and wholesalers who made and distributed Perfector piano rolls.

LORDIER & CAUCHIS   36 rue de Petits-Champs, Paris. Advertised in 1912 as successors to Baron u. de Maillet. Makers of piano rolls.

LIRON, GORDO Y GONZALEZ (successors to Salvi)   12–14 calle Sevilla, Madrid, Spain. Maker of mechanical pianos and piano rolls, *fl.*1930.

LYRAGRAPH MUSIC ROLL CO.   19 Gainsborough Gardens, Golders Green, London, NW, *fl.*1914.

'Having been on the market a few months, but their excellent musical arrangement, high class finish, most durable paper and low price has obtained us extensive orders from a great number of piano dealers and manufacturers'.

MASTER   *See under* ALTOONA.

MASTERTOUCH PIANO ROLL COMPANY   Canterbury, New South Wales, Australia. George Harry Horton founded G. H. Horton & Co. Ltd, which was the original proprietor of the Mastertouch label in 1919. Horton was born in Chicago, USA, and his brother, Henry B. Horton, was an early organette inventor who patented a music roll system for playing a reed organ in 1878. G. H. Horton went to Australia with the Aeolian Company to set up the Australian marketing organisation and then set up his own business, designing a pneumatic carbon-ribboned piano player recording machine which is claimed to have given a most reliable reproduction of the player's performance. In 1957 the company took over the ANGLO-AMERICAN PLAYER ROLL COMPANY (q.v.) and its Broadway label and since 1961 has traded as Mastertouch. Still in business producing piano rolls.

MEL-O-ART   *See* BRAITERMAN FEDDER COMPANY.

MEL-O-DEE MUSIC ROLL COMPANY   New York and Chicago. Formerly the UNIVERSAL MUSIC CO. (q.v.), a subsidiary of the Aeolian Corporation, this name was adopted from around 1920. Several series were made including song rolls, Hand-Played, and the uninspired-sounding Mel-O-Dee Mathematically Arranged Music Roll. Became MELOTO (q.v.) in Great Britain.

MELOGRAPHIC ROLL COMPANY, THE   25 Jewett Avenue, Buffalo, New York, USA. Piano roll manufacturers who advertised as a selling point their 'lint paper' in a circular imprint stamped onto the roll above the label.

MELOTO   Name used by Universal Music Co., London.

MENDELSSOHN MUSIC CO.   171 Tremont Street, Boston, Massachusetts, USA. Makers of the Mendelssohn music roll. Claimed to make 'the only truly synchronized word rolls'.

MICHAEL, PREUSS & CO., GmbH.   12 Warschauer Str., Berlin, Germany. Makers of player piano rolls, *fl.* 1930.

MORANCHO, F.   67 Urgel, Barcelona, Spain. Maker of mechanical pianos and also piano rolls, *fl.* 1930.

MOYA HERMANOS, S. EN C.   476, Cortes, Barcelona, Spain. Makers of piano rolls, *fl.* 1930.

MUNDELL, DAVID   High Road, Chadwell Heath, Essex. Advertised as maker of piano rolls for pianos in 1930, but probably an agent.

MURDOCH, MURDOCH & CO.   Hatton House, Hatton Garden, London, EC. In April 1912 advertised Suprema Golden Tube Music Rolls, a type of piano roll which was made without a spool to save cost and weight. In use, one spool was all the user required. This had one detachable flange and a fluted core onto which the Golden Tube roll was slid for use.

MUSIC ROLL CO., THE   78 Great Portland Street, London. Makers of player piano rolls. The surviving part of the once great Perforated Music Co. (q.v.). Still *fl.* 1930. Was also some time at 92 Great Portland Street, London, W. *See* UP-TO-DATE MUSIC ROLL COMPANY.

MUSICNOTE ROLL COMPANY   106–8 River Street, Dixon, Illinois, USA. Makers of Keynote song rolls.

NATIONAL MUSIC ROLL COMPANY   St Johnsville, New York, USA. Subsidiary of the National Electric Piano Company. Makers of music rolls under the names 'Master Record', 'Hand Played', 'Auto Inscribed', and 'Peerless'.

NAGLER BRUDER   Gera (Reuss), Germany. Maker of spools for piano rolls, *fl.* 1930.

NEW-PHONO   35 y 37 Ancha, Barcelona, Spain. Maker of music rolls, *fl.* 1930.

NIAGARA MUSIC CO.   198 Terrace Street, Buffalo, New York, USA. Makers of piano rolls, *fl.* 1908.

N.O.S.   *See under* CAPITOL MUSIC ROLL CO.

OPÉRA-PARIS   10 rue Coquillière, Paris. Makers of music rolls, *fl.* 1920.

ORPHEUS   Music rolls made by the Roll Music Co. Ltd.

PERFECTA   Name used by Universal Music Co., London.

PERFECTA   5 Avenue de l'Opéra, Paris. Makers of music rolls advertised as 'Exclusively French'. Director was René Savoye and the factory was at 51 Avenue Galliéni, Bagnolet (Seine). Succeeded Heni Zacconi, *fl.* 1920.

PERFECTOR MUSIC ROLLS   Manufactured and distributed by Lockwoods, 76 & 78 City Road, London EC, *fl.*1915, 1920.

PERFORATED MUSIC CO.   197–203 City Road, London EC. The largest firm of music-roll manufacturers in the British Isles, founded in 1903. By 1913, the annual output had risen to 300,000 rolls, a ton of paper being consumed each week in their manufacture. Rolls for almost every make of player piano and organ were manufactured. In the early hours of 16 March 1918, the entire premises took fire and were destroyed, the insurance value being put at £48,750. For several years after that, the company continued in business in a small way at 6 St Bride Street, London EC. At the height of their success the firm had offices at 94 Regent Street with a music-roll library at 81 Beak Street off Regent Street, London.

PERFORATED MUSIC CO. LTD   99 Princes Street, Edinburgh, Scotland. Branch of the London company of the same name, *fl.*1912.

PHILAG   Name used by Frankfurter Musikwerke-Fabrik J. D. Philipps & Sohne for music rolls. Formed from abbreviation of name Philipps A.-G.

PHILIPPS A.-G.   Aschaffenburg, Germany. Makers of music rolls under the name Philag, *fl.*1930.

PIANOSTYLE COMPANY   Brooklyn, New York, USA. Founded in 1913 to produce piano rolls under this name. Some 100 people were employed by the company which built up a major export trade to South America and Europe and was finally absorbed into the Q.R.S. (q.v.) organisation.

PICTUROLL   Music rolls made by Filmusic Company of Los Angeles, California, intended for use with photo-players. These offered a variety of musical selections and a catalogue issued in November 1918 advertised rolls 'indexed as to Dramatic and Emotional character'.

PISTORIA, ENRICO, E CIA (SOCIETA ITALIANA COMMERCIO PIANOFORTI E STRUMENTI MUSICALI)   12 r.c. Andrea Podesta, Genoa, Italy. Agent and distributor for player pianos and music rolls, *fl.*1930.

PLAY-RITE   Music rolls for player and reproducing pianos, orchestrions and band organs produced by Play-Rite Music Rolls, Inc., Turlock, California. Business founded c.1960 by John and William Malone. Uses one-to-one digital electronic mastering process and creates a music roll from an artist's performance on magnetic tape via a teletype machine to program a computer.

PLAZA MUSIC CO.   10 West 20th Street, New York, USA. Makers of music rolls. One brand name was Winner advertised as 'the only perfect 10¢ roll on the market'. Another was the Ideal which was made to sell at 25¢. Both roll types had a special one-piece metal spool which united core with ends into a single fabrication.

PLEYEL, LYON ET CIE   22 rue Rochechouart, Paris. Makers of piano rolls, *fl.*1920.

POCH, JUAN   7 Condesa de Orleans, Garcia, Barcelona, Spain. Maker of piano rolls, *fl.*1930.

QRS CANADIAN CORPORATION LTD   259 Spadina Avenue, Toronto, Canada. Makers of piano rolls, *fl.*1930. See following.

QRS MUSIC ROLLS INCORPORATED   Founded in 1900, QRS is the most famous name in piano rolls and is still in operation today. The company had its beginnings as part of the Melville Clark Piano Company in Chicago and DeKalb, Illinois, and by 1920 it had succeeded so well in marketing its product that it had become by far the largest concern of its type in the world (writes Harvey Roehl). Although it remains something of a mystery as to the true meaning of the initials QRS, it is considered to stand for Quality Real Service. Significantly, one of the companies acquired by QRS early on was the UNITED STATES MUSIC CO. (q.v.) with its trade mark of a capital letter Q. The company became established in its own right in the late 'teens, while the CLARK ORCHESTRA ROLL COMPANY (q.v.) continued to make coin-piano rolls at that location and eventually the DeKalb factories were absorbed into the Wurlitzer organisation. While the popularity of the player piano was at its zenith in 1923, the roll business peaked in 1926 and during that year QRS produced and sold almost 10 million rolls. This production was aided by the acquisition of some 25 smaller roll-making concerns with names such as Vocastyle, US, Imperial, Pianostyle, International and Angelus. One of the larger companies acquired, United States Music Company, cost QRS around half a million dollars. The decline in music roll sales in the late 1920s pushed QRS into other ventures including radio valves (QRS Red-Top Tubes), motion-picture cameras and projectors in conjunction with

DeVry, and neon signs. However, with the collapse of the stock market, QRS as a company faced liquidation. One of the staff artists, Max Kortlander, bought the company and renamed it Imperial Industrial Corporation and moved it to New York City where it remained for some 30 years. The business remained as makers of QRS rolls but in a very small way with the lowest market being in 1952, when a mere 200,000 or fewer rolls were made. Kortlander died on 11 October 1961 and for the next few years the company was operated by his brother and widow but, in April 1966, piano roll collector, lawyer and former manager of the Buffalo Philharmonic Orchestra, Ramsi P. Tick, took over the business, forming a new company called QRS Music Rolls, Inc. He moved the company from the Bronx to his home town of Buffalo where it remains in operation today at 1026 Niagara Street. At present the company is making more than 500,000 rolls a year.

RECORDO PLAYER ROLL COMPANY   Chicago, Illinois, USA. Makers of piano rolls for use with Gulbransen reproducing and expression pianos. In the early 1920s it took over the IMPERIAL MUSIC ROLL COMPANY (q.v.) and shortly afterwards was absorbed into the QRS (q.v.) organisation.

REGENT   Name used by Universal Music Co., London.

REPUBLIC PLAYER ROLL CORPORATION   645–51 West 51st Street, New York, USA. President was Paul B. Klugh. Makers of Republic hand-played song music rolls.

RESOTONE GRAND   Rolls 9^{11}/$_{16}$ in. wide for a chrysoglott by Resotone Grand Company, New York. Uneven hole spacing.

RICORDI & CO., G.   Querstr. 6, Leipzig H, Germany. Established in 1808. Makers of piano rolls under the title 'F.I.R.S.T.'

RIESSNER BR.   Schmiederberg Bz., Halle, Germany. Maker of piano rolls, fl. 1930.

ROLL MUSIC CO. LTD.   92 Worship Street, London, EC. Makers of music rolls, fl. 1914. Later at 1 & 3 Sun Street, Finsbury Square, London, EC. Makers of Orpheus music rolls.

ROLLA-ARTIS   Piano rolls made by Zacharias of Leipzig.

ROLLOS ERA S.A.   5 Alvarado, Madrid, Spain. Maker of piano rolls, fl. 1930.

ROSE VALLEY CO.   Media, Pennsylvania, USA. Makers of the Ideal music roll. Trade mark was a horizontal diamond shape enclosing the letters IDEAL.

ROYAL MUSIC ROLL CO.   Main Street and Hertel Avenue, Buffalo, New York, USA. Makers of Royal brand music rolls.

RYTHMODIK MUSIC CORPORATION   Belleville, New Jersey, USA. Associate company of the American Piano Company of 437 Fifth Avenue, New York, at which address the recording studios were. Makers of rolls which were said to be of unusually high interpretational standard.

S. & P. Music Roll Co. Ltd   27 Lots Road, Chelsea, London SW19. Music roll makers.

SCHULLER A.-G., FELIX   22 Sedanstr., Leipzig, Germany. Makers of piano rolls who were in business in 1930.

SEYBOLD, RENÉ   45 rue des Vosges and 22 rue Oberlin, Strasbourg, France. Makers of music rolls for orchestrions and electric pianos, specifically Clavitist, Phonoliszt, Fratinola and Pneuma. Brand name 'd'Artists'.

SOC. AN. BREVETTI BARBIERI PER APPLICAZIONI ELETTRO-MUSICALI   26 via S. Vincenzo, Milan, Italy. Maker of music rolls, fl. 1930.

STAFFNOTE   Music rolls made by Billings Player Roll Co.

STANDARD MUSIC ROLL COMPANY   29–35 Central Avenue, Orange, New Jersey (factory and main office) and 225 Fifth Avenue, New York, USA. In business making music rolls prior to 1908. Made song rolls under the names 'ARTO Word Rolls' and 'VOCO Word Rolls'. Later introduced the Play-A-Roll and made the 'SingA' word rolls introduced in 1916. By 1917 the company had addresses at 1437 Broadway, New York, 431 William Street, Buffalo, and 1129 Chestnut Street, Philadelphia. Also produced the Electra music roll 'made upon electric perforators developed in the Edison Works, at Orange, New Jersey'.

STOPPA, L. CAV   c. Garibaldi 108, Milan, Italy. Agent for player pianos and music rolls, fl. 1930.

SUPERBA   See under ALTOONA.

SYMPHONIA   Piano rolls made by Eugene de Roy in Anvers, Belgium.

THEMODIST   *See under* AEOLIAN CO.

TRIUMPH   Name used by Universal Music Co., London.

TRIUMPH AUTO LTD   Triumph House, 185–91 Regent Street, London W1. Makers of music rolls.

U.M.E.C.A.. SOC. AN.   4 Doctor Santero, Madrid, Spain. Maker of music rolls, *fl.*1930.

UNION PLAYER MUSIC CO.   Jamestov˥, New York, USA. Advertised as makers of 'the only perfect music roll'.

UNITED STATES MUSIC COMPANY   Factory and general offices 1951–9 Milwaukee Avenue, Chicago; retail store: 154 Wabash Avenue, Chicago, Illinois, USA. Manufacturers of music rolls 'for all makes of player-pianos', *fl.*1910, then

UNITED STATES MUSIC COMPANY   2934–8 West Lake Street, Chicago, Illinois, USA (factory) and 122 Fifth Avenue, New York. Roehl (*Player Piano Treasury*) states that this company was founded *c.*1906, yet no directory entries can be traced until 1910. Makers of player piano rolls with the label US and the slogan 'The Best Player Music Rolls'. Introduced spools of hard rubber. By 1913, the company had adopted the trade mark of a letter Q and a music roll in a box with the legend 'Perforated Quality Music Rolls'. In 1926 the company was absorbed into QRS (q.v.).

UNIVERSAL MUSIC CO.   29 West 42nd Street, New York and 425 South Wabash Avenue, Chicago, Illinois, USA. Advertised as the 'Oldest and largest manufacturers of music rolls in the world'. Subsidiary of the Aeolian Corporation. Around 1920 the company changed its name to MEL-O-DEE (q.v.). In 1916 the company advertised a Canadian branch at 10½ Shuter Street, Toronto.

UNIVERSAL MUSIC CO.   Meriden, Connecticut, USA. Makers of piano rolls, *fl.*1908.

UNIVERSAL MUSIC CO. LTD   1–2 Goldsmith Street Buildings, Drury Lane, London, WC. Makers of the Meloto Full-Scale music rolls with factory at Hayes, Middlesex. Offshoot of the Aeolian Company. In 1910 the company published a two-volume catalogue containing 1,300 pages. The music roll activities of the company and all rights thereto were acquired by Gordon B. Iles of ARTONA MUSIC ROLLS (q.v.) in 1947.

UNIVERSAL   Name used by Universal Music Co., London.

UP-TO-DATE MUSIC ROLL COMPANY   King Street, Hammersmith, London. Formed by Stanley Mukle and his brother F. G. Mukle of Imhof & Mukle fame. By 1934, this firm, which manufactured player-piano rolls including those for the Harper Electric Piano, had moved to 4 Leysfield Road, London W12, at which premises they remained until 1938, when they moved to Netherwood Place, Netherwood Road, W14. In 1947 they changed their name to the MUSIC ROLL COMPANY, finally going out of business in 1949.

VERHERTBRUGGE, VVE. F.   125 Boulevard de Ménilmontant, Paris. Makers of piano rolls *c.*1920. By 1930 was described as maker of organs and orchestrions.

VICTORIA   Music rolls made by Blancafort, La Garriga, Barcelona, Spain. Very important Spanish maker. Made rolls for Kastner.

VICTORY   *See under* ALTOONA.

VOCASTYLE MUSIC COMPANY, THE   412–26 East Sixth Street, Cincinnati, Ohio, USA. Makers of piano rolls with the trade mark of a bird superimposed on a letter V in a solid disc and the slogan 'Look for the bird'. Pioneers of the song roll as early as 1908. Introduced a series of thematic rolls – one of the very first if not the first so to do – including Home Minstrel (Negro songs), Children's Game, Nursery Rhymes, Slumber Songs for Children, a group of vaudeville-style rolls, and a series based on James Whitcomb Riley's poetry as Riley Recitation Rolls. The company was ultimately acquired by QRS (q.v.).

VOIGT, ADOLF ERNST   9 Koenigsberger Str., Berlin, Germany. Maker of piano rolls, *fl.*1930.

WILLRATH, E., & BARNICK, A.   28 Ferdinandstr., Berlin-Lichterfelde-Ost, Germany. Makers of player piano rolls, *fl.*1930.

ZACHARIAS, P.   Weststrasse 28, Leipzig, Germany. Makers of Kunstler-Noten-Rolle (artists' piano rolls) for pianos under the name Rolla-Artis. In the 1923 roll catalogue, rolls are numbered from 4200 to 5648. By 1930 was at 31, Inselstr., Leipzig, Germany.

ZIEGLER-THOMA, J.   Todtnau, Schwarzwald, Germany. Makers of paper for player rolls, *fl.*1930.

APPENDIX B

List of Trade Names

The number of manufacturers who made player pianos was truly enormous. Apart from the products of special companies set up to market instruments, usually, in such cases, instruments of the same name as the company, there were the instruments contrived by regular piano and organ makers. The variety of names which they used for their creations was even greater, with many makers using more than one brand name or style title. Even the name on the fall-board is no positive identification of the originator of an instrument.

On the following pages appears a list of names which relate to player pianos, piano players and the occasional player organ and harmonium where any confusion might arise. Some of the names are listed more than once where they applied to more than one maker or the application was otherwise duplicated. Wherever possible the name of the maker is given.

The large number of instruments whose names end in the suffix '-ola' indicates that the sincerest form of flattery – and best commercial sense – was to produce a name which sounded something like 'pianola'. If Aeolian could succeed with its '-ola', then others might follow suit with their own versions.

Some names are strange to say the least. 'Invisible' must have been a perplexing name to see on a player piano, while 'The Finest' just did not live up to its name. As for 'Convertola' and 'Acktotest', the former must have been inspired by the automobile industry while the latter was probably spawned by someone trying to read poorly written piano names on the sales orders.

Other names range from the incredible to the fanciful. 'Metalnola' and 'Accompano', 'U'nette' and 'Marveola' may be bad enough, but who would relax at an instrument with a name like 'Primavolta' or, come to that, as mundane as 'Albert'? What, one wonders, about the cunning side of an 'Artonola' . . .

ACCENTIOLA   Adalbert Piano Co., London
ACCOMPANO   Emerson Piano Company, Boston, Massachusetts
ACKOTIST   Pianora Co., New York
ACKTOTEST   Acktotest Player Piano Co., Fall River, Massachusetts
ACOUSTIGRAND   Aeolian-American Corporation, New York
ADAPTO   Name of action by Lindenberg Piano Co., Columbus, Ohio
ADEK   Adek Manufacturing Co., New York (also made PIANOTIST in USA)
AEOLIAN   Orchestrelle Company, later Aeolian Corporation
AERIOL   Theodore P. Brown (1897), later part of Aeolian
AERIOLA   Jenkins Music Co., Kansas City, Montana
AERO-TONE   Aero-Tone Player Piano Co., New York

AIRMATIC   Simplex Player Piano Co.
AIR-O-PLAYER   National Piano Co., Boston, Massachusetts
ALBERT   Mansfield Piano Co., New York
ALTONA   Made in Chicago; maker unknown
AMERICAN ELECTRELLE   American Piano Co.
AMPHION   Amphion Co.
AMPICO   American Piano Co.
ANGELUS   Hallet & Davis Piano Co.
ANGELUS   Premier Grand Piano Corp., Los Angeles, California
ANGELUS   Wilcox & White Co., Meriden, Connecticut (later bought by Simplex)
ANTIPHONEL   Debain, Paris
APOLLO   Melville Clark Piano Co., De Kalb, Illinois
APOLLO   Apollo Piano Company, Ohio
ARCADIAN   British Player Action Company
ARIA DIVINA   M. Schulz Co., Atlanta, Georgia
ARISTANO   A. B. Chase Co.
ARISTOS   Bansell & Sons, London
ARROW   Direct Pneumatic Action Co., London
ARTECHO   Amphion Co.
ARTENIS   Steger & Sons Piano Manufacturing Co., Chicago, Illinois
ARTIST   Wilhelm Hedke
ARTISTANO   A. B. Chase Co.
ARTO-GRAND   C. A. Ahlstrom & Co., Jamestown, New York
ARTO-REPRODUCING   C. A. Ahlstrom & Co., Jamestown, New York
ARTOLA   Wurlitzer
ARTONOLA   C. S. Ahlstrom & Co., Jamestown, New York
ARTRIO-ANGELUS   Reproducing pianos made by Simplex
ARTROLA   Artrola Player Co., Chicago
ARTRONOME   Straube Piano Co.
ATLANTIC   Hupfeld, Leipzig
AUTO PNEUMATIC   Kohler Industries, New York
AUTOGRAND by Kastner & Co., London
AUTO-GRAND   Krell's Auto-Grand Piano Co.
AUTOFORDE   Hardman, Peck, New York
AUTOLA   Horace Waters & Co., New York
AUTOLECTRA   Auto-Electric Piano Co., New York
AUTOLYON   Louis George Lyon, 116 Camberwell Road, London SE
AUTO-MANUAL   Bacon Piano Co., New York
AUTO-NAMIC   Clark Pneumatic Action Co., Wisconsin
AUTOPIANISTE   Thièble, Paris
AUTOPIANO   Autopiano Co., New York
AUTOPIANO   Kastner & Co., London
AUTOPLAYER   Boyd Ltd, London
AUTO-PLAYER   Krell Auto Grand Co., Connersville, Indiana
AUTO-PLAYER   Werner Industries, Cincinnatti
AUTOSTYLE   John Church Co., Cincinnatti
AUTOTONE   Hardman, Peck & Co., New York
BANJ-O-GRAND   Nelson-Wiggen Piano Co., Chicago
BEHNING   Behning Piano Co., New York
BEHR   Behr Brothers & Co., New York

BELLWOOD   Players made in New York by an unidentified company
BRABO   Gebruder Weber, Waldkirch, Black Forest
BRAUMULLER   Braumuller Piano Co., New York
BRUNOPHONE, LE   J. M. Brun, St. Étienne, France
CÄCILIA   Frankfurter Musikwerke-Fabrik J. D. Philipps & Sohne
CALAME   Roberto V. Calame, Uruguay
CARL SCHIRMER   Henry G. Johnson Piano Manufacturing Co., Bellvue, Iowa
CAROLA   Cable Company, Chicago, Illinois
CECILIAN   Bush & Lane Piano Co., Holland, Michigan
CECILIAN   Farrand & Votey, Detroit, Michigan
CELCO   Amphion Co.
CELCO REPRODUCING MEDIUM   United Piano Corporation, Norwalk, Ohio (name used on instruments under brand names A. B. Chase, Emerson, Lindeman & Sons)
CELESTE   Kohler & Campbell, New York
CELLOTONE   S. A. Hawke & Co., Malden, Massachusetts
CHALET PLAYER   Made in America by unidentified maker
CHICAGO ELECTRIC PIANOS   Smith, Barnes & Ströhber
CHILTON   Aeolian Co.
CHRISTMAN   Christman Piano Co., New York
CLARENDON   Haddorff Piano Co.
CLASSIC   Classic Player Action Co. (T. H. Poyser, Harringay, London)
CLAVIOLA   Claviola Company, New York (controlled by Kindler & Collins, New York)
CLAVIOLA   Stichel, Leipzig
CLAVITIST   Hupfeld, Leipzig
CLAYTON   Grinnell Brothers, Detroit, Michigan
CLINTON   Martin Brothers, Rochester, New York
CLUB   Hegeler & Ehlers, Oldenburg, Germany
COINOLA   Operators' Piano Co., Inc., Chicago, Illinois
COLONIA   Colonia Player Piano Co., London (Colonia-Menzel)
CONCERTO   Polyphon Musikwerke, Leipzig
CONNOISSEUR   Murdoch, Murdoch & Co., London
CONOVER SOLO CAROLA   Cable Company, Chicago, Illinois
CORONA   Frankfurter Musikwerke-Fabrik J. D. Philipps & Sohne
CONTINENTAL   Continental Musikwerke Hofmann & Czerny, Vienna
CONVERTOLA   Lindenberg Piano Co., Columbus, Ohio
COPLEY   H. P. Nelson (on players made for department store Wookey & Co. of Peoria, Illinois)
CREMONA   Marquette Piano Co., Chicago, Illinois
CYLINDRICHORD   Courcell
DALE LECTRONIC   Dale Electronics, USA
DANCO-O-GRAND   Nelson Wiggen Piano Co., Chicago, Illinois
DEA   Hupfeld, Leipzig
DELPHIN   Player piano by Kessel's Kon. Ned. Fabriek van Muziekinstrumenten (N.V.) Ceciliastraat D. 24/25, Tilburg, Netherlands. Possibly factored.
DELPHIN   Albert Melnik, Trautenau, Austria
DIRECT ARROW   Direct Pneumatic Action Co., London
DUCA-LIPP   Lipp & Söhn
DUCANOLA   J. D. Philipps & Sohne
DUCARTIST   Frati, Berlin
DUCHESS   Werner Industries, Cincinatti
DUO-ART   Aeolian

126

DUOLA Player action patented 1925 by Broadwood
DYNACHORD ART EXPRESSION PLAYER Amphion Co.
DYNACORD Amphion Player Co., Syracuse, New York
DYNAVOICE Dynavoice, Inc., Plymouth, Michigan
ELBURN J. W. Jenkins' Sons, Kansas City, Montana
ELDORADO Etzold & Popitz
ELECTRA Kohler & Campbell
ELECTORA Separate player pump made by Motor Player Corporation
ELECTRATONE Waltham Piano Co., Milwaukee, Wisconsin
ELECTRELLE Electrelle Co.
ELECTRELLE Hopkinson Ltd, London
ELECTROVA Electrova Company, Bronx, New York
ELECTROVE Jacob Doll, New York
ELLWOOD Wurlitzer
EMMETT Coolidge Piano Co., Boston, Massachusetts
EMPRESS ELECTRIC Operators' Piano Co. for Lyon & Healy
EUPHONA Cable Company, Chicago, Illinois
EUPHONA HOME ELECTRIC Cable Company, Chicago, Illinois
EUTERPE Albert Gast & Co.
EVOLA Frelburger Musikapparate-Bauanstalt, GmbH, Freiburg, Germany
EXCELTONE Chase-Hackley Piano Co., Muskegon, Michigan
FINEST, THE Western Electric Piano Co.
FLEXOTONE-ELECTRELLE American Piano Co.
FOX Fox Music Co., Kansas City, Montana (assembled from bought-in parts)
FRATINOLA Frati & Co., Berlin
GASONELLA Diego Fuchs, Prague
GEHLING Douillet, Paris
GEHLING Ehrhardt, Altenburg
GEHRLING Gehrling Piano Co.
GRANDETTE Kranich & Bach, New York
GRANDEZZA Gebruder Weber, Waldkirch
GREGORIAN Orchestrelle Co., London
GUEST Guest Piano Corp., Burlington, Iowa
GULBRANSEN Gulbransen-Dickinson Co., Chicago
FOTOPLAYER American Photoplayer Co., San Francisco, California
HAPECO Peters & Co., Leipzig
HARALD Waldkircher Orchestrionfabrik
HARCOURT MOTO-PLAYO Conservatory Player Actions Co.
HARMONIST Peerless Player Co.
HARMONIST Roth & Englehardt (owned by Peerless), New York
HARMONISTA Emil Müller (harmonium player)
HARMONOLA Price & Teeple Co., Chicago, Illinois
HARP-O-GRAND Nelson-Wiggen Piano Co., Chicago, Illinois
HARWOOD PLAYER J. W. Jenkins' Sons Music Co., Kansas City, Montana
HILLIER Hillier Player Piano & Organ Co., London
HOPKINSON PLAYER Hopkinson Ltd, London
HUMANA J. H. Marshall, London
IDEAL Kohler & Campbell, New York
INVISIBLE Milton Piano Co., New York
KASTONOME Kastner & Co.

KELLER, GEO. F.   Laffargue Co., New York (name used on pianos for Keller, a Scranton, Pa, dealer)
KINGSBURY   Cable Co., Chicago
KOHLMANN   Kohlmann Piano Co., New York
KONZERT-CLAVITIST   Hupfeld, Leipzig
KONZERT-PHONOLISZT   Hupfeld, Leipzig
KOSMOS   Lehmann & Co., Berlin
KRELL AUTO-PLAYER   Krell Auto-Grand Piano Co., Connersville, Indiana
LAFAYETTE   H. Lehr & Co., Easton, Pennsylvania
LIEBMANNISTA   Liebmann (harmonium player)
LINDENBERG   Lindenberg Piano Co., Columbus, Ohio
LINGARD   Wurlitzer
LIVINGSTON   Weaver Piano Co., Inc., York, Pennsylvania
LORRAINE   Field-Lippman Piano Stores, St Louis, Montana
LYRAPHONE   Smith Lyraphone Co., Hanover, Pennsylvania
LYRIST   Klingmann & Co., Berlin
MACEY & CAMP   Goldsmith Piano Co., Chicago, Illinois
MAESTREL   Triumph-Auto Pianos Ltd, London (later Barratt & Robinson)
MAESTRO   Maestro Co., Elbridge, New York
MAESTRO   Mustel, Paris (agent's name for Welte-Mignon)
MAGIC FINGERS   Gribble Music Co.
MALCOLM   John Malcolm & Co., Ltd
MANUALO   Baldwin Piano Co., Cincinnati, Ohio
MARQUE   Ampico Co.
MARQUETTE   Marquette Piano Co., Chicago, Illinois
MARVEOLA   Weser Brothers Inc., New York
MASCOT   Western Electric Piano Co., Chicago, Illinois
MASSILIA   Guerin et Cie, Marseilles, France
MAXFIELD   Maxfield Co., London
MAYTONA   May & Co., Cleveland, Ohio
MELL-O-TONE   Becker Bros, New York
MELOGRAPH   Carpentier, France
MELODANT   Marshall, London
MELOSTRELLE   Steger & Sons Piano Mfg Co., Chicago, Illinois
MELOTONE   Field-Lippman Piano Stores, St Louis, Montana
MELOTROPE   Carpentier, France
MENDEL   Copplestone & Co., London
MERCER   Weaver Piano Co., York, Pennsylvania
METALNOLA   Higel Co.
MIGNON   Welte
MINERVA   John G. Murdoch Co., London
MINSTRELLA   Barratt & Robinson, London
MINSTRELLO   McPhail Piano Co., Boston, Massachusetts
MIRANDA   Automatic Musical Instrument Co., London
MIRANDA PIANISTA   Automatic Musical Instrument Co., London
MITANOLA   Koth-Bayer Co., Poughkeepsie, New York
MODELLO   Baldwin Piano Co., Cincinnati, Ohio
MONOLA   Société des Pianos Pneumatiques Français, Paris
MULTITONE   Operators' Piano Co.
MUSETTA   Calmont Co., London (mfg by A. Buff-Hedinger, Leipzig)
MUSICUS   Musicus Player Piano Co., London

MUSOLA   Musola Co.
NEOLA   Neola Piano & Player Co., London
ORIGINAL   Original Musikwerke Paul Lochmann
ORPHÉE   Gustin Whright & Cie, Paris
ORPHEUS   Dawkins, London
ORPHOBELLA   Ehrlich's Musikwerke Emil Ehrlich
PACKARD   The Packard Co., Fort Wayne, Indiana
PAGANINI VIOLIN PIANO   Wurlitzer
PANELLA   Keyboardless café piano made by Seybold
PARAGON   Needham Piano Co., New York
PARAGON   Ambridge & Son, London
PEDALEON   Barratt & Robinson, London
PEERLESS   Englehardt Piano Co.
PENNYANO   Keith, Prowse & Co., London
PER OMNES   Capra, Rissone & Detoma, London
PERFECTS   Morton & Co., London
PERRYOLA   Ludwig & Co., New York
PHILLIPS, H. L.   Cable-Nelson Piano Co. for Knight-Campbell Music Co., Denver, Colorado
PHONEON   Murdoch, Murdoch & Co., London
PHONOBELLA   Hupfeld, Leipzig
PHONOLA   Hupfeld, Leipzig
PHONOLISZT   Hupfeld, Leipzig
PIALO   Singer Piano Co., Chicago, Illinois
PIANAUTO   Karn-Morris Piano & Organ Co. (Woodstock, Canada, and London)
PIAN-AUTO   Krell
PIANETTE   Otto Manufacturing Co., New Jersey
PIANEX   Pianex Co., London
PIANO MELODICA   Giovanni Racca, Bologna, Italy
PIANIST   Spaethe
PIANISTA   Autopiano Co., London
PIANISTA   Thibouville-Lamy, Paris
PIANO EXECUTANTE   Gavioli, Paris
PIANO EXECUTANTE ARTISTE   Ullmann, Paris
PIANOCORDER   Pianocorder Divn, Marantz Corp., USA
PIANOHARPA   Andersson, also Nilsson, Sweden
PIANO-JAZZ   Pierre Eich, Belgium
PIANOLA   Aeolian Co.
PIANOLA   Votey (original user of name)
PIANOLIN   North Tonawanda Musical Instrument Works
PIANO ORCHESTRA   Wurlitzer
PIANOSONA   Chase & Baker
PIANOTIST   Pianotist Co., Leipzig, also Emil Klaber (ADEK), New York
PISTONOLA   Boyd Ltd, London
PLAYANO   Playano Manufacturing Co.
PLAYERNOLA   Becker Bros, Inc., New York
PLAYETTA   Philip Cohen & Co.
PLAYOLA   Playola Piano Co., Chicago, Illinois
PLAYOTONE   Hardman, Peck & Co., New York
PLAYTONA   Grinnett Bros, Detroit, Michigan
PLEYELA   Pleyel, Paris

PNEUMA   Kuhl & Klatt, Berlin
PNEUMATIST   Kuhl & Klatt, Berlin
PREMIER   Harper Electric Piano Co., London
PREMIER   Neue Leipziger Musikwerke Adolf Buff-Hedinger
PRIMATONE   Foster-Armstrong (The Foster Co.), Rochester, New York
PRIMAVOLTA   Neue Leipziger Musikwerke Adolf Buff-Hedinger
PUREATONE   Name used by Chicago maker, unidentified
PUTNAM   Otto Wissner, Brooklyn, New York
RADI-O-PLAYER   Weydig Piano Corporation, New York (incorporating radio receiver!)
READ-HAWKE   S. A. Hawke & Co., Malden, Massachusetts
REGAL   Wright Piano Co.
REGINAPIANO   Marquette on product for Regina, New Jersey
REPRODUCO   Operators' Piano Co.
REPROPHRASO   Story & Clark, Chicago
RIDGEWAY   Unidentified maker for the O.K. Houck Piano Co., Memphis, Tennessee
SERENATA   Etzold & Popitz
SILWOOD   Unidentified maker for Cincinatti department store
SIMPLEX   Theodore P. Brown, Massachusetts
SLAVIA   Fuchs, Prague
SOLO VIRTUOSO   Unidentified Boston maker
SOLOPHONE   Pierre Eich, Belgium
SOLOPHONOLA   Hupfeld, Leipzig
SOLOTIST   Choralian Co., Berlin (Aeolian)
STANDARD   Schiller Piano Co., Oregon
STARR   Starr Piano Co.
STECK   Aeolian Co.
STELLA   Popper & Co., Leipzig
STERLING   Sterling Piano Corporation, Shelton, Connecticut
STROUD PIANOLA   Aeolian
STUYVESANT PIANOLA   Aeolian
SUBLIMA   Regina, Rahway, New Jersey
SYMPHONIA   Kohler & Campbell, New York
SYMPHONIA   Eugene De Roy, Belgium
SYMPHONIOLA   Symphonion-Fabrik, Leipzig
SYMPHONOLA   Price & Teeple Piano Co.
SYMPHONY   Paul G. Mehlin & Sons
SYMPHONY   Wilcox & Whight, Meriden, Connecticut (player reed organs)
TECHNOLA   Aeolian subsidiary, Technola Piano Co., New York
TEL-ELECTRIC   Tel Electric Co., Pittsfield, Massachusetts
TELEKTRA   Tel-Electric Co.
TERPRETOR   Boyd Ltd, London
TERRACE   Spector & Son Piano Co. Inc., New York
THIEBER   Unidentified American maker
TOCCAPHON   Neue Leipziger Musikwerke Adolf Buff-Hedinger
TONE-OLA   Hasbrouck Piano Co., New York
TONK   William Tonk & Brothers, New York
TONOPHONE   DeKleist
TRIPHONOLA   Hupfeld, Leipzig
TRIUMPH   Kastner and the Autopiano Co., London
TRIUMPHOLA   Rachals & Co.

TROUBADOUR   Haddorff Piano Co., New York
U'NETTE   Th. B. Thompson, Chicago, Illinois
UNETTE   Thompson-U'Nette Piano Co., Chicago
UNIKA   Gebruder Weber, Waldkirch
UNIVERSAL PIANO PLAYER   Bansell & Sons, London
VAN DYKE   Van Dyke Piano Co., Scranton, Pennsylvania
VERDI   Giovanni Racca, Bologna, Italy
VICHORD   Unidentified Baltimore, Maryland, maker
VIOLANO-VIRTUOSO   Mills Novelty Co.
VIRTUOLA   Hallet & Davis Piano Co., Boston, Massachusetts
VIRTUOS   Heilbrunn
VORSTELLER   Kuhl & Klatt, Berlin
VOSE   Vose & Sons, Boston, Massachusetts
WARDELL   J. & C. Fischer, New York
WAUD   R. H. Waud pianos made by Foster-Armstrong subsidiary of American Piano Co., Rochester, New York
WEBER   Aeolian Co.
WELTE-MIGNON (LICENSEE)   Auto Pneumatic Action Co., New York
WESLEY   Raudenbush & Sons Piano Co., St Paul, Minnesota
WHEELOCK PIANOLA   Aeolian Co.
WONDERTONE   Lindenberg Piano Co., Columbus, Ohio
XYLOPHON-KLAVIER   Neue Leipziger Musikwerke Adolf Buff-Hedinger

Some serial numbers of Player Pianos

The following is a list of piano serial numbers given under the name of the maker. This list refers only to the more common types of instrument which the collector may find, and the serial numbers are those relating to the years during which that maker may have produced player pianos.

Always check the make of a piano by the name cast into the iron frame and do not rely on the name on the fall-board – this may have been altered at some time. The name and number usually appears on upright pianos at the top right-hand side of the piano frame and is visible by the lifting of the piano top. Grand pianos display name and serial number cast into the iron frame, again on the right-hand side. Raise the lid to find this. The author offers grateful acknowledgement to *Michel's Piano Atlas* (by N. E. Michel, USA).

AEOLIAN-WEBER PIANO CO. and PIANOLA CO. (Worcester, Massachusetts, USA)

1903 – 1900	1911 – 27000	1919 – 59000	1927 – 82000
1904 – 3000	1912 – 31000	1920 – 63000	1928 – 85000
1905 – 5400	1913 – 35000	1921 – 67000	1929 – 88000
1906 – 9000	1914 – 39000	1922 – 70000	1930 – 91000
1907 – 12000	1915 – 43000	1923 – 73000	1931 – 94000
1908 – 15000	1916 – 47000	1924 – 76000	1932 – 97000
1909 – 19000	1917 – 51000	1925 – 78000	1933 – 98000
1910 – 23000	1918 – 55000	1926 – 80000	

ALLISON PIANOS LTD (50 New Bond Street, London W1)

1910 – 38000	1917 – 43600	1924 – 48400	1931 – 52500
1911 – 39800	1918 – 44400	1925 – 49200	1932 – 53000
1912 – 40600	1919 – 45200	1926 – 49800	1933 – 53400
1913 – 41000	1920 – 46000	1927 – 50200	1934 – 53800
1914 – 41600	1921 – 46600	1928 – 50800	
1915 – 42000	1922 – 47200	1929 – 51200	
1916 – 42800	1923 – 47800	1930 – 52000	

AMPICO (AMERICAN PIANO CO., East Rochester, New York)

1920 – 81000	1923 – 84900	1926 – 88800	1929 – 93700
1921 – 82900	1924 – 86600	1927 – 89600	1930 – 94000
1922 – 83900	1925 – 87800	1928 – 91500	1931 – 97000

APOLLO PIANO CO. (Dekalb, Illinois, USA – successors to Melville Clark Piano Co.)

1903 – 5700	1911 – 17800	1919 – 36000	1927 – 80000
1904 – 7000	1912 – 19600	1920 – 40000	1928 – 87000
1905 – 8700	1913 – 22000	1921 – 45000	1929 – 95000
1906 – 10000	1914 – 23200	1922 – 49000	1930 – 106000
1907 – 11500	1915 – 24400	1923 – 53000	1931 – 112000
1908 – 13000	1916 – 26800	1924 – 58000	1932 – 118000
1909 – 14500	1917 – 29000	1925 – 63000	1933 – 126000
1910 – 16000	1918 – 32800	1926 – 77000	1934 – 130000

AUTOPIANO CO. (12th Avenue, 51st and 52nd Streets, New York)

1904 – 36000	1910 – 75000	1916 – 112000	1922 – 155000
1905 – 45000	1911 – 85000	1917 – 118000	1923 – 165000
1906 – 52000	1912 – 89000	1918 – 125000	1924 – 185000
1907 – 56000	1913 – 98000	1919 – 133000	1925 – 195000
1908 – 60000	1914 – 105000	1920 – 137000	1926 – 205000
1909 – 66000	1915 – 108000	1921 – 145000	

BENTLEY PIANO CO. (Woodchester, Gloucestershire – made by STROUD)

1919 – 3400	1923 – 13000	1927 – 25200	1931 – 32900
1920 – 10000	1924 – 15800	1928 – 27300	1932 – 34700
1921 – 10800	1925 – 18500	1929 – 29200	1933 – 36300
1922 – 11800	1926 – 21800	1930 – 31300	1934 – 38400

BERRY, NATHANIEL & SONS (15a The Grove, Crouch End, London)

1907 – 11004	1915 – 13743	1923 – 19057	1931 – 28253
1908 – 11246	1916 – 14265	1924 – 19945	1932 – 29229
1909 – 11467	1917 – 14860	1925 – 20684	1933 – 30153
1910 – 12159	1918 – 16000	1926 – 21713	1934 – 31547
1911 – 12437	1919 – 16460	1927 – 22638	1935 – 32977
1912 – 12676	1920 – 17000	1928 – 24159	
1913 – 12865	1921 – 17865	1929 – 25598	
1914 – 13347	1922 – 18272	1930 – 26699	

BIESE, W. (Weigand, Vier 18, Berlin)

1912 – 22300	1917 – 24000	1922 – 26000	1927 – 27000
1913 – 22400	1918 – 24500	1923 – 26100	1928 – 28000
1914 – 22600	1919 – 25000	1924 – 26200	
1915 – 23000	1920 – 25300	1925 – 26400	
1916 – 23500	1921 – 25600	1926 – 26700	

BLUTHNER, JULIUS (Friedrich – Ebertstrasse 69, Leipzig)

1912 – 87000	1918 – 97000	1924 – 107000	1930 – 115000
1913 – 90000	1919 – 98000	1925 – 109000	1931 – 115500
1914 – 93000	1920 – 100000	1926 – 111000	1932 – 116000
1915 – 94000	1921 – 101500	1927 – 112000	
1916 – 95000	1922 – 103000	1928 – 113000	
1917 – 96000	1923 – 105000	1929 – 114000	

BORD, A. (1 rue François, Paris – Made by PLEYEL)

1920 – 129100	1924 – 131000	1928 – 133000	1931 – 134800
1921 – 129500	1925 – 131500	1929 – 133500	1932 – 135300
1922 – 130000	1926 – 132000	1930 – 134100	
1923 – 130500	1927 – 132500		

BOSENDORFER, L. (Canduagass 4, Vienna, Austria)

1914 – 21100	1920 – 22530	1926 – 24160	1932 – 25530
1915 – 21370	1921 – 22800	1927 – 24490	1933 – 25560
1916 – 21660	1922 – 23060	1928 – 24850	1934 – 25600
1917 – 21870	1923 – 23300	1929 – 25120	1935 – 25700
1918 – 22070	1924 – 23580	1930 – 25350	
1919 – 22330	1925 – 23880	1931 – 25470	

CECELIAN (made by FARRAND in Holland, Michigan, USA)

1908 – 5000	1913 – 13000	1918 – 23000	1923 – 33000
1909 – 6500	1914 – 15000	1919 – 25000	1924 – 35000
1910 – 8000	1915 – 17000	1920 – 27000	
1911 – 9500	1916 – 19000	1921 – 29900	
1912 – 11000	1917 – 21000	1922 – 31000	

CHALLEN PIANOS, CHARLES H. (Omega Works, Hermitage Road, Finsbury Park, London N4)

1908 – 30423	1915 – 33778	1923 – 36630	1930 – 43205
1909 – 30852	1916 – 34170	1924 – 37761	1931 – 45346
1910 – 31309	1917 – 34675	1925 – 38152	1932 – 47684
1911 – 31842	1918 – 35362	1926 – 38608	1933 – 49673
1912 – 32356	1920 – 35814	1927 – 39060	1934 – 52424
1913 – 32767	1921 – 36167	1928 – 39885	
1914 – 33522	1922 – 36280	1929 – 41306	

CHAPPELL PIANO CO. (50 New Bond Street, London W1)

1916 – 59000	1921 – 66000	1926 – 71400	1931 – 75800
1917 – 60500	1922 – 67000	1927 – 72300	1932 – 76400
1918 – 62000	1923 – 68000	1928 – 73200	1933 – 77200
1919 – 63500	1924 – 69000	1929 – 74100	1935 – 77600
1920 – 65000	1925 – 70500	1930 – 75250	1936 – 78400

CHICKERING & SONS (Chickering Hall, Fifth Avenue & 18th Street, New York)

1911 – 117200	1916 – 126000	1921 – 133400	1926 – 141600
1912 – 120000	1917 – 127500	1922 – 134400	1927 – 143900
1913 – 121000	1918 – 128500	1923 – 137500	1928 – 145400
1914 – 122500	1919 – 130000	1924 – 137600	1929 – 147700
1915 – 124000	1920 – 132500	1925 – 139700	1930 – 148400

COLLARD & COLLARD (50 New Bond Street, London W1)

1917 – 185220	1921 – 188080	1925 – 190630	1929 – 192850
1918 – 186360	1922 – 188580	1926 – 191390	1930 – 193320
1919 – 186980	1923 – 189010	1927 – 191805	1931 – 193580
1920 – 187505	1924 – 189960	1928 – 192310	

DANEMANN, W. & CO. LTD. (Northampton Street, Essex Road, London N1)

1918 – 38300	1922 – 39900	1926 – 43000	1930 – 45400
1919 – 38700	1923 – 40600	1927 – 43500	1931 – 46000
1920 – 39100	1924 – 41500	1928 – 44000	1932 – 47000
1921 – 39300	1925 – 42500	1929 – 44600	

ERARD (or **GAVEAU-ERARD**) (45–7 rue de la Boetie, Paris)

1912 – 101200	1917 – 106500	1922 – 110000	1927 – 116300
1913 – 103000	1918 – 107000	1923 – 111000	1928 – 117600
1914 – 105000	1919 – 107500	1924 – 112500	1929 – 118900
1915 – 105500	1920 – 108000	1925 – 113800	1930 – 120000
1916 – 106000	1921 – 109000	1926 – 115000	

FARRAND (Detroit, Michigan)

1910 – 61000	1920 – 73000	1928 – 81000
1915 – 68000	1925 – 79000	

GROTRIAN-STEINWEG (Simmerstrasse 24, Braunschweig, Germany)

1912 – 28150	1918 – 35069	1924 – 47337	1930 – 61235
1913 – 30169	1919 – 36390	1925 – 50250	1931 – 61903
1914 – 31541	1920 – 38076	1926 – 52506	1932 – 62268
1915 – 32100	1921 – 39802	1927 – 55788	
1916 – 33162	1922 – 42075	1928 – 58238	
1917 – 34134	1923 – 44698	1929 – 60121	

GULBRANSEN CO. (2050 Ruby Street, Melrose Park, Illinois, USA)

1915 – 90000	1920 – 140000	1925 – 218000	1930 – 301000
1916 – 101000	1921 – 150000	1926 – 240000	1931 – 303000
1917 – 110000	1922 – 165000	1927 – 265000	1932 – 304500
1918 – 120000	1923 – 182000	1928 – 282000	
1919 – 130000	1924 – 195000	1929 – 300000	

HARDMAN-PECK & CO. (33 West 57th Street, New York, USA)

1906 – 60000	1913 – 73500	1920 – 86000	1928 – 93400
1907 – 61500	1914 – 75000	1921 – 88000	1929 – 94000
1908 – 63000	1915 – 77200	1922 – 89300	1930 – 94200
1909 – 65400	1916 – 78900	1923 – 90000	1931 – 94600
1910 – 68100	1917 – 81000	1924 – 91000	1932 – 94700
1911 – 70000	1918 – 82500	1925 – 91500	
1912 – 72000	1919 – 84000	1927 – 92700	

HOPKINSON (Paxton Piano Works, Paxton Road, London N17) (See also ROGERS, GEORGE & SON)

1912 – 66000	1918 – 70800	1924 – 75000	1930 – 80400
1913 – 67000	1919 – 71600	1925 – 75800	1931 – 81200
1914 – 68000	1920 – 72400	1926 – 76400	1932 – 82100
1915 – 68800	1921 – 73000	1927 – 77200	
1916 – 69600	1922 – 73700	1928 – 78900	
1917 – 70200	1923 – 74600	1929 – 79750	

KIRKMAN & CO. (50 New Bond Street, London W1) (Associated with COLLARD & COLLARD)

1924 – 49020	1926 – 49050	1928 – 49064	1930 – 52100
1925 – 49030	1927 – 49060	1929 – 49070	

KNABE & CO. (Baltimore, USA)

1912 – 72000	1918 – 84000	1924 – 95000	1930 – 107300
1913 – 74000	1919 – 86000	1925 – 97400	1931 – 108200
1914 – 76000	1920 – 88000	1926 – 99600	1932 – 109000
1915 – 78000	1921 – 90000	1927 – 102000	
1916 – 79000	1922 – 92800	1928 – 104400	
1917 – 82000	1923 – 93900	1929 – 106100	

KOHLER & CAMPBELL (401–425 East 163rd Street, New York, USA)

1910 – 116000	1916 – 179000	1922 – 215000	1928 – 258000
1911 – 127000	1917 – 190000	1923 – 223000	1929 – 264000
1912 – 137000	1918 – 198000	1924 – 230000	1930 – 266000
1913 – 150000	1919 – 203000	1925 – 237000	1931 – 267000
1914 – 155000	1920 – 206000	1926 – 240000	1932 – 268000
1915 – 165000	1921 – 210000	1927 – 250000	

LABROUSSE PIANOS (33 rue de Rivoli, Paris)

1910 – 7700	1918 – 9000	1923 – 11000	1928 – 14000
1911 – 8000	1919 – 9500	1924 – 11800	1929 – 14500
1912 – 8300	1920 – 9800	1925 – 12500	1930 – 15000
1913 – 8500	1921 – 10100	1926 – 13000	1931 – 15500
1914 – 8800	1922 – 10500	1927 – 13500	1932 – 16000

MARSHALL & ROSE (SIR HERBERT MARSHALL CO., Conduit Street, London W1)

1910 – 700	1918 – 2400	1925 – 24100	1932 – 32000
1913 – 1200	1920 – 3200	1928 – 28000	1935 – 35000
1915 – 1800	1923 – 3700	1930 – 30000	

MELVILLE CLARK CO. (Grand Haven, Michigan, USA)

1901 – 2075	1909 – 14500	1917 – 29000	1925 – 63000
1902 – 4000	1910 – 16000	1918 – 32800	1926 – 77700
1903 – 5700	1911 – 17800	1919 – 36000	1927 – 80000
1904 – 7000	1912 – 19600	1920 – 40000	1928 – 93000
1905 – 8700	1913 – 22000	1921 – 45000	1929 – 112000
1906 – 10000	1914 – 23200	1922 – 49000	1930 – 118000
1907 – 11500	1915 – 24400	1923 – 53000	1931 – 126000
1908 – 13000	1916 – 26800	1924 – 58000	

MONINGTON & WESTON LTD. (Piercefield Street, Malden Road, London NW5)

1915 – 41234	1925 – 44900	1935 – 56200
1920 – 43101	1930 – 49100	

NIENDORF, GEBR. (Luckenwald, Germany)

1920 – 18500	1923 – 22000	1926 – 26300	1929 – 31000
1921 – 19500	1924 – 23100	1927 – 28200	1932 – 34500
1922 – 20700	1925 – 24700		

PIANOLA (AEOLIAN CO.) (New York and Hayes, Middlesex)

1904 – 3000	1911 – 27000	1918 – 55000	1925 – 78000
1905 – 5400	1912 – 31000	1919 – 59000	NEW SERIES
1906 – 9000	1913 – 35000	1920 – 63000	1960 – 16800
1907 – 12000	1914 – 39000	1921 – 67000	1961 – 17400
1908 – 15000	1915 – 43000	1922 – 70000	1962 – 20000
1909 – 19000	1916 – 47000	1923 – 73000	1963 – 22700
1910 – 23000	1917 – 51000	1924 – 76000	1964 – 24700

ROGERS, GEORGE & SON (Paxton Piano Works, Paxton Road, London N17)

1912 – 25900	1918 – 28500	1924 – 34000	1930 – 40500
1913 – 26000	1919 – 29000	1925 – 35200	1931 – 41200
1914 – 26500	1920 – 30000	1926 – 36400	1932 – 42000
1915 – 27000	1921 – 31000	1927 – 37600	
1916 – 27500	1922 – 32000	1928 – 38800	
1917 – 28000	1923 – 33000	1929 – 40000	

STECK, GEO. & CO. (650 East 132nd Street, New York, USA)

1910 – 43000	1918 – 58900	1926 – 75000	1934 – 128400
1911 – 45100	1919 – 61000	1927 – 79000	1935 – 130700
1912 – 47200	1920 – 63300	1928 – 81000	1936 – 133100
1913 – 49300	1921 – 65000	1929 – 83000	
1914 – 51400	1922 – 67000	1930 – 85000	
1915 – 53500	1923 – 69000	1931 – 121000	
1916 – 54600	1924 – 71000	1932 – 125000	
1917 – 56700	1925 – 73000	1933 – 127000	

STEINWAY & SONS (New York and Hamburg)

1910 – 140000	1916 – 180000	1922 – 210000	1928 – 260000
1911 – 150000	1917 – 185000	1923 – 220000	1929 – 265000
1912 – 155000	1918 – 190000	1924 – 225000	1930 – 271000
1913 – 160000	1919 – 195000	1925 – 235000	1931 – 273000
1914 – 165000	1920 – 200000	1926 – 240000	1932 – 274000
1915 – 170000	1921 – 205000	1927 – 255000	

WEBER & CO. (East Rochester, New York, USA)

1910 – 64500	1916 – 72500	1922 – 77600	1928 – 79600
1911 – 66000	1917 – 74000	1923 – 78200	1929 – 80000
1912 – 67500	1918 – 74700	1924 – 78600	1930 – 81300
1913 – 69200	1919 – 75400	1925 – 78900	1931 – 82300
1914 – 70100	1920 – 76000	1926 – 79100	1932 – 82600
1915 – 71900	1921 – 77200	1927 – 79300	

WHEELOCK PIANO CO. (New York, USA)

1912 – 27800	1917 – 32400	1922 – 36000	1927 – 41500
1913 – 28400	1918 – 33000	1923 – 37100	1928 – 42700
1914 – 29200	1919 – 33700	1924 – 38200	1929 – 44000
1915 – 30000	1920 – 34300	1925 – 39300	1930 – 45100
1916 – 31700	1921 – 35100	1926 – 40400	

Bibliography

Ampico Reproducing Piano: *Inspector's Reference Manual (1923)*, facsimile reprint by Frank Adams, Seattle, Washington, USA, 1973.

Ampico Service Manual 1929, facsimile reprint, Frank Adams, Seattle, Washington, 1973.

Armstrong, Durrell, *Player Piano Co. Inc., Catalogue* (a most valuable source of reference for the American player piano), Kansas, 1981.

Association des Amis des Instruments et de la Musique Mécanique, *Bulletin*, Le Vesinet, 1976, *et seq.*

Barbour, J. Murray, *Tuning and Temperament, A Historical Survey*, Michigan State College Press, 1951.

Bowers, Q. David, California, USA: private collection of mechanical music ephemera.

British Patent Office, *Musical Instruments, 1694–1933*, Abridgement Class 88, London.

Conservatoire Nationale des Arts et Métiers, *Automates et Mécanismes à Musique*, Paris, 1960.

Das Mechanische Musikinstrument, journal of the Gesellschaft der Freunde Mechanischer Musikinstrumente E.V., Baden-Baden, 1975 *et seq.*

Dolge, Alfred, *Pianos and their Makers*, Covina Publishing Company, California, 1911 (facsimile, Dover Publications, Inc., New York, 1972).

Dolge, Alfred, *Men Who Have Made Piano History* (described as Vol. 2 of *Pianos and their Makers*), Covina, California, 1913 (facsimile, Vestal Press, New York, 1980).

Drake, Harry, 'The Pneumatic Player', *Musical Opinion*, London, 1921.

Drake, Harry, 'The Player Piano Explained', *Musical Opinion*, London, 1922.

Duo-Art Reproducing Piano Service Manual, 1925, facsimile reprint, Frank Adams, Seattle, Washington, USA, 1973.

Duo-Art Reproducing Piano Service Manual, 1927, facsimile reprint, Tuners Supply Co., Boston, Massachusetts, USA (n.d.).

Edgerton, Bill, Darien, Connecticut, USA: Private collection of ephemera.

Ellis, Alexander J., and Mendel, Arthur, *Musical Pitch* (a series of monographs), Frits Knuf, Amsterdam, 1968.

Givens, L., *Rebuilding the Player Piano*, New York, Vestal Press, 1963.

Harding, Rosamond E. M., *The Piano-Forte: Its History traced to the Great Exhibition of 1851*, Cambridge, England, 1933.

Heinitz, Wilhelm, Extract: 'Mechanische Musikinstrumente der Instrumentenkunde', in *Handbuch der Musikwissenschaft*, Potsdam, 1928.

Howe, Alfred H. *Scientific Piano Tuning and Servicing*, American Piano Supply Co., New Jersey, 1941 (revised edn 1966).

Journal of the Musikhistorische Gesellschaft für selbstspielende Instrumente in Deutschland, E. V., Hannover, 1978 *et seq.*

McCombie, Ian, *The Piano Handbook*, Scribner's, New York, 1980.

McFerrin, W. V., *The Piano – Its Acoustics*, Edward Lyman Bill, 1925 (facsimile, Tuners Supply Co., Boston, 1971).

Marini, Marino, *Museo di Strumenti Musicali Meccanici*, Marino Marini, Ravenna, Italy, *c.*1972.

Matetzki, J., *Uber die Behändlung und Instandsetzung von Pneumatischen Musikwerken*, Leipzig, 1913.

Mathot Library, Brussels, Belgium: private papers, catalogues and ephemera.

Michel, N. E., *Michel's Piano Atlas*, USA, *c.*1963.

Music Industries Directory, London, 1914, 1924 and 1929.

BIBLIOGRAPHY

Musical Box Society of Great Britain, *The Music Box* (journal), London, 1962–82.
Musical Box Society International of America, *Bulletin* (journal), USA, 1966–82.
Musique Adresses Universel, Paris, 1919–20 and 1930.
Musical Opinion, London, 1877–1930.
Ord-Hume, A. W. J. G., *Player Piano*, London, Allen & Unwin, 1970.
Ord-Hume, A. W. J. G., *Clockwork Music*, London, Allen & Unwin, 1973.
Ord-Hume, A. W. J. G., *Mechanics of Mechanical Music*, London, Ord-Hume, 1973.
Ord-Hume, A. W. J. G., *Barrel Organ*, London, Allen & Unwin, 1978.
Ord-Hume Library, London: piano roll catalogues, early advertising literature, player piano and related material, US, UK and European patent extracts (collection, shelfmark 2/87.b to 3/24.b inclusive).
Ottenheimer, Paul D., Thorofare, New Jersey, USA: private collection of catalogues and ephemera.
Perry, Adelaide Trowbridge, *Compendium of Piano Material*, Schirmer Music Stores, Los Angeles, 1929 (copy in Logan Library, Philadelphia).
Player Piano Group, *Newsletter*, London, 1964–82.
Player Piano Review, Birmingham, 1912–14.
Player Piano Supplement, *The Gramophone*, London, 1924–5.
Presto Buyer's Guide (to) Pianos, Players, Reproducing Pianos and their Manufacturers 1926, facsimile edition, Frank Adams, Seattle, Washington, 1972.
Reblitz, Arthur A., *Piano Servicing, Tuning and Rebuilding*, Vestal Press, New York, 1976.
Reblitz, Arthur A., and Bowers, Q. David, *Treasures of Mechanical Music*, Vestal Press, New York, 1981.
Roehl, H., *Player Piano Treasury* (1st edn), Vestal Press, New York, 1961.
Roehl, H., *Player Piano Treasury* (2nd edn), Vestal Press, New York, 1974.
S. G. E(arl), 'How to Repair the Player Piano', *Musical Opinion*, London, 1920.
Shead, Herbert, *The Anatomy of the Piano*, Unwin Brothers, Old Woking, 1978.
Spillane, Daniel, *History of the American Pianoforte; Its Technical Development, and the Trade*, New York, 1890.
Stephen, James Leslie, *Collection of Miscellany on Pianos, 1876–1947* (collection, British Library, Shelfmark 07902.b.1/1 to 1/12 inclusive).
Suidman, Peter, Speetjens, Frits, and Mathor, Gustave, *Pianolas*, Nederlandse Pianola Vereniging, Holland, 1981.
Travis, John W., *A Guide to Restringing*, Middleburg Press, 1961.
Weiss-Stauffacher, H., and Bruhin, R., *Mechanische Musikinstrumente und Musikautomaton*, published by the author, Seewen, Switzerland, 1973.
Welte-Mignon, *Instructions for Testing and Regulating the Original Welte-Built Welte-Mignon Reperforming Instrument* (n.d.), facsimile reprint by Frank Adams, Seattle, Washington, USA, 1973.
White, W. B., *Piano Playing Mechanisms*, 1st edn, Lyman Bill Inc., Chicago, 1925.
White, William Braid, *A Technical Treatise on Piano Player Mechanism*, New York, Edward Lyman Bill, 1908.
White, William Braid, *Regulation and Repair of Piano and Player Mechanisms*, New York, Edward Lyman Bill, 1909.
White, William Braid, *The Player Piano Up to Date*, New York, 1914.
Wilson, David Miller, *An Introductory Book on The Piano-Player and Player-Piano*, c.1918, London.
Wilson, David Miller, *Instruction Book on the Piano-Player and Player-Piano*, J. M. Kronheim & Co., London, 1911.
Wilson, David Miller, *The Player-Piano, Its Construction and How to Play*, London, Pitmans, 1923.
de Wit, Paul, *Weltadressbuch der Musikindustrie*, Leipzig, 1903 and 1909.
de Wit, Paul, *Zeitschrift für Instrumentenbau*, Leipzig, 1881–1890.
Wolfenden, Samuel, *A Treatise on the Art of Pianoforte Construction*, Unwin Brothers, Old Woking, 1977.
Woodman, H. Staunton, *How To Tune a Piano*, New York, Corwood Publishers, 1960.

* Service manual reprints and related literatures can be obtained from The Vestal Press, PO Box 97, Vestal, New York, 13850, United States of America, or through The British Piano Museum, 368 High Street, Brentford, Middlesex.

Picture Credits

I would like to express my thanks to those who have let me photograph instruments in their collections for publication in this book. These include Graham Webb; Gustave Mathot, Belgium; Michael Woolf, New Zealand; National Technical Museum, Prague; Christie's, South Kensington; Ron Benton, Isle of Wight; Sotheby's, Belgravia; Simon Haskell, Putney; Mary Belton, Brighton; Frank Holland, British Piano Museum; Harvey Roehl, Vestal Press, New York.

The following have graciously supplied illustrations for my use: Christie's, South Kensington, Sotheby's, Belgravia, Paul Ziff, Gustave Mathot, Werner Baus, Nationaal Museum van Speelklok tot Pierement, West Cornwall Museum of Mechanical Music (Douglas Berryman), Harvey Roehl. The attributions are:

Paul Ziff – 1; Sotheby's, Belgravia – 2, 14; Graham Webb – 3, 5; Werner Baus – 20; West Cornwall Museum of Mechanical Music – 22; Harvey Roehl – 55; Nationaal Museum van Speelklok tot Pierement – 54.

All other pictures are from my own collection or from instruments which have passed through my workshop during the past quarter of a century.

Index

This index does not include references to Player Piano makers and Piano Roll makers which are self-indexed in the Appendices. It does, though, contain reference to names within these Appendices which are not self-indexed. Plates are indicated in bold type.

789.72   86371
Or2r
     Ord-Hume, Arthur W. J. G.
     Restoring Pianolas

      SEP 11 92
      DEC 3 93